Reclaiming the Public Sphere

Palgrave Studies in Communication for Social Change

Series Editors: **Pradip Ninan Thomas**, The University of Queensland, Australia and **Elske van de Fliert**, The University of Queensland, Australia.

Advisory Board: **Silvio Waisbord**, George Washington University, USA, **Karin G. Wilkins**, University of Texas at Austin, USA, **Thomas Tufte**, Roskilde University, Denmark, **Zaharom Nain**, University of Nottingham, Malaysia Campus, **Rico Lie**, Wageningen University, The Netherlands, **Claudia Mitchell**, McGill University, Canada, **Jo Tacchi**, RMIT University, Australia, **Nicholas Carah**, The University of Queensland, Australia, **Zala Volcic**, Pomona College, Claremont, USA

Communication for Social Change (CSC) is a defined field of academic enquiry that is explicitly transdisciplinary and that has been shaped by a variety of theoretical inputs from a variety of traditions, from sociology and development to social movement studies. The leveraging of communication, information and the media in social change is the basis for a global industry that is supported by governments, development aid agencies, foundations, and international and local NGOs. It is also the basis for multiple interventions at grassroots levels, with participatory communication processes and community media making a difference through raising awareness, mobilising communities, strengthening empowerment and contributing to local change.

This series on Communication for Social Change intentionally provides the space for critical writings in CSC theory, practice, policy, strategy and methods. It fills a gap in the field by exploring new thinking, institutional critiques and innovative methods. It offers the opportunity for scholars and practitioners to engage with CSC as both an industry and as a local practice, shaped by political economy as much as by local cultural needs. The series explicitly intends to highlight, critique and explore the gaps between ideological promise, institutional performance and realities of practice.

Titles include:

Tina Askanius and Liv Stubbe Østergaard (*editors*)
RECLAIMING THE PUBLIC SPHERE
Communication, Power and Social Change

Pradip Thomas and Elske van de Fliert
INTERROGATING THE THEORY AND PRACTICE OF COMMUNICATION
AND SOCIAL CHANGE
The Basis for a Renewal

Palgrave Studies in Communication for Social Change
Series Standing Order ISBN 978-1-137-36166-0 (hardback)
(*outside North America only*)

You can receive future titles in this series as they are published by placing a standing order. Please contact your bookseller or, in case of difficulty, write to us at the address below with your name and address, the title of the series and the ISBN quoted above.

Customer Services Department, Macmillan Distribution Ltd, Houndmills, Basingstoke, Hampshire RG21 6XS, England

Reclaiming the Public Sphere

Communication, Power and Social Change

Edited by

Tina Askanius
Lund University, Sweden

and

Liv Stubbe Østergaard
Roskilde University, Denmark

THE EUROPEAN UNION
The European Regional Development Fund

Interreg IVA
ÖRESUND – KATTEGAT – SKAGERRAK

First published 2014 by
PALGRAVE MACMILLAN

Palgrave Macmillan in the UK is an imprint of Macmillan Publishers Limited,
registered in England, company number 785998, of Houndmills, Basingstoke,
Hampshire RG21 6XS.

Palgrave Macmillan in the US is a division of St Martin's Press LLC,
175 Fifth Avenue, New York, NY 10010.

Palgrave Macmillan is the global academic imprint of the above companies
and has companies and representatives throughout the world.

Palgrave® and Macmillan® are registered trademarks in the United States,
the United Kingdom, Europe and other countries.

ISBN: 978–1–137–39874–1

This book is printed on paper suitable for recycling and made from fully
managed and sustained forest sources. Logging, pulping and manufacturing
processes are expected to conform to the environmental regulations of the
country of origin.

A catalogue record for this book is available from the British Library.

A catalog record for this book is available from the Library of Congress.

Transferred to Digital Printing in 2014

Contents

List of Illustrations

Figures

Tables

Notes on Contributors

Måns Adler founded the video service Bambuser in 2007. It enables anybody to live stream video from mobile phones or webcams. His professional portfolio includes projects for Linden labs (Second life) in San Francisco and the set-up of a lab environment at Medea, Malmö University. He was awarded the Royal Swedish Academy of Engineering Sciences Ambient Award in 2010.

Tina Askanius is a post-doctoral researcher in the department of Communication and Media, Lund University. Her research concerns social movement media practices, with a particular focus on contemporary forms of video activism in online environments. Her recent work within this area has been published in international journals such as *Research in Social Movements, Conflict and Change* and *Interface: A Journal for and about Social Movements*.

Jyothsna Latha Belliappa is Associate Professor of Gender Studies at Azim Premji University, India. In addition to sexual harassment, her research interests include gender, modernity, and work and personal life. She is the author of *Gender, Class and Reflexive Modernity in India* (2013). She is currently engaged in a qualitative research project on the career narratives of women in the teaching profession in India.

Nick Couldry is Professor of Media, Communications and Social Theory at the London School of Economics and was previously Professor of Media and Communications at Goldsmiths College, University of London. He is the author or editor of 11 books, including *Ethics of Media* (2013), *Media, Society, World* (2012) and *Why Voice Matters* (2010). He has led funded research on citizens' 'public connection' (see http://publicconnection.org.uk/) and story exchange in community engagement (http://www.firm-innovation.net/portfolio-of-projects/storycircle/). He is currently working on a new book on the mediated construction of reality.

Martin Davies is a broadcast and media specialist on Africa. After nearly 20 years of broadcasting to the continent with the BBC World Service he ran the broadcast element of a global campaign to make educational change, before setting up the media production company 'Between the Posts Productions'. The successful delivery of a Slum Radio Project for Amnesty International led to a value exchange model to Tanzania where it has been running media campaigns to support advocacy on issues around disability and elderly people. In 2013 Davies was commissioned by the BBC to produce a radio documentary about life in the Accra slums.

Ingrid Elam is a literary critic, author and Associate Professor of Comparative Literature. She has worked as the Chief Editor of the culture section of *Göteborgs-Tidningen* and *Göteborgs-Posten*, and at the Stockholm daily newspaper, *Dagens Nyheter*. She was Head of the School of Arts and Communication (K3), Dean of the Faculty of Culture and Society, and Vice Chancellor for international affairs at Malmö University. Between 2006 and 2012 she was a member of the board of the Swedish Arts Grants Committee. She is currently dean at the Faculty of Fine, Applied and Performing Arts at Gothenburg University.

Ylva Ekström holds a PhD in Media and Communication Studies from Uppsala University, Sweden, where she is currently based at the Department of Informatics and Media. Her research has taken her on many long journeys to Tanzania where, since the late 1990s, she has conducted research about young people and their relation to media and popular culture. Questions about social change through communication, media and culture, and meetings between people and cultures are central to her research.

Thomas Hylland Eriksen is Professor of Social Anthropology at the University of Oslo and a prolific author in many genres. His research is focused on cultural complexity, globalization and identity politics, and he has carried out field research in Trinidad, Mauritius, Australia and Norway. He is currently directing a research project on the three crises of globalization: economic, environmental and cultural. His books published in English include: *Ethnicity and Nationalism, Small Places: Large Issues, Globalization: The Key Concepts, Engaging Anthropology* and *Tyranny of the Moment*. His most recent book in Norwegian (2013) is a biography of the anthropologist Fredrik Barth.

Jorge A. Gonzalez is Senior Researcher at CEIICH, Universidad Nacional Autónoma de México. He won the first ISA Worldwide Contest for Young Sociologists in 1990, and has worked for Catedrático UNESCO, Universitat Autónoma de Barcelona (2000) and as Tinker Professor at the University of Texas, Austin (2002). He is a Member of the Mexican Academy of Science, the International Sociological Association and the New York Academy of Sciences. His research concerns contemporary cultures in Latin America. Since 2001, he has been researching and facilitating cybercultur@. His most recent publication is *Entre cultura(s) e cibercultur@(s): Incursões e outras rotas não lineares* (2012).

Oscar Hemer is Professor of Journalistic and Literary Creation at Malmö University, Sweden, where he has headed the master's programme in Communication for Development since its inception in 2000. He is also a co-director of the transnational research group Ørecomm, based at the universities of Malmö and Roskilde. His research interests are situated in the crossroads of literature and ethnography. He is the author of six novels and several books of essay and reportage, and holds a Dr. Philos. degree in Social Anthropology from the University of Oslo, Norway

Carsten Jensen is a Danish writer and critic. As a writer, Jensen has brought the classic essay genre into the modern media era and filled it with critical awareness. He has been engaged in the domestic debate on Denmark's participation in the Afghanistan war. In 2010 he received the prestigious Olof Palme Prize and in 2012 the Søren Gyldendal Prize.

Rikke Frank Jørgensen is a researcher and senior adviser at the Danish Institute for Human Rights. She has specialized in the field of communication technology and human rights. Her experience includes ICT policymaking for the Danish Government, international advocacy and board positions in the field of 'Internet rights', and numerous presentations and writings on the topic. Since 2012, she has been an appointed expert on the Council of Europe's working groups on Internet Users' Rights. She holds a PhD in Communication from Roskilde University. Her thesis, 'Framing The Net: The Internet and Human Rights', was published in 2013.

Nicky Morrison is a lecturer at the University of Cambridge and a senior associate at the Cambridge Centre for Housing and Planning Research. Her research focuses on comparative housing and urban planning issues, in particular on community engagement in housing-related initiatives. She has collaborated on a number of housing and neighbourhood renewal projects across Europe, China and, more recently, Africa. She is currently involved in the EcoHouse Initiative, which seeks to create a platform for exchange between academic and industrial innovators as well as development organizations with the aim of developing permanent, sustainable housing for low-income communities worldwide.

Liv Stubbe Østergaard works for the Danish Refugee Council and is associated with the Department of Communication, Business and Information Technologies, Roskilde University.

Cicilia M. Krohling Peruzzo is Associate Professor in the Graduate Programme in Social Communication at Universidade Metodista de São Paulo. Her main research interests are communication in social movements, participatory communication, alternative public relations and organizational communication in the third sector. She was president and resident member of the Board of Trustees of INTERCOM, the Brazilian Society of Interdisciplinary Studies in Communication Studies, in 1999–2002, and Coordinator of the Working Group 'Popular, Alternative and Community Communication for Citizenship' for the Latin-American Association of Communication Researchers in 1996–2010.

Geetanjali Sachdev is a faculty member at the Srishti School of Art, Design and Technology. Her interests lie in art and design pedagogy and in developing tools for assessment within the context of art and design education. Her recent focus has been on the areas of public pedagogy and botanical art. She holds an MA in Education from Oxford Brookes University and the Westminster Institute of Education, UK. She has a BSc in Industrial Management and Graphic Communications with a minor in Visual Communication from Carnegie-Mellon University, Pittsburgh, US.

Linda Helgesson Sekei obtained her PhD in Social and Economic Geography from Umeå University, Sweden. She has been living in Tanzania for the past 13 years and is currently working as a research consultant at Development Pioneer Consultants in Dar es Salaam. Her research has to a large extent focused on youth development, with livelihood as a central theme in the context of self-employment, entrepreneurship, rural-urban linkages and mobility.

Thomas Tufte is Professor in Communication at Roskilde University (2004–) and Co-founder and Co-director of the Bi-national Research Centre *Orecomm – Centre for Communication and Glocal Change.* Tufte's research covers media ethnography, health communication, media and globalization, and communication for development and social change. He directs the international research project *Critical Perspectives on New Media and Processes of Social Change in the Global South* (2013–2017). Recent publications include *Handbook of Development Communication and Social Change* (2014) and *Speaking Up and Talking Back? Media, Empowerment and Civic Engagement among East and Southern African Youth* (2013).

Karin Gwinn Wilkins is Professor of Media Studies, Director of the Center for Middle Eastern Studies and Chair of the Global Studies Bridging Disciplines Program at the University of Texas, Austin. She has won numerous awards for research, service and teaching, and chaired the Intercultural/Development Division of the International Communication Association. Her work addresses scholarship in the fields of development communication, global communication and political engagement. Selected works include *Handbook of Development Communication and Social Change* (2014), *New Agendas in Global Communication* (2013) and *Questioning Numbers: How to Read and Critique Research* (2011).

Introduction

Tina Askanius and Liv Stubbe Østergaard

There has been a dramatic increase in the attention paid to the role of media and communication technologies in processes of social change around the world in the immediate aftermath of the so-called Arab Spring that began to unfold at the end of 2010. Surrounded by hype and buzzwords such as the 'Twitter or Facebook revolution', media and communication technologies have been celebrated as vehicles for rapid political mobilization and alleged to have made a considerable impact on political life, agency and the public sphere. Some of these debates have sparked renewed energy and interest in the longstanding issues and questions at the heart of Communication for Development and Social Change (CDSC). Others, however, have been haunted by techno-determinism, media-centrism and a lack of analytical sensitivity towards the contingencies of the geopolitical and cultural contexts of these events and the specificities of how media and communication practices are appropriated by different groups of citizens. Looking back at these 'years of protest' and social unrest, as they have been labelled, calls for a deeper moment of critical reflection.

The concept of the public sphere is intrinsic to an understanding of the arenas and power dynamics linked to these events. This book offers a space for critical analysis of how media and communication practices for social change, on the one hand, and analytic conceptions of public spheres and participation, on the other, are currently being reconfigured in both conceptual and rhetorical terms. It offers insights into how new arenas and agents in the public sphere are challenging conventional wisdom on the relation between communicative practices, power and social relations among all stakeholders involved in the processes of communication for social change.

It is possible to add a question mark or a plural to the notion of 'reclaiming the public sphere' as it is framed in the title of this book. Rather than retrieving the public sphere in a traditional Habermasian sense, we wish to consider how new means of communication and political action shape and constitute emerging public spheres in the plural. What are the implications of this ongoing shift? Who are the new agents in the public arenas of today? What processes of power-brokering are taking place? How do communicative practices, the negotiation of power, and the formation and negotiation of social relations come together in and around mediated public spheres? How do public spheres relate to public spaces – be they physical cityscapes or virtual environments? The negotiation of power is not only connected to formal institutional processes of elections and the formation of representative democracies, but is just as much about the processes of governmentality in everyday life. We negotiate power in our everyday social and cultural practice – and thus also in our participation in public spheres, be they mediated or not. These processes of power-brokering have implications for who influences processes of social change.

This book offers both conceptual frameworks and analytical insights into some of these developments, the various actors involved in claiming voice and the communicative means of participation in public spaces, as well as the media practices in which they engage to these ends. Of critical concern to this volume are questions of how developments in media technologies and communicative practices are contributing to the long-term transformation of the institutions of democracy, the public sphere and citizens' modes of participation within these spaces. The book thus positions media on the frontlines of current transformations of the public sphere by arguing that media play a significant, albeit complex and never unequivocal, role in the dynamics of social change. In so doing, it seeks to avoid media-centrism by situating media and communication technologies within a larger set of reciprocal factors in which the complex interplay between media and social change should be considered. Such an approach takes into account the contingency of the socio-cultural contexts under study. It asks not only what possibilities new media technologies can bring, but also what constraints and obstacles may impinge on the socio-political realities and everyday practices of communication for social change projects.

While media technologies are frequently celebrated for enlarging the possibilities for democratic engagement and advancing human rights standards across the world, this book raises critical and sobering questions about the communicative practices of various state and civil society actors, and offers an examination of how such actors really use and appropriate media in concrete contexts for specific political or social ends. In this book, we wish to juxtapose optimistic rhetoric on media technologies with critical reflections on the processes and powers that may be seen to undermine access to free, democratic media and arenas for participation. Thematically organized around the intellectual horizons and conceptual frames of the public sphere, the issues raised in this book range from the role of the public intellectual and artistic practices in reinterpreting the public sphere, to the ways in which social movement actors and disadvantaged groups in developing countries seek visibility in the public sphere and use different forms of media to forge social change and enlarge their opportunities for participation in an expanded democracy.

The notion of the public sphere lies at the heart of a longstanding tradition of scholarship that interrogates the nexus between the media, democracy and civic engagement. In recent years, an extensive body of literature has emerged from this tradition. It contests the boundaries of what constitutes 'the political' and questions how we might broaden our understanding of what it means to participate in democracy and political processes. Much of this work coalesces in a joint critique of the shortcomings of the model of deliberative democracy for understanding the various ways in which citizens engage politically beyond the confinements of the representative system (see e.g., Fraser, 1992; Mouffe, 2005, 2013; Rosanvallon, 2008 for a few examples of this extensive body of literature). Key to this critique is a reaction to the idealized view, inherent in the Habermasian model of deliberative democracy, of political interaction as based on consensus and communicative rationality. As alternative conceptual categories to that of the public sphere (Habermas, 1989), scholars have offered notions such as counter-public spheres (Fraser, 1992), public sphericules (Gitlin, 1998) agonistic public spaces (Mouffe, 1999, 2007, 2013) or civic cultures (Dahlgren, 2009, 2013). This by now extensive body of literature criticizes the rationalistic bias of the public sphere framework and instead emphasizes the messy, polemical and affective nature of contemporary political struggle and expression. Moreover, another more recent literature has begun to explore the various technical, political, economic and sociocultural contingencies of digital media, adding these dimensions to the discussions about their potential and limitations in facilitating democratic participation (Carpentier, 2011; Dahlgren, 2013; Morozov, 2011; Papacharissi, 2010).

In short, the aim of this book is to connect the field of CDSC to theoretical thinking on the changing notions of the public sphere, in order to identify and analyse new arenas for participation and voice. Such an endeavour will not only enrich our understanding of the possibilities and limitations of CDSC as an academic discipline, but also contribute to improving practice in the field. Although dialogue and participation are at the heart of both CDSC and the broader public sphere tradition, there is a remarkable gap in the literature when it comes to linking the two fields and bridging the gap between the predominantly 'prescriptive recipes of communication *for* development' (Hemer and Tufte, 2012, p. 235) in CDSC and critical analysis of the broader contexts and structures into which these projects and initiatives inscribe themselves. Apart from contributions from Alfaro (2003), Barbero (2001) and Barranquero (2005), which establish some preliminary links between the two trajectories, most CDSC literature tends to treat communication in terms of strategic communication interventions by Western NGOs, largely neglecting the plethora of other academic disciplines that direct attention to the relationship between media, participation in public life, and processes of social change more broadly. These disciplines go beyond the field of CDSC to include political communication, human rights studies, social movement studies and the broad field of media sociology.

Although these studies are often devoted to similar research questions and analytical objects, the insights derived from them have a tendency to circulate in disciplinary silos without ever crossing paths. The ambition of this book is to bring the disciplines together, intellectually as well as in a highly concrete manner in the following pages. The volume therefore foregrounds contributions that connect and contextualize the dispersed scholarship conducted across the wide array of academic disciplines and practitioners' fields that are currently engaged with questions of how the transformation of the public sphere and developments in the global mediascape are reorganizing political agency and the social realms in which citizens make claims for representation, recognition and voice.

To this end, this volume brings together a range of different actors in the arts and cultural industries, as well as academics and public intellectuals. In so doing, the book links and contextualizes these multifaceted areas and arenas, academic as well as practice-based, to the methodologies, themes and current theorizing in the field of CDSC. The collection combines theoretical perspectives on the wider transformation of the public sphere with critical essays, debates and empirical case studies of collective action, public interventions and CDSC initiatives in public spaces – both online and offline, in old and new media contexts. The dual focus on theory and practice makes the book relevant to scholars and students in the fields of media and communication, sociology, anthropology, political science, international affairs and development studies who may wish for a broad introduction and interdisciplinary approach to the field of CDSC. Furthermore, we hope the book will be of interest and inspiration to activists, educators and practitioners involved in the current upsurge of political action, social movement organizations and communication for change projects that are currently being scrutinized so eagerly by academics across the world. This book is a valuable resource for readers interested in gaining a critical understanding of the theory and practice of CDSC from the perspective of the public sphere, past and present movements involved in communication for social change, women's empowerment, the role of media and communication in human rights, the pedagogic dimensions of CDSC, and the concrete implementation and evaluation of CDSC initiatives.

The structure of the book

The book project was initiated at the second Örecomm Festival, which took place in Roskilde and Copenhagen, Denmark and Malmö, Sweden, in September 2012.[1] The four-day, multi-location festival, which combined a range of academic keynote speakers, presentations of papers, presentations by artists and cultural events, was jointly organized by the department of Communication, Business and Information Technology at Roskilde University and the School of Arts and Communication (K3) at Malmö University. The panels, their presentations and the debate provoked during these four intensive days form the backbone of this volume.

The book is organized in three thematic parts. In part I of the book, 'Theorizing Communication for Change and the Transformation of Public Spheres', a range of theoretical contributions highlight the relationship between the changing notion of public spheres and current developments in the field of CDSC. The chapters engage in various ways with some wider political currents and structures, such as the broad schemes of neoliberalism, consumerism and globalization, that shape and impinge on citizens' opportunities for engaging in society and gaining power over their lives. In this way, the chapters provide valuable insights into the conditions and contexts in which contemporary CDSC projects and initiatives should be understood and analysed.

Nick Couldry opens the volume with a discussion of the possibilities for and constraints on citizens gaining voice in contemporary Western democracies under conditions of neoliberalism. Couldry demonstrates how neoliberal states have become increasingly 'voiceblind' to the spaces where democratic voice emerge. He explores how neoliberal states, in the face of the most serious financial crisis in more than a century, are caught in a complex legitimacy deficit that affects both how they reflect and how they perform the act of governing. Against this backdrop, he proposes a number of possible solutions for how state and society can be reorganized in ways that better recognize citizens' knowledge and experience in order to improve conditions for a more vital democratic life.

Based on comparative field studies conducted in Mexico and Brazil, Jorge González explores in Chapter 2 how *'glocal' knowledge communities* can revive and empower citizens in poor, marginalized regions. Gonzalez introduces and develops the notion of 'Cybercultur@' as a prism for understanding and theorizing on how multiple voices, self-governance and bottom-up organization in situated local contexts can reactivate the public sphere in countries and regions in which this space has been 'abandoned' by its citizens.

At the heart of Chapter 3, by Karin Wilkins, is a concern with *advocacy communication,* understood as strategic public communication from a Communication for Social Change perspective. Wilkins argues for the importance of including political communication in the field of Communication for Social Change and conceiving advocacy communication as a comprehensive approach to communication technologies and processes for social change in a global context. She argues that studies of advocacy communication should focus analytical attention on notions of social justice, in order to recognize how differences in access to resources create spaces through which some groups have more power to assert their perspectives than others. The framework of advocacy communication proposed by Wilkins builds on a critical understanding of the public sphere not as an idealized pluralistic space, but as a site for struggle and resistance.

In Chapter 4, 'The Public Sphere and the Dialectics of Globalization', Thomas Hylland Eriksen outlines some of the central parameters of globalization in order to highlight the implications of the process of transnational integration for 'global conversations among citizens' at a time when they no longer face any material impediments. Eriksen argues that the understanding of public spheres has been intimately linked with the nation state and the consolidation of national identities, democratic values, language communities and civil society. He asks what becomes of the public sphere in an era of transnational mobility and communication, porous boundaries and destabilized national identities. Eriksen shows that the ideological tensions characterizing the public spheres of the early 21st century are fundamentally framed by the tension between the global and the local, the universal and the particular, and the different subject positions taken on by citizens vis-a-vis these schemes. He suggests that the public sphere can be read as a dramatization of the dialectics of globalization that play out on national stages that are structured by a global grammar.

Whereas Part I of the book concentrates on theoretical perspectives on the fluctuating nature of public spheres and questions of how the structural mechanisms underpinning these transformations might impinge on practice and opportunities in the field of CDSC, Parts II and III of the book examine concrete cases of public interventions, technologies and arenas for participation in public spheres. Part II, 'Contemporary Drivers of Social Change: Art, Technology and Public Pedagogy', contains contributions from a wide range of stakeholders, including public intellectuals, educators in the arts and the cultural industries, and media professionals involved in the practical implementation or political discussions of the issues covered in this volume on a day-to-day basis. The contributions all highlight the opportunities for and constraints on participation and intervention in today's changing public spheres. The chapters build on the diverse personal and professional experiences of writers, public intellectuals and media entrepreneurs. In this sense, Part II breaks with traditional academic conventions to offer a number of non-traditional takes on the subject area, such as essays, moderated roundtable discussions and interviews. By turning these practitioner perspectives into chapter contributions, which the reader will find to be in more of a colloquial or verbatim form compared to the rest of the volume, we have sought to pass on some of the interesting cultural and intellectual exchanges and debates that emerge when theoretical and practical perspectives are brought together.

Part II opens with three subsequent chapters evolving around the changing role of the intellectual in the contemporary public sphere and increasingly complex mediascape. The chapters draw on a debate, which took place between three of Scandinavia's leading public intellectuals at the 2012 Ørecomm Festival; Ingrid Elam (Sweden) and Carsten Jensen (Denmark), who each gave an introductory address, and Thomas Hylland Eriksen (Norway) as the discussant. In Chapter 5 Ingrid Elam opens the discussion by posing the question: 'What is an intellectual, anyway?' Elam takes her point of departure from two seminal writings on the role of the public intellectual: Noam Chomsky's *The Responsibility of Intellectuals* and Edward Said's

Representations of the Intellectual, to provide a historical account of the role of the public intellectual and to discuss what can be learned from Chomsky's demand to take sides and speak truth to power compared with Said's advocacy of amateurism and the benefit of 'an exile position'. Elam suggests that in an increasingly fragmented public sphere, many intellectuals have moved away from the more traditional arenas, and today some of the most interesting contributions to the public debate on social and political change are to be found in the intersection between interactivity and public interventions in contemporary art.

In Carsten Jensen's contribution to the discussion, 'What I Think about When I Think about Being an Intellectual' (Chapter 6), he reflects on what constitutes a public intellectual today and the role intellectuals play in societies. He argues that an intellectual is distinct from a decision maker, but plays a role in engaging in public debate and reasoning based on rational arguments. Furthermore, he discusses why freedom of expression is not the same as freedom of information, and why the crisis of the latter undermines the meaning of the former. Particular attention is paid to the role of the Internet in the fragmentation of the public sphere, enabling more people to express their opinion without necessarily creating a more democratic debate among publics. On the basis of the contributions by Elam and Jensen, Thomas Hylland Erikson engages in a debate with the two authors. In chapter 7 this debate is contextualised by Professor Oscar Hemer under the heading: 'The Flattening of the Public Sphere and the Loss of Respect for Knowledge'. Hemer positions the debate within a broader discussion of the distinction between public and private spheres and the general watering down of political agency and participation in the public spheres of liberal democracies.

In Chapter 8, 'The Democratization of Live Streaming Tools', the development of the live video streaming platform Bambuser is described. The interview with the founder of Bambuser, Måns Adler, provides a wide range of empirical examples of how live mobile video broadcasting is changing the political landscape and power dynamics across the world.

The final contribution of this section revolves around the role of public educators in the arts and the cultural industries, and their professional use of new communication technologies in processes of social change and empowerment. Geetanjali Sachdev, from Srishti School of Art, Design and Technology in Bangalore, India, shares her experiences of a range of interventionist projects carried out with students in public spaces in Bangalore. Her chapter, 'Beyond Polemical Practice: A Tribute to Henry Gireoux', (Chapter 9) focuses on artistic practices and design methods, critical and public pedagogy, and the transformative potential of art in public spaces.

Part III, 'Practitioners and Practices: New Communication for Social Change Perspectives and Initiatives', contains empirical case studies and evaluations of specific CDSC initiatives, in which a diverse range of media forms and practices, from reality game shows in Tanzania to slum radio in Kenya, are critically assessed in relation to their implementation in local development projects and programmes around the world. The authors all connect their studies to questions of how their particular cases and findings reflect broader processes of change in the nature of publics and notions of 'publicness'.

Jyothsna Latha Belliappa (Chapter 10) examines public discourses on gender and modernity in the light of a recent series of sexual and physical assaults on young women (and men) in Mangalore, a coastal town in southern India. Examining the public responses to these assaults as reported in the media, she argues that while women's presence and participation in the public sphere are applauded in late modern societies, they also give rise to anxieties regarding women's sexuality in certain cultural contexts. This results in attempts to control and circumscribe women's participation in the public realm through punitive measures that include brutal physical and sexual assaults. However, the popular protests against these assaults, from public squares across India to viral campaigns online, suggest that young women in urban India continue to claim their right to move around freely in public spaces and have voice in the public sphere by challenging established gender hierarchies and the boundaries between religious communities.

In her capacity as senior adviser to the Danish Institute for Human rights, Rikke Frank Jørgensen has specialized in questions of how ICTs can strengthen or weaken human rights standards across the world. Jørgensen challenges the conventional wisdom on how the use of new media will automatically advance standards on human rights, in particular with regard to the rights to freedom of expression, freedom of information and freedom of assembly. Instead, she draws attention to how recent policy initiatives and enforcement have undermined the idea of and ideology behind a free and open Internet. In her chapter, 'Participation in the Internet Era', (Chapter 11), Jørgensen discusses the state of human rights on the Internet and the ongoing battle between openness and control of the Internet, widely referred to as the 'Third World War'. She uses current examples from the field of human rights and human rights policymaking to shed light on key developments and tensions related to how civil society organizations mobilize to fight against Internet regulation from a human rights perspective.

In Chapter 12, Cecilia Peruzzo offers a framework for considering 'the right to communication' as part of a third generation of human rights. In so doing, she offers a perspective that moves beyond traditional notions of civil, political and social rights – the so-called first and second generations of human rights – to examine how we may consider access to media and communication critical components in processes of change and an intrinsic part of citizens' universal rights. Based on a discussion of both historical and contemporary social movements in Brazil, Peruzzo explores the potential for a 'communication rights perspective' to understand community communication and questions of how different types of social movement across the world seek to enlarge their citizenship status and opportunities to express civic engagement in public spheres, where their freedom of expression is restricted by the national system of communication.

Ylva Ekström and Linda Helgesson analyse participatory media practices in the specific context of mobile phones and the possibilities for communicating for change afforded by SMS services. Their chapter, 'Citizen Engagement through SMS? Audiences 'Talking Back' to a Reality TV Edutainment Initiative in Tanzania' (Chapter 13), is based on a case study of a reality television entrepreneurship competition, *Ruka Juu*, initiated by a civil society organization and media platform in Tanzania, Femina HIP. Their case study scrutinizes the opportunities and obstacles in relation to the use of mobile phone messaging as a tool for participatory communication in an edutainment context.

Martin Davies and Nicky Morrison's Chapter 14, 'Accessing the Public Sphere in Africa through a Slum Radio Project', examines and evaluates the Slum Radio project funded by Amnesty International in Kenya. The project, which was launched in 2012 and targeted some of the poorest communities in the country, gives them a platform to engage and debate in the public sphere within the cities in which they live. The authors share their experiences with setting up and running the Slum Radio project and provide concrete guidelines on how the approach could be adapted and implemented elsewhere. Drawing on related fieldwork carried out with the BBC and the 1GOAL campaign, the authors highlight the possibility of creating debate and raising awareness in the public sphere in Africa.

Note

1. Örecomm, the Centre for Communication and Glocal Change, was founded in 2008. It is a transnational platform for research in Communication for Development and Social Change shared by K3, Malmö University (Sweden) and CBIT, Roskilde University (Denmark). The Örecomm Festival is a recurring four-day conference organized by the Örecomm universities that combines academic, artistic and cultural events.

References

Alfaro, R. M. (2006) 'State and Civil Society: A Collaboration or Cautionary Relationship?' in Alfonso Gumucio-Dagron and Thomas Tufte (eds), *Communication For Social Change Anthology: Historical and Contemporary Readings* (New Jersey: Communication For Social Change Consortium Inc.), pp. 905–911.

Barranquero, A. (2005) 'From Freire and Habermas to Multiplicity: Widening the Theoretical Borders of Participative Communication for Social Change', unpublished conference paper presented at IAMCR 2005, Taipei.

Calhoun, C. (ed.) (1992) *Habermas and the Public Sphere* (Cambridge, MA: MIT Press).

Carpentier, N. (2011) *Media and Participation* (Bristol: Intellect Ltd.).

Dahlgren, P. (2009) *Media and Political Engagement: Citizens, Communication and Democracy* (Cambridge: Cambridge University Press).

Dahlgren, P. (2013) *The Political Web: Media, Participation and Alternative Democracy* (London: Palgrave).

Fraser, N. (1992) 'Rethinking the Public Sphere: A Contribution to the Critique of Actually Existing Democracy' in Craig Calhoun (ed.), *Habermas and the Public Sphere*. (Cambridge, MA: MIT Press), pp. 109–142.

Gitlin, T. (1998) 'Public Spheres or Public Sphericules' in Tamar Liebes and James Curran (eds), *Media, Ritual and Identity* (London: Routledge), pp. 168–174.

Gumucio-Dagron, A. and Tufte, T. (eds) (2006) *Communication for Social Change Anthology: Historical and Contemporary Readings* (New Jersey: Communication for Social Change Consortium Inc.).

Habermas (1989) *The Structural Transformation of the Public Sphere: An Inquiry into a Category of Bourgeois Society* (Cambridge, MA: MIT Press).

Hemer, O. and Tufte, T. (2012) 'ComDev in the Mediatized World' *Nordicom Review* 33, pp. 229–238.

Martín-Barbero, J. (2006 [2001]) 'Communicational Reconfigurations of the Public Sphere: Globalization and the Crisis of Representation' in Alfonso Gumucio-Dagron and Thomas Tufte (eds), *Communication For Social Change Anthology: Historical and Contemporary Readings* (New Jersey: Communication For Social Change Consortium Inc.), pp. 912–919.

Morozov, E. (2011) *The Net Delusion: The Dark Side of Internet Freedom* (New York: Public Affairs).

Mouffe, C. (1999) 'Deliberative democracy or agonistic pluralism?', *Social Research* 66(3), pp. 746–758.

Mouffe, C. (2005) *On the Political* (London: Taylor & Francis Ltd).
Mouffe C. (2007) 'Artistic Activism and Agonistic Spaces', *Art & Research* 1(2), pp. 1–5.
Mouffe, C. (2013) *Agonistics: Thinking the World Politically* (London: Verso).
Papacharissi, Z. (2010) *A Private Sphere: Democracy in a Digital Age* (Cambridge: Polity Press).

Part I

Theorising Communication for Social Change and the Transformation of Public Spheres

1
Voiceblind: Beyond the Paradoxes of the Neoliberal State

Nick Couldry

This book revolves around the idea of *reclaiming* the public sphere. When land is reclaimed from the sea, a common story in Denmark, the United Kingdom and many other countries, major work must be done to redirect the sea's flow and to plan and build new types of foundations strong enough to support life on land that has been damaged. So, too, with democracy. In many countries, the experience of democracy has been eroded for decades by flows that once seemed supportive of democratic expression, but which have damaged its very basis. I refer to what I call the 'crisis of voice' in neoliberal democracies (Couldry, 2010). To survive this crisis and rebuild a democratic culture 'after' neoliberalism, we need to be attentive to where the energies of democracy are flowing right now, and to where they might be redirected. The circumstances of that rebuilding will be unstable. They will require clear-sightedness as to the conditions for new voices to be sustained, overcoming the paradoxical state of voice-blindness that characterizes the present. How we might start to do this is the main topic of this chapter.

The problem of neoliberalism[1]

Let me start with the problem: the multi-level crisis of voice in which we find ourselves in neoliberal democracies. By neoliberal democracies, I mean states with the formal properties of democracy, which have been dominated for decades by neoliberal doctrine. By a crisis of voice I mean a situation in which, in many domains, voice is continually offered and yet retracted, endorsed but then made empty. The contradictions of late modern democratic politics are multiple and complex, and I do not mean to understate that complexity. I do, however, want to insist, as one element in the mix, on the specific intent of neoliberal doctrine for over three decades to make market functioning the overriding principle of social and political organization. The core of neoliberal doctrine – popularized by Milton Friedman and others in the US and the UK in the 1970s but with roots going back almost two centuries – is stated most clearly by Michel Foucault in his lectures on *The Birth of Biopolitics*, in which he identifies a deep rethinking of liberal governmentality that 'does not ask the state what freedom it will leave to the economy, but asks the economy how its freedom can have a state-*creating* function' (Foucault, 2008, pp. 94–95).

Here are the seeds of the idea, now so familiar, that *markets themselves* provide a principle of *social* organization, and therefore in turn a preferred model for transforming politics. Neoliberal discourse is an attack not just on particular conditions of political speech (or 'voice' in the familiar sense of political expression), but on the very idea that the opinions, desires and goals of human beings might *matter* in the organization of social and economic resources. Familiar here is the intellectual imperialism of a certain type of economic thought that, as Wendy Brown puts it, 'while foregrounding the market, is not only or even primarily focused on the economy; rather it involves extending and disseminating market values to all institutions and social action' (2005, pp. 39–40).

What do I mean by voice, the term that I diagnose as in crisis? I mean, first, the process whereby people give an account of the world within which they act (for a more detailed account see Couldry, 2010, chapter 1). This process is reflexive; that is, it is embodied and requires a material form, which may be individual, collective or distributed. The *process of voice* also relies on socially produced resources and is oriented to social exchange, which is why it can be undermined by an organizational rationality that takes no account of voice. So models for organizing life that *place no value on voice* undermine it by crowding out alternative narratives that *would* authorize us to value voice. I call any such model 'a voice-denying rationality'.

Neoliberalism is just such a voice-denying rationality. It operates with an account of the social, as a space for expanding freedom modelled only on economic competition, which lacks most of the features associated with social life. If it is ever to be resisted, neoliberal rationality must be opposed by what Wendy Brown calls a 'counter-rationality – a different figuration of human beings, citizenship, economic life, and the political' (2005, p. 59). This is what must be established if democratic culture is to be rebuilt, although, as yet, we have few clear signs about how to do this.

You may say, however, that things are much more complicated than that – and of course they are. The current crisis of democracy in Europe, for example, is much more than a cultural construction. It is a profoundly *practical* crisis – a crisis of economic and political management. Neoliberalism's slogan that 'markets are always right' has been intensely contested, if not exploded, ever since the financial collapse and banking crisis of the autumn of 2008 – and yet the crisis of democratic functioning continues. That democratic crisis has only deepened in the past year to a point where whatever voter majorities say in Greece, in Spain, in France, and so on, the same measures (budget cuts, labour market flexibilization, public service privatization) are imposed on the basis that global markets and 'economic reality' demand it.

Today's crisis of voice, then, is shaped not just by neoliberal doctrine, but by the independent practical reality that the means available to national governments to manage their national economies have been drastically reduced during three decades of expanding global financial markets. As Colin Leys pointed out over a decade ago, the 'internationalized state' is characterized not just by its exposure to the huge growth in global capital markets but, just as importantly, by the huge increase in the dependence of national economies on foreign direct investment. The process has only intensified, particularly in the UK.

Leys uses 1997 figures (Leys, 2001, p. 16; and note 25). Using 2010 UNCTAD figures (www.unctad.org), the UK's inward foreign direct investment as a percentage of GDP increased from 19 per cent in 1997 to 48 per cent in 2010. As a result, national governments face increasing pressures to adopt policies that are favourable to global markets.

What we call 'the economy' – nationally, regionally, globally – seems beyond democratic control. The theorist of the market-state, Philip Bobbitt, makes the same point more vividly. For him, attempts by the contemporary nation-state to control global markets are like those of 'a bear chained to a stake, trying to chase a shifting beam of light' (2003, pp. 220–221). During the unresolved euro crisis of the past year, intergovernmental meetings have become, we might add, like a sad circus of trapped animals gesturing at democratic freedom, but with little effect.

We have become accustomed to the idea that democracy does not work – and on many levels. We are already accustomed to this on a smaller scale in the organizations in which we are employed, which are dominated by what the UK financial sociologist, Michael Power, has called 'audit culture'. This culture supplants the internal democratic processes of organizations and replaces them with the demands of apparent economic necessity. Whatever its apparently democratic motivation, 'the audit process', according to Power (1997, p. 117), 'requires trust in experts and is not a basis for rational public deliberation. It is *a dead end in the claim of accountability*...audit is in this respect *a substitute for democracy* rather than its aid' (My emphasis added).

Yet celebratory theorists of the market-state, such as Bobbitt, may be more alive to its contradictions than conventional political commentary. Writing in 2003, Bobbitt announced the replacement of the nation state by the 'market state' as world markets are restructured along supranational lines. The aim of national governments shifts from maximizing the welfare of citizens to maximizing the opportunities for the population to participate in global markets. The *offer* of participation in government cannot be completely abandoned, however, if government is to retain any democratic legitimacy. Instead, that offer becomes contradictory: 'there will be more public participation in government, but it will count for less' (2003, p. 234).

There is a deeper contradiction. The *legitimacy* of the market state has its roots in the public goods necessary for any quality of life – goods that, as Bobbitt admits, the market 'is *not* well adapted to creating or maintaining'. Bobbit lists these public goods as 'Loyalty, civility, trust in authority, respect for family life' (2003, p. 814). This is the underlying paradox of neoliberal politics: that neoliberal doctrine requires social goods that its market principles disavow and even undermine. If today's crisis of voice involves a genuine impasse, namely how to manage economic life democratically *at all* on *any* level, then the only way forward must be a great deal of collective practical effort to rethink how populations manage what we call 'the economy'. Efforts in that direction have only just started.

Again we must complicate our analysis, since this impasse in democratic management in all economies has much in common with deeper historical problems that have afflicted the modern concept of democracy itself. Drawing on the French political theorist, Pierre Rosanvallon, and his recent book, *Political Legitimacy* (2011), one way of reading today's crisis of democratic management is as a conflict between *the time of the global markets*, which can move within *minutes* against a national economy through the yields demanded on its government's bond offerings, and *the time of democratic decision-making*, which can never be synchronized with the changing demands of market processes. If the democratic crisis *within* the euro crisis is such a conflict between different temporalities, then, Rosanvallon notes, we can find just such a contradiction in the early discussions on democracy that followed the French Revolution.

It was the Marquis de Condorcet, Rosanvallon points out (2011, p. 128), who realized in 1790 that popular deliberation in a democracy requires a reflective context, the time for which must always extend beyond the moment of an election, or the moment when an elected government has to make a difficult decision. As a result, democracy inevitably involves multiple temporalities, and the role of 'popular will' is somehow to connect up those temporalities into something more coherent. Only in this way can we restore the dimension of polit-ical legitimacy that Rosanvallon calls 'legitimacy of reflexivity'. Here, Rosanvallon notes, civil society organizations make a vital contribu-tion to government's response to such contradictions by 'denouncing discrepancies between the fundamental principle of democracy and the reality', and by 'reintroducing the people *as principle*...into the political arena' (2011, p. 148). We can understand the Occupy movement and its attempt to interrupt the policy process in this way. Today's democratic crisis has historical roots that long predate neoliberalism.

Rosanvallon sees another problem of legitimacy that runs alongside the difficulty of organizing democratic reflection to match the accel-erated speed of government decision-making. This additional problem Rosanvallon calls 'the legitimacy of proximity', that is, the conflict between the *distance* from everyday life necessary if complex societies are to be governed at all and the *proximity* to everyday life experience needed if governing is to have any *legitimacy* over the long-term. Rulers must, within this new model, be 'present' to the people. Contemporary media of course provide practical ways for politicians to be 'present' to the people, and for the experiences of particular people to be 'presented' to government. There is a risk, however, Rosanvallon argues, of this media interface between government and people collapsing into an empty spectacle, which obstructs decision-making.

In response to this problem, Rosanvallon argues that we need new forms of democratic *experimentation* that allow citizens to become involved in government through new types of engagement that enable a better 'exchange of information between government and society' (2011, p. 209). Through his rich analysis, Rosanvallon opens our eyes to the continuing value of democratic *experiment*, and the possibility of *new* forms of democratic invention that might point beyond the current crisis. The static notion of the 'general will' in earlier democratic theory needs to be refreshed by what Rosanvallon calls 'a constant generaliza-tion of the social' (2011, p. 215), but without collapsing into a pure localism that ignores the very real coordination problems in contempo-rary societies.

How should we respond?

Rosanvallon's recognition of democratic creativity provides a link to my focus on how we as citizens might *respond* to the difficult challenges that face the practice of democracy today. I want to make three points: first, on the importance of saying no; second, on the importance of saying yes; and, third, on the importance of reorienting ourselves away from false arenas of democratization towards other, more promising, ones.

My first point is that future democratic experimentation cannot succeed unless it is prepared to say no to the forces that negate democracy. Saying no does not, of course, require an act of violence: its negation operates at the level of discourse. In Jose Saramago's wonderful novel *Ensaio sobre a Lucidez* (*Seeing*) (2007), published one year after the deeply undemocratic decision of some countries to go to war in Iraq, 'saying no' takes the form of submitting a blank ballot paper. This simple rejection of what is on offer – ambiguous as to its underlying reasons but completely clear in its enunciation, especially if, as in the novel, it is repeated a second time – works as if it were an act of symbolic violence against the principle of government. In the novel, it is interpreted as an act of violence by a government that is blind to the new act of 'seeing', or democratic vision, that is under way. As a leader of a local council says to the Minister of the Interior: 'Whether you like it or not, minister, it is night now, pitch-black night, we know that something is happening that goes far beyond our understanding, that exceeds our meagre experience, but we are behaving as it were the same old bread, made with the usual flour and cooked in the usual oven' (2007, p. 95).

What, more specifically, must we say no to in today's crisis of voice? First, to the idea, so often insisted on by governments, that market values – and the overall necessity of market functioning – can and should *override* other important values, such as voice and democratic functioning. In the wake of the near collapse of the global financial system, we are beginning to see, even from mainstream sources, an insistence on some limits to the dominance of market values. It is surely worth taking note when Elizabeth, the daughter of Rupert Murdoch, in a speech to the Royal Television Society, argues that we should reject the idea that 'the free market is the only sorting mechanism' for organizing public life (Sabbagh, 2012).

More substantially, the Harvard philosopher, Michael Sandel, argues in his recent book, *What Money Can't Buy*, that market reasoning empties public life of moral argument, and that when 'the logic of buying and selling ... increasingly governs the whole of life, it is time to ask whether we want to live this way' (2012, pp. 14, 6). Sandel quite directly says no to the expansion of market mechanisms as the sole regulator of, for example, the distribution of health and other public goods, but he is weaker on the political causes of the moral blind spots he identifies. He condemns the general 'moral vacancy of contemporary politics' (2012, p. 13) as if all of us were somehow to blame for the principle that markets override other public values. Rather oddly, he accuses both the US Tea Party and the Occupy movement of failing to pay moral attention to 'the role and reach of markets'. This ignores both the contradictory moralism of the US right-wing and the clear moral rejection by the Occupy movement of the excessive dominance of the global market over everyday life.

We need to say *no* also to those specific forms of politics, not all of them explicitly neoliberal (think of Tony Blair), that refuse to say no to markets, and are based on *translating* markets' supposed 'necessity' into political and cultural reality. A paradox of the neoliberal state, particularly but by no means only in the UK, has been that in order to ensure the spread of markets, governments have *interfered* massively in the regulation of social and economic life. One example is the creeping marketization of Britain's national health service, which has generated the most chaotic attempt by the UK government to change how health goods are produced and distributed. By transforming consortia of local doctors into the main allocators of health goods, doctors will become the chief buyers from drug companies and health insurers. No democratic mandate was obtained for those reforms, and there is widespread opposition within the health professions, but the process of reform goes on under the banner of 'modernization'.[2]

My argument, however, is not about the details of the British case, but about a wider point: that reforms such as the health privatization under way in the UK are attempts to enclose for private gain decision-making processes that should be accountable to public values. As with the audit culture, new types of expertise gain power – particularly the vast consultancy industry that 'serves' health provision – obscuring the fact that they operate in what was once a zone for *public* deliberation that remains largely *subsidized* by public money through taxation. As in the economy generally, we must get better at saying no to the authority of economic commentators, and spokespersons for business and corporate power, who dominate debate on the economy and the management of public resources. It is a question not of rejecting genuine expertise (we need it), but of rejecting the illegitimate claims of certain types of experts to *control* decisions that are properly *public* decisions – decisions that relate to the distribution of social goods and social resources.

This takes me to my next point: that, to be effective, any strategy of saying no needs to be based on alternative possibilities of saying yes: new ways of organizing resources, decision-making and democratic representation. To quote Elizabeth Murdoch again, 'profit without purpose is a recipe for disaster'. But what sort of purpose? Whose purpose? Generating such alternatives is very difficult, but they are essential to escape today's impasse in democratic government. Longer term alternatives require us to grasp, that is, to say yes to, useful democratic experiment wherever it occurs.

As I note above, the Occupy movement was an attempt to form Rousseau's concept of the 'general will' in new ways. As such, it was a fundamental contribution to the contemporary crisis of democracy. The Occupy movement *interrupted* the bleak routine of what Rosanvallon calls 'counter-democracy': the many ways, strengthened by social media, in which we can now undermine the reputation of politicians and undermine trust in the possibility of government. Occupy operated on at least two levels. First, it said yes to the possibility of thinking differently about the political consequences of global markets. Occupy stepped around the supposed necessity of what the markets 'say' to assert a more basic truth: that 'the economy', on whatever scale, remains our way as human beings of organizing our resources for a better life.

Amartya Sen (1987) insisted 25 years ago in his book, *On Ethics and Economics*, that we restore economics to the domain of the political and the ethical: the common pursuit of the elements of a good life. Until recently, however, this aspect of his work has had little influence outside academic circles, because to do so would require *rethinking ourselves* as political subjects and as political actors, that is, saying yes to *our* possible role in deciding how the economy should be.

Nothing could be harder than this: that is, trying to see the economy once more 'as a site of decision' (Gibson Graham, 2006, p. 87) and as a process open to democratic accountability. This, in Engin Isin's terms, requires new acts of citizenship (Isin, 2008) as well as new habits of treating ourselves, and those around us, as citizens with a valid contribution to make on how the economy *should* be run. This is where the collectives of the Occupy movement – both the permanent residents and those who visited – and their improvised educational resources, were, like the educational experiments of the Transition Town movement that began a few years earlier, important ways of 'generalizing the social', as Rosanvallon puts it. And this is the second level at which Occupy operated – bringing a different range of people into the processes through which we enact a 'social' that can represent us.

Occupy is of course only one, and not necessarily the most successful, of the attempts across the world in the past to challenge existing forms of neoliberal democracy and to offer at least glimpses of a different way of doing politics: important also, of course, have been the *Indignados* movement in Spain and the *Aganaktismenoi* movement in Greece that challenged the implementation of neoliberal reforms, and the longer history of alternative democracy movements, particularly in Latin America (surveyed in de Sousa Santos, 2005).

Such important experiments are not enough, however, unless they are recognized by government and by a significant body of citizens not directly involved. If governments and most citizens remain blind to the fact that these new processes of democratic voice are going on and require a *political* response, then they will not progress very far. That is the risk of us remaining 'voice blind': that is, blind to the wider conditions needed to sustain new and effective forms of voice.

This brings me to a final point. In developing such experiments in forming the general will, we must not be misled by false offers of collectivity. Nearly four decades ago, the geographer Henri Lefebvre wrote, in his book *The Production of Space,* of the 'mirage effect of capitalism', and the 'illusion of transparency' that capitalist spaces of exchange create. If we keep our eyes and ears fixed only within those spaces, 'real life', as he put it, 'appears [but is not really] quite close to us' (1991, p. 189). This warning is a good antidote to much of the rhetoric that surrounds today's social media platforms. The importance of these platforms in everyday habit and their role as a context for some historic moments of mobilization are not in doubt. But what is the long-term price that these platforms demand in return for the sense of immediacy they provide?

The space that we are in when on a platform such as Facebook is a space whose very design, gradients and signals are organized to one primary end – the ever more precise and continuous tracking of individual actions and choices to generate income for data collectors, content providers, platform owners and, of course, advertisers. As the most perceptive analyst of the 'revolution' under way in the digital public world, Joseph Turow, notes in his book, *The Daily You,* 'the centrality of corporate power is a direct reality at the very heart of the digital age' (2011, p. 17).

If we still, even in small part, believe in Habermas's vision of the 'public sphere' – in the positive historical reference point of the 18th century English coffee house as a place where a certain limited male elite spoke freely, and without censorship, on the basis of circulated content called 'newspapers' – then we know immediately that we live today in a radically different space of possibility. Nearly all of us – or at least

955 million of us, according to Facebook's latest figures – may be 'there' in the potential public space that social media represent, but (keeping to the metaphor of the coffee house) this is a space where every gesture we make, every sip from our coffee cup, our every movement as we scan the news, is tracked and, by being tracked, provides the basis for slightly different content, perhaps slightly different coffee, too, to be delivered to us next time – all against an ever-adapting backcloth of advertisements delivered to us wherever we go.

We need to be careful before we rush to claim that 'the people' are gathered in this or that place online. The lateral social network – the collective voicing of what appears to be, in Lefebvre's phrase, 'real life close to us' has *itself* become the main focus of meaning-production in today's emerging media industries (for related concerns see Dean, 2010; Lovink, 2012).

This complicates things as the citizens of today's nation states and world enter what is potentially an era of huge collective experiment in the forms of democracy. Such experiments will have no choice but to use social media platforms on their way to other discoveries. Thus, it is not a matter of ignoring the standard forms that everyday sociality takes, and still less of retreating from them into some realm of pure thought, but rather of judging them clear-sightedly for whether they really contribute to the development of democratic forms.

For this, I suggest we have two guides that are especially useful. First, the value of voice, which has found expression in the economic and development policy fields through the recommendations of Amartya Sen and others,[3] although much more work needs to be done. Second, as is mentioned above, the fables of the late Jose Saramago. Saramago's novel *Seeing* is double-edged. It is not just governments but all citizens who need to see clearly before them the new possibilities of voice now emerging and the tough preconditions that must be met if these possibilities are to be sustained. This transformation – this shift in our current ways of seeing and not seeing – is difficult. We may hear voices of protest, but remain voice-blind, blind to the conditions of and potentials for a wider and more sustained transformation. The challenge, as expressed by Saramago, is to end this blindness and see right in front of us the ground both of our despair and of our new experiments of hope.

Notes

1. The first part of this section draws in condensed form on the arguments in Couldry (2010, chapters 1 and 2).

2. See especially the work of Alison Pollock (2008) and Colin Leys (Player and Leys, 2011).
3. See the report of the Commission on the Measurement of Economic Performance and Social Progress (lead authors Fitoussi and Sen), http://www.stiglitz-sen-fitoussi.fr/documents/rapport_anglais.pdf, date accessed: 21 September 2009.

References

Bobbitt, P. (2003) *The Shield of Achilles: War, Peace and the Course of History* (Harmondsworth: Penguin).

Brown, W. (2005) 'Neo-liberalism and the End of Liberal Democracy' in Wendy Brown (ed.), *Edgework: Critical Essays on Knowledge and Politics* (Princeton: Princeton University Press).

Couldry, N. (2010) *Why Voice Matters: Culture and Politics After Neoliberalism* (London: Sage).

Dean, J. (2010) *Blog Theory: Feedback and Capture in the Circuits of Drive* (Cambridge: Polity Press).

Foucault, M. (2008) *The Birth of Biopolitics: Lectures at the Collège de France, 1978–1979* (Basingstoke: Palgrave Macmillan).

Gibson-Graham, J. K. (2006) *A Post-Capitalist Politics* (Minneapolis: University of Minnesota Press).

Isin, E. (2008) 'Theorizing Acts of Citizenship' in E. Isin and G. Nielsen (eds), *Acts of Citizenship* (London: Zed Books).

Lefebvre, H. (1991) *The Production of Space* (Oxford: Blackwell).

Leys, C. (2001) *Market-driven Society: Neoliberal Democracy and the Public Interest* (London: Verso).

Lovink, G. (2012) *Networks without a Cause: A Critique of Social Media* (Cambridge: Polity Press).

Player, S. and Leys, C. (2011) *The Plot against the NHS* (London: Merlin).

Pollock, A. (2008) *NHS PLC* (London: Verso).

Power, M. (1997) *The Audit Society: Rituals of Verification* (Oxford: Oxford University Press).

Rosanvallon, P. (2011) *Democratic Legitimacy: Impartiality, Reflexivity, Proximity* (Princeton: Princeton University Press).

Sabbagh, D. (2012) 'Elizabeth Murdoch Rounds on Brother in McTaggart Lecture', *The Guardian*, 23 August.

Sandel, M. (2012) *What Money Can't Buy: The Moral Limits of Markets* (London: Allen Lane).

Saramago, J. (2007) *Seeing* (New York: Vintage).

Sen, A. (1987) *On Ethics and Economics* (Blackwell: Oxford).

de Sousa Santos, B. (ed.) (2005) *Democratizing Democracy: Beyond the Liberal Democratic Canon* (London: Verso).

Turow, J. (2011) *The Daily You: How the New Advertising Industry is Defining Your Identity and Your Worth* (New Haven, CT: Yale University Press).

2
Researching and Developing *Cybercultur@*: Emerging Local Knowledge Communities in Latin America

Jorge A. Gonzalez

This chapter puts forward the concept of 'cybercultur@' (KC@) as a different and complementary approach to mainstream research on the relationship between society and technology. Mainstream approaches tend to consider digital technologies and computer-mediated communication to be the key to increasing social development in low-income countries. The KC@ approach rejects the idea that access to computers, the Internet and its content is the key to educational and social empowerment. On the contrary, initial comparative fieldwork research on experiences in Mexico and Brazil shows that information and communication technologies (ICTs) operate as knowledge platforms in a 'k'-continuum of social representations.[1] A threefold transformation can develop into a small group social organization for the enacting of an emergent local knowledge community (ELKC) as a strategy for coordinating actions (communication) and reordering their symbolic relations with their conditions (information) in order to construct new plausible relationships (knowledge) that help to confront ignorance and mystified notions of the group's social conditions. Knowledge is action. This process, when connected through adequate technology to the dynamics of other experiences of ELCKs confronting similar situations, activates another process – that of increasing empowerment linked to a network that generates emergent situated knowledge.

This chapter is divided in four sections. The first shows how a number of significant 'local' problems have a neglected 'global' dimension when looked at from a world-systems perspective. The disconnection between tough local situations and the world scale tends to mystify several cognitive *differentiations* operating in local perceptions and actions. The second part argues that technology should be understood as a *social vector*. When dealing with ICT, a missing 'K' must be added for the knowledge dimension (IC+KT). The third section delimits the Western concept of the 'public sphere' when applied to other national and regional realities in the world-system. The fourth section presents a conceptualization of *'cybercultur@'* as a different and complementary theoretical development of the current concept of cyberculture.

Global problems, local consequences, mystified conditions

Billions of people live their lives confronting and coping with serious situations just to survive: food insecurity, hunger, violence, poverty, water insecurity, drought, discrimination, ignorance, and so on. These are specific problems that can be resolved with adequate social policies and a better distribution of social energy.[2] These conditions and their costs are by no means 'natural'. Nonetheless, many people tend to take for granted that 'this is the way it is'. When understood against a backdrop considered on a world scale, there are no such things as poor countries or poor people, but only historically impoverished geo-economic zones. Within this world structure, a considerable part of the total collectively produced social energy goes to a few agents in a well-known cycle of accumulation. This process operates as a pattern of self-similarity [that is, *fractal*] at different scales, such as countries, regions and cities.

Being poor is not a natural condition but an outcome of a set of powerful relations and tensions that historically de-energize large groups of the world population, not because they are less talented or cognitively inferior, but because of their position in a set of social and historical relations. As a part of these 'misconceptions', the social representations of concrete problems tend to consider them only in quite a narrow and proximal scale. A number of strategic actions are conveyed to cope with these conditions, but the unresolved, permanent situations in everyday life push citizens in these impoverished regions to believe that it really is their individual problem. A large part of human social activity is engaged in designing strategies for re-energizing through different tactics (De Certau, 1998), confronting a deeply uneven and unfair social order enacted at all scales.

All the major problems experienced by any society, even if they appear purely 'natural' such as earthquakes, floods, epidemics and droughts, maintain a systemic relationship of *interdefinability*[3] with the type of social organization that exists to contain, overcome, heighten or avoid them (see García, 2000, p. 47). Rolando García (1981) showed how what might initially be considered 'natural disasters', such as the famine that affected the world and especially the Sahel in Africa in 1972, have geopolitical causes. By introducing a different question into his research, he concluded that 'nature pleads not guilty'. The disaster was not triggered by lack of rain. The same applies to problems with their origins in tense social coexistence in conditions of inequality and greed, such as exploitation, ignorance, war, urban violence, preventive or punitive invasions, abuse, ethnic intolerance, air and water pollution, environmental degradation, financial speculation, theft, feminicide, and so on. These are problems precisely because they have no immediate or simple solution. Solutions are considered too expensive or beyond the scope or possible space for action, and problems simply impossible to overcome or avoid.

Placed in such situations, people pay a high price: uprooting, hopelessness, marginalization, loss of rights, water and food insecurity, and death. The conception of these problems often operates as a set of cognitive negative feedback loops, because they form a kind of continuous cyclic situation with no end. All relations seem to operate as closed loops, enduring social representations (Moscovici, 2000) that give the sensation that socio-historical problems are just natural: 'Social representations are about different types of collective cognitions, common sense or thought systems of societies or groups of people. They are always related to social, cultural and/or symbolic objects, they are representations of something'. (Höijer, 2011, p. 4) The process by which structural characteristics are mistaken for personal properties is what Bourdieu termed 'social illusionism' (Accardo, 1987; Bourdieu, 1993).

The international flows of capital, people, images and information that spread all around the world put such problems in global perspective. Their amount, intensity and speed give life to and organize a *world-system* (Wallerstein, 2001; Fossaert, 2003; Taylor, 1986). With some nuances, each of these authors recommend that the study of society is explored as an integrated but contradictory whole, as a totality that is a complex set of multiple relations and processes that shape interactions and every natural disaster. Thus, we have an interesting contradiction: world scale problems, such as for example, water insecurity,[4] experienced and described as a *local*, almost *personal* situation.

One of the most effective social representations of capitalism as a world-system is the individual's lived experience of being isolated

Figure 2.1   Global water issues
Source: http://www.waterforum.jp/twj/eng/ws/index.html

and disconnected from social organization. To cope with this, people develop actions that are by no means linked to a global scale perspective. A structurally interconnected problem happening in disconnected localities, such as northeast Brazil and northern Mexico, in some cases produces similar solutions but with no related connections between them. In a way, it is a matter of poor cognitive differentiation and loose integration – that is to say, the very roots of *knowledge construction*, as Piaget (2012) so brilliantly demonstrated in his work on genetic epistemology. Differentiating/integrating information from objects are the two dialectic parts of the process of creation of human knowledge.

Technology, society and the missing 'K'

The study of the relationship between technology and society is a constant in the history of science. The very formation of the human species coincides with the invention of special tools, the utility of which was crucial for survival. These special tools served not only to accomplish a particular task, but to generate other tools. As Cirese (1984) pointed out, the ability to produce meta-instruments, that is, tools for manufacturing other tools, is uniquely human. Archaeological findings of sharp stone flakes (tools to cut with) document both the material tool and the emergence of another unique human capacity – to produce meta-languages, a special language able to 'talk' about other languages. Without this capability, which was at the same time organic, linguistic and social, it is hard to imagine how designing different angles in the carved stone adapted to different functions would be possible. Coinciding with the emergence of this two-fold process, palaeontologists have dated strong changes in the need for association, that is, the 'birth' of human society.

Technologies are not just 'tools'. They are instrumental forms of 'know-how' (Ellul, 1980). Like all knowledge processes, they also generate power (Foucault, 1979) as this knowledge is not only instrumental. Its design and its uses also involve a specific form of relating to the world. Any technology operates like a force that has an origin, an orientation and a target, and can therefore be understood as a social vector. Could it be possible to re-orientate and reuse the strength of this social force? I believe that it is.

Technology as a social vector

Using the concept of a technological vector, I would like to outline the socio-historical processes and effects of *forces-with-orientation* that have been identified in processes to do with the adoption, adaptation, imposition or rejection of technological complexes and devices between societies with resources and asymmetric and uneven positions in the unequal structure of worldwide social space. ICT cannot resolve the serious economic, political or educational problems that exist everywhere, but especially among that part of the world population that has been labelled poor.

As in everyday social life, there is a widespread overestimation of the role of ICT in society, and as a theoretical and empirical object of study. There have been multiple speculative and journalistic writings on digital and computer-mediated communication, but scarcely any interdisciplinary theoretical and field research on them as a complex and contingent objects of study. Nobody can deny that ICT and Internet technology have a key relevance in society. However, there is a missing knowledge dimension that must be related to its two inseparable relatives: information and communication. The intertwined set of information-communication-knowledge is the conceptual and methodological key to understanding the processes that forge any *symbolic ecology* (González, 2012). Neglecting the bonds with knowledge, especially within conceptual and empirical ICT research, tends to convert such technology into technologies of confusion, bewilderment, uncertainty and disorientation. By ignoring the 'K' factor, ICT operates as a powerful support for *agnogenesis*: the deliberate induction of ignorance (Proctor and Schiebinger, 2008; Sullivan and Tuana, 2007).

Knowledge is not just about accessing or handling information created and diffused by others, about others – the informational poor who – 'obviously' – cannot produce knowledge because they can only participate as objects of study. Knowledge is simultaneously a complex process of neurological, psychological and social activity that increases our capacity to differentiate and integrate the lived experience (García, 2000). This implies that knowing maximizes the power to construct and establish relations over non-relational (or previously related) experiences (Piaget, 2012). Knowledge has always been a strategic weapon for survival and increasing our quality of life. As an emergent property, it has a highly practical function, supporting an endless process of resilience. It has been, and still is, the key to breaking multiple dependencies on nature, and by weaving and constructing new relationships, it gives the power to elucidate between what is produced by social and historical conditions and what is produced by natural causes. Paraphrasing John Lennon's famous song, knowledge 'is like a warm gun',[5] and so is its crucial relation with technologies.

I am particularly interested in two of the more acute dimensions that have led to hyperbolic hopes being invested in this vector: digital technologies and the processes of computer-mediated communication. These two processes have had a large-scale diffusion and high penetration in the everyday life of contemporary societies, and worldwide initiatives are trying to include people as much as possible.[6] The advantages and potentialities of the digital form of processing, packaging, sending, receiving and collecting data are increased by instant communication through networks of computers. The access to knowledge and experience that they necessarily require for their functional operation allows the more (or less) skilful coordination and orientation of the direction and meaning of flows of all symbolic forms.

These socio-technical complexes shape a crucial part of the technological springs that trigger both the appearance and the global dispersion of a 'fourth world' – that of the excluded and disposable social agents that have been designed top-down by the system as *dumb* terminals. At the same time, however, they facilitate enormous peer-to-peer interaction out of the industrial media system:

> … the network society constitutes socialized communication beyond the mass media system that characterized industrial society. But it does not represent the world of freedom sung by the libertarian ideology of Internet prophets. It is made up both of an oligopolistic business multimedia system controlling an increasingly inclusive hypertext,

and of an explosion of horizontal networks of autonomous local/global communication – and, naturally, of the interaction between the two systems in a complex pattern of connections. (Castells and Cardoso, 2005, p. 13)

There is no *pure* periphery and no *immaculate* centre in this truly global process of social exclusion prompted by technology that, far from being mere mechanical utilities, is a constituted force with direction and multidimensional constituent effects beyond mere technique (Ellul, 1980). These aspects and nuances have scarcely been studied as radical social innovations. The technological vector is an outcome of the movement of world-scale society, but at the same time it forms and helps to produce the aberrant and unexpected social worlds that touch and progressively transform and generate multiple resistances.

This is precisely why the current unequal power structures should not be understood in terms only of a planned conspiracy organized for the domination and submission of the world by the 'evil forces of the centre'. Historically, once it takes off, technological development has generated its own laws, and its own relative autonomy and impulses, with costs and benefits that have never been enjoyed in an equitable way in world history (White, 1964). The images of the Internet as a global village, also understood as the imagined open society of information and pristine communication, where everyone can connect and have access to any kind of content, is not only a beautifully patterned graphic – it is also a myth (See Figure 2.2a and 2.2b).

Given the inequalities of world geopolitics, Figure 2.2b gives us a more nuanced picture of the social texture of the Internet. We can see a large area of 'void' zones within the patterns of the wired centres (Figure 2.2b).[7] Internet use has been growing since the beginning of the 21st century with some traits that challenge our 'traditional' view of technology appropriation and use. The processes of the appropriation and use of network facilities and services have evolved, and at first glance give us a contradictory image. Of the top ten countries for Facebook users in 2012, seven are located in the 'void' zone show in Figure 2.2b.

We are probably facing contradictions that can only be understood if we focus on the process of technological appropriation in countries that are not considered to have a strong, democratic public sphere, as is the case for many states in Latin America. 'The explosion of blogs, vlogs, podding, streaming, and other forms of interactive, computer-to-computer communication sets up a new system of global, horizontal

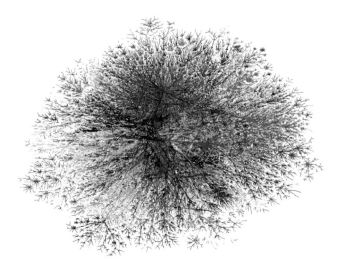

Figure 2.2a   Symmetric and fractal beauty of the Internet

Source: http://cheswick.com/ches/map/gallery/wired.gif (used by permission).

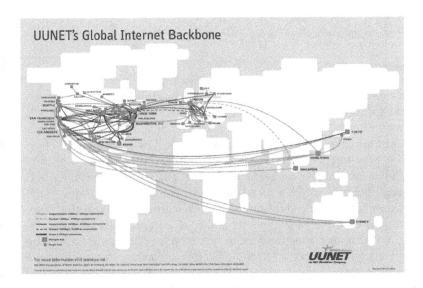

Figure 2.2b   Asymmetrical and geopolitical appearance of the Internet

Source: http://personalpages.manchester.ac.uk/staff/m.dodge/cybergeography/atlas/uunet_global_99_large.gif (used by permission).

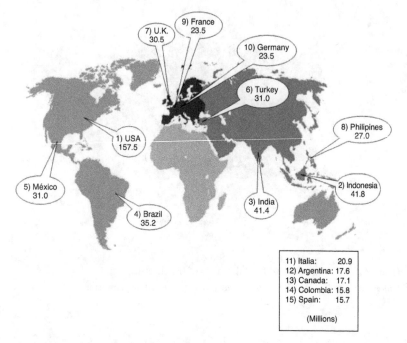

Figure 2.3 Facebook users: top ten countries in 2012

Source: Author's elaboration from: http://www.fortunecat.it/facebook-statistics/#eng.

communication networks that, for the first time in history, allow people to communicate with each other without going through the channels set up by the institutions of society for socialized communication' (Castells and Cardoso, 2005, p. 13). When, with whom, and how does this horizontal virtual communication become part of a social movement? There have been recent examples that deserve our attention.

Such movements represent the major challenges of building and imagining new 'societies' faced by people within the 'void zones' of the Middle East, Africa and Latin America. Schachtner (2012) questions how far trans-territorial public spheres can develop in Arab networks as social movements that effectively bring out diverse political views, and the role digital media played in the processes dubbed by the media as the Arab Spring.

In East Africa, Wildermuth (2011) has developed the outline of a theoretical critique of simplified conceptualizations of 'ICT for development', based on the findings of his empirical field research carried out in Nairobi between the autumn of 2009 and the spring of 2011. He focuses on the role of digital network media, both mobile and online, in facilitating the empowerment and social inclusion of excluded Kenyan youth.[8] In Mexico, Galindo and González-Acosta (2013) have undertaken a unique field research analysis of the '#YO_SOY_132' movement, an 'aesthetic community' that challenged the usual demonstrations against electoral fraud during the most recent Mexican presidential election in 2012.[9]

From a broader perspective, Castells (2012) has studied the protests of the Arab Spring, the 'Indignados' in Spain, and the Occupy Wall Street movements, providing interesting chronologies and connecting those uprisings with other social protests 'powered' by ICT. A number of new social uses of technologies by social movements are demonstrating the complex dynamics of use and appropriation to power social protest at an increasing global scale.

The public sphere from the perspective of geopolitics

The concept of the public sphere comes from the European liberal tradition of the 19th century. It makes a neat distinction between private and public life in so-called modern societies. In ideal terms, as Habermas (1989) stated, the public sphere is a space where citizens get together to discuss common problems in their own society, and through that discussion open up opportunities to correct or criticize political actions by public authorities. According to Odugbemi (2008), the process that occurs between the private sphere made up of citizens, households and firms, on the one hand, and the institutional powers of any state, on the other, models public opinion as a trait of what he calls the national democratic public sphere. Several criticisms must be made, however, of such a clean and colonial notion of the public, which excludes the colonized and women, among others (Fraser, 1990).

The distinction between private and public is no longer – and arguably never has been – universally valid (Hardt and Negri, 2009). Issues of ethnocentrism, andro-centrism and socio-centrism have undermined such a clear separation (González, 2012, pp. 233–235). Discussion of social policies and social issues of coexistence are at the core of the public sphere, but in many countries, people still have a long way to go to reach the status of citizens. Even in so-called liberal democracies, citizens experience problems and limitations in various ways. Discrimination is not a legacy of underdeveloped countries and nation states.

Couldry (2010) highlights the importance of voice as a key strategy of resisting neoliberalism and constructing another possible world based on ordinary people speaking out and being heard on what affects their own lives:

> I offer 'voice' as a connecting term that interrupts neoliberalism's view of economics and economic life, challenges neoliberalism's claim that its view of politics as market functioning trumps all others, enables us to build an alternative view of politics that is at least partly oriented to valuing processes of voice, and includes within that view of politics a recognition of people's capacities for social cooperation based on voice. (p. 2)

Indeed, voice matters – especially of those who historically have been silenced and neglected. In many impoverished countries, the prerequisites for having the ideal model of a democratic public sphere are found wanting. Neoliberal capitalism and democracy seems to be an oxymoron. We need to re-weave the social tissue in order for more diverse voices to be heard.

The geopolitical system of 'distributed ignorance' helps to perpetuate the social but assumed condition of people's 'self-perception' as objects, or subjected subjects. A lack of differentiation and weak integration mean not knowing, and thus, given the current state and historical distribution of the capacity to generate knowledge, distributed ignorance.

Figure 2.4 Geopolitical map of scientific collaborations
Source: http://olihb.com/wp-content/uploads/2011/01/collabo_links-medium.jpg.

If we take a closer look at the map of worldwide scientific collaborations made by Olivier Beauchesne,[10] the issue of a global missing
'K' stands out more clearly (see Figure 2.4). The shape drawn by the
relationships, and the flows of capital, people, information and images
of the world-system seems to be consistent with the image of scientific collaboration. Very few peripheral regions of the world are in a
position to generate and exchange scientific knowledge. At the same
time, billions of people are not considered citizens with rights, duties
and voices coming from the bottom-up that allow them to confront
ignorance and develop first local, and then, situated knowledge. This is
precisely the aim of KC@.

KC@ as an object of study of value for development and social empowerment

In parallel with current conceptions of cyberculture (Levy, 2001;
Piscitelli, 2002; Galindo, 2005, 2006),[11] and without ignoring the relevance of the intense transformation of global cultural dynamics that
is currently happening, I propose a step back in order to conceptualize
the process. From this vantage point, the meaning of KC@ is not necessarily related to the universe of computers and the Internet. Instead, I
emphasize three meanings in my composite neologism: the Greek prefix
'Κψβερ' (cyber), the Latin word *'cultur'*, and, analogically, the spiral form
of the sign '@'.

First, I take from the word 'Kyber' the original meaning of *driver*,
because developing KC@ means generating, increasing, perfecting,
improving and sharing the ability to steer, direct and govern, from this
root, and to 'pilot' social relations in an exercise of collective, horizontal
and participative self-steering. In other words, *cyber* has nothing to do
with computers. It is the media and science fiction that have linked
computers to the word.

Second, I take the original agricultural meaning of *culture*, understood
as the action of cultivation, of taking care of, paying attention to, and
motivating transformations from the soil. The first junction between
Kyber and *Cultur* highlights the ability to govern ourselves and to journey
with others towards more intelligent solutions, and face the huge challenges of the 21st century. KC@ makes it possible to learn, share and
cultivate with others and for others.

Third, the sign '@', in place of a simple 'e', has today become familiar
to e-mail and twitter users. It is precisely for its graphical similarity to the
helicoid, a three dimensional spiral, that I use the sign '@' to represent a

positive feedback loop – an open and adaptable process that generates a range of emergent answers which arise from the density of relations in a system that cannot be reduced to the sum of its parts. This is precisely the meaning of intelligence, as an emergent capacity to solve problems using the intellect.

Against this backdrop, I propose the neologism *cybercultur@* to mean a series of specific processes that imply two complementary and simultaneous qualities: first, KC@ understood as an *object of study*; and, second, KC@ understood as a *value for development* and social empowerment (González, 2003).

Cybercultur@ as an object of study

As an object of analysis, cybercultur@ means the study of complex phenomena at the social, historical, symbolic and contextual levels than can be described, analysed and explained by multi-level processes of relations between the *symbolic ecologies* of specific societies and their *technological vectors*.

By the notion of *symbolic ecologies* I mean the total set of relations of meaning that is constructed in every specific society throughout history, in physical, biological, psychological, social and cultural environments, through cognitive activity in its more complex dimensions, such as the mind, speech and the modelling and adaptive activity of social identities. This vast cognitive and symbolic dimension can only be generated as an emergent process from a kind of *ecosystem of material support* that make possible the activity of symbolic representation in any society. Without it, the efficacy of culture in the construction of identities, the reproduction of society, and the establishment of traditions and avant-garde movements would be unthinkable. The human species is unique in that, in addition to the satisfaction of material needs, such as for water, food, clothes and shelter, it *must* generate a meaningful 'second nature' in order to survive. Composite simple and complex signs, texts and discourses shape this human interpretative activity.

For this reason, *the history of the material ecosystems of culture* must be understood in relation to the *history of the generation of its audiences*, that is, the *history of the social distribution of the cognitive dispositions* operating in those ecosystems. The concept of *symbolic ecologies* accounts for both *systemic forms* (structured and ordered) and *enactive forms* (in structuring processes) of 'signicity' (*segnicitá*), as defined by Cirese (1984) from Italian cultural anthropology.

I am interested in the intense interrelation between meaning, norms and power from the perspective of the societies that have been removed or excluded from the social space, which means that they have been – or are a being – economically *exploited*, politically *dominated* and culturally *directed*. Excluded from the beginning from the benefits of globalization, enormous and dispersed social sectors have been globalized by misery and degradation, and have become 'the black holes of informational capitalism' (Castells, 2010). The proposed perspective implies intense work on describing, analysing and explaining the social and historical processes of the genesis and development of the symbolic modulations of the relation between the two dimensions outlined above. It is crucial to harness any scientific development that, besides interpreting and theorizing the social world, looks to *transform that world* in order to empower the numerous depressed social sectors.[12]

This first meaning of *KC@*, as an object of study, makes several assumptions. First, on a wider scale, we depart from a *cognitive complex* characterized by the inequality of the structure of relations in the world-system, in which we can observe many vast multi-distributed zones of the planet, historically colonized and impoverished by social relations of exploitation, domination and exclusion, that nourish and provide social energy (capital) to different cities that operate as *attractors*. These 'city nodes' of the world-system, in addition to the concentration of immense volumes of capital, increasingly concentrate or attract millions of people, some poor and others not *so* poor,[13] who migrate to such nodes for a better life. At the same time, these special cities also operate like producers and massive diffusers of permanent and global flows of technologically mediated information and images that serve as basic raw material for metabolizing and representing the world: that is, who is who, and how various actors become visible or invisible in the arena of public life (Thompson, 2005).

These processes of discursive and symbolic elaboration are indispensable both for narrating the threads and communicating the *value* and meaning of landmarks of social memory, definitions of the current situation, and the feasibility and density of other *possible worlds*. With and from these symbolic processes, relations are established, contested and transformed in history. These are social relations of hegemony, subalternity and alterity with many sorts of resistance. In some cases, counter-hegemonic projects emerge along with new relations that require and generate new forms of organization of symbolic strategies to modulate the social discourse and steer the intellectual and moral direction of society, as Gramsci (1994) illustrated so well.

KC@ as value for development

The second meaning of KC@, as a strategy for development, is a form of empowerment that, as is stated above, engages on three strategic fronts: information, knowledge and the ability to create networks of action to use the information and knowledge in specific projects. KC@ does not just mean intensive and uncritical use of computers and digital technologies, nor should these technologies be politically or ideologically rejected because of their 'central' or 'northern' origin.

To develop KC@ means, instead, to enact the capacity for building and using dialogically every technique submitted for social reflexivity, built and shared within horizontal networks. These issues arise once we enter into processes of distributed intelligence in constant movement and growth. It is a strategy through which it is possible to design and generate dialogic and mobilizing knowledge. It is complex because it requires a high degree of interaction, processes and feedback. These features force us to use and design an interdisciplinary meta-language, especially open to cognitive sciences and complex system-thinking.

To develop KC@ really means redesigning collectively – and from the bottom up – a different attitude to and way of relating to technology and social problems. This change is based on the incorporation of precise and transferable skills and dispositions, which allow participants to operate intelligently by mastering and using any kind of technology. In this way, it is possible to address information needs, to generate and evaluate knowledge and to coordinate communication actions that can break the vicious circle of technological dependence and subaltern representations that conform to symbolic ecologies. Developing KC@ requires a complex communication strategy from the 'periphery' of the world-system that aims to break the vicious circle of technological dependence. It will entail a coordinated effort to reweave the unbalanced social bonds.

Investigating KC@ means focusing attention on the structures and processes that have occurred, are occurring and could occur between the socio-historical specificity of our symbolic ecologies and the technological vector. A kind of negative feedback loop has been created where top-down imposed policies and ICTs generate limited and disconnected information about unresolvable social problems linked to fixed representations or memes. These memes operate pretty well and function according to technology policies, and so on. Developing KC@ creates a positive feedback loop that brings the 'k' factor to the uses of digital technologies and computer-mediated communications. The aim is the creation of local knowledge. Once this has been generated, possible connections with other ELKCs coping with global situations open the door to the creation of situated knowledge from the bottom up.

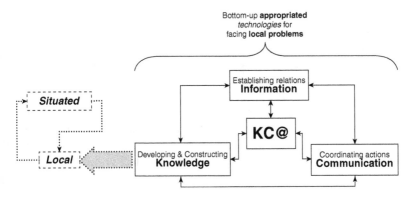

Figure 2.5   Positive feedback loop between problems and their representation
Source: Author's personal elaboration.

Last words, first experiences: new questions and open horizons

I propose the framework of KC@ as a tool to develop self-determined answers to and actions on relevant problems by means of collective intelligence. Its immediate outcome is the formation of an emergent local knowledge community. A strategy to counter designed and assumed isolation is combined with ways to creatively confront *agnogenesis* – ignorance of, and indifference about, communitarian problems.

In the San Luis Potosi highlands, in the middle of the Great Desert of Chihuahua, México, several initiatives have been launched in both the city and the countryside arising from a small number of KC@ workshops. Charcas is the name of both a municipality and a mining city, founded in 1567 after the discovery of gold and silver. Since then, mining activity has not ceased. Immense riches have flowed for almost five centuries, first to Spain and Europe and now to large corporate Canadian mining companies. Unfortunately, none of these riches have stayed in Charcas. A number of problems directly linked to mining and the semi-arid weather, combined with social decomposition, have created a location for the activities of 'the Zetas' drug cartel.

Critical situations such as water insecurity, pollution, public health problems, alcoholism, migration and drug violence, among others, began to be acknowledged, explored and documented by an ELKC. It is composed of a variety of people, by age, gender, social condition and profession, and its members have chosen the name La otra Min@ de

Charcas,[14] a 'very different mine' in which the knowledge produced belongs to and is used by all Charquenses. Several other initiatives have emerged: rural cooperatives to breed goats and build an organic cheese factory at Tinajuelas,[15] cultural animation organizations (Charcas en Escena)[16] and workshops on human rights, gender and other issues decided and documented by Charquenses.

Five years of continual facilitation work have produced interesting initiatives since the expected creation of local knowledge began in January 2007. By October 2010, it was time to try to connect with others who experience similar conditions. The semi-arid regions of Brazil, especially the Polo da Borborema,[17] were selected for initial comparison. Strategically selected, these two cases are both semi-arid zones. Whereas Charcas could be seen to have zero or a negative degree of organization, Borborema has more than 30 years of experience of mobilizing for its rights and demanding respect for productive organization. The outcomes of long-standing processes of resistance and mobilization have created sustainable and efficient organization and a clear political position.

We are just at the beginning of this second order task of facilitating a weave of networks of ELKCs as a material way to generate shared and situated knowledge. This is a kind of knowledge that is always based on local knowledge, but enriched by an extended scale that emerges by sharing diverse local knowledge with other ELKCs. In so doing, KC@ activates agents who can take the next step forward, that is, reconsidering their own ways of using IC+KTs, which means the appropriation of complex tools for generating and organizing information, and a serious transformation of their initial cultures and ecologies of information. Only by transforming their own cultures of *Information (I), Communication (C) and Knowledge (@)* can the process of intelligent appropriation of technology become possible. This means redirecting the orientation and targeting of the technological vector, and, finally, enacting the transformation of their symbolic ecologies. This is the aim of the initial comparative research that has been undertaken and will be carried out in the future

The people will decide what their approach will be to digital technologies and computer-mediated communication, as well as how, where and when – not only for 'consulting' content or accessing accumulated knowledge, but also to be able to re-narrate their past, rebuild their memory and relocate their current conditions, and finally to be able to redefine other possible connected dialogical and 'better' worlds.

Notes

1. The continuous but non-linear interplay between *ignorance, local* knowledge and *situated* knowledge.
2. Social energy, understood as the force that is generated in social relations. The structural configuration of these relationships 'designs', that is, produces, distributes and consumes, the bodies and minds of social actors and even their scenarios, scripts and issues of social life. See Bertaux (1977).
3. A concept from Propositional Logic in which each term is mutually defined by its relationship with the others.
4. For Grey and Sadoff (2007), water security is 'the reliable availability of an acceptable quantity and quality of water for health, livelihoods and production, coupled with an acceptable level of water-related risks'.
5. Lennon, J. (1968) 'Happiness is a warm gun'. *The Beatles* (London: Apple Records).
6. That is, for instance, the aim of the World Summit on Information Society, http://www.itu.int/wsis/index.html.
7. More recent maps are not available, but both images were produced in the same period (1999–2000).
8. The study, which is part of the Danish-East African MEDIeA (Media, Empowerment and Democracy in Eastern Africa) research project, seeks to develop a comparative, contextual understanding of the dialectical relation between the two dominant dimensions of digital media appropriation that are observable.
9. Immanuel Wallerstein (2011) also looks at this kind of unexpected and emergent mobilization, analysed as part of the World-System crises, stating that the Occupy Wall Street movement should be considered 'the most important political happening in the United States since the uprisings in 1968'. Crisis is everywhere, not only in the world 'periphery'.
10. An amazing work of geovisualization by Beauchesne, http://olihb.com/2011/01/23/map-of-scientific-collaboration-between-researchers/, accessed February 2013 and used by permission.
11. Different authors conceptualize – with some nuances – *cyberculture* as a new modulation of contemporary culture linked to digital technologies and telecommunication networks, the site of *cyberspace*. Galindo (2006) offers an analytical and critical perspective tracing the conceptual space of the neologism, which was originally coined in literature.
12. 'The philosophers have only interpreted the world, in various ways: the point is to change it', Karl Marx, 11th *Thesis on Feuerbach*, http://www.marxists.org/archive/marx/works/1845/theses/theses.htm, accessed February 2013.
13. The existing excess of cheap and unskilled handwork with little 'cosmopolitism' that has historically moved in migrant flows by means of forced 'globalization' has been 'enriched' by the flight of 'qualified professionals', either unemployed or with grim wealth expectations, from their original countries, as documented by the 'educated' migration from Ecuador and other Latin American countries to Spain and to Europe in general (Pellegrino, 2004).

14. Initially, a blog was created as an instrument of coordination (http://laotramina.blogspot.mx/) but slowly Facebook and other resources were used (http://www.youtube.com/watch?v=bFotxgE7g-Q). Bicycle parades are a recent mechanism for contacting and sharing several aspects of the knowledge creation process with the inhabitants of Charcas, as in the case of 'unseen' river pollution. At the same time, however, this tactic operates as a part of a strategy for recovering the public space abandoned because of fear of 'halcones', young Charquenses recruited by the Zetas as enforcers and local informants.
15. With almost no way to overcome poverty in rural areas, for instance, half the population of Charcas survives deep in poverty; the formation of a cooperative began to give good results in several areas, see: http://www.youtube.com/watch?v=Tc_O7GNaoL8
16. http://www.diariodelaltiplano.com/index.php?option=com_k2&view=item&id=551:charcas-en-escena-guerreros-en-combate-sigue-promoviendo-eventos&Itemid=561. Check the campaign organized by 'Charcas en escena' at: http://www.youtube.com/watch?v=yOHRX-HWrV8
17. In a semi-arid zone of the state of Paraíba, a social organization of farmers has been attempting to adapt to the environment with a clear political position against mono-crops, agro toxins, chemical poisons and intensive agriculture. See http://www.agriculturesnetwork.org/magazines/latin-america/4-experiencias-que-duran/polo-de-borborema-las-redes-de-experimentadores-se

References

Accardo, A. (1987) *Initiation à la sociologie de l'illusionisme social: Invitation à la lecture des oeuvres de Pierre Bourdieu* (Bordeaux: Le Mascaret).
Bertaux, D. (1977) *Destins personneles et structure de classes. Pour une critique de l'anthroponomie politique* (Paris: Presses Universitaires de France).
Bourdieu, P. (1993) *El sentido práctico* (Madrid: Taurus).
Castells, M. and Cardoso, G. (eds) (2005) *The Network Society: From Knowledge to Policy* (Washington, DC: Johns Hopkins Center for Transatlantic Relations).
Castells, M. (2010) *The Information Age: Economy, Society and Culture, Volume III: End of Millennium* (New York: Willey-Blackwell).
Castells, M. (2012) *Networks of Outrage and Hope. Social Movements in the Internet Age* (Cambridge: Polity Press).
Cirese, A. M. (1984) *Fabrilitá, Segnicitá, Procreazione: Appunti Etnoantropologici* (Roma: CISU).
Couldry, N. (2010) *Why Voice Matters: Culture and Politics After Neoliberalism* (London: Sage).
De Certau, M. (1998) *La Invención de lo Cotidiano* (México: Universidad Iberoamericana).
Ellul, J. (1980) *The Technological System* (New York: Continuum).
Fossaert, R. (2003) *El mundo en el siglo XXI: Una teoría de los sistemas mundiales* (México: Siglo XXI).
Foucault, M. (1979) *Microfisica del Poder* (Buenos Aires: La Piqueta).
Fraser, N. (1990) 'Rethinking the Public Sphere: A Contribution to the Critique of Actually Existing Democracy', *Social Text* 25(26), pp. 56–80.

Galindo, J. (2005) 'Fuentes conceptuales de la cibercultura' en *Cuadernos de Patrimonio Cultural y Turismo* 11 (México: CONACULTA).

Galindo, J. (2006) *Cibercultura: un mundo emergente y una nueva mirada* (Toluca: CONACULTA-Instituto Mexiquense de Cultura).

Galindo, J. and González-Acosta, J. I. (2013) *#Yosoy 132: La primera erupción visible* (México: Global Talent University Press).

Garcia, R. (1981) *Drought and Man: Nature Pleads Not Guilty* (London: Pergamon Press).

Garcia, R. (2000) *El Conocimiento en Construcción: De las Formulaciones de Jean Piaget a la Teoría de los Sistemas Complejos* (Barcelona: Gedisa).

González, J. A. (2003) *Cultura(s) y Cibercultur@(s): Incursiones no Lineales entre Complejidad y Comunicación* (México: Universidad Iberoamericana).

González, J. A. (2012) *Entre Cultura(s) e Cibercultur@(s): Incursões e Outras Rotas não Lineares* (São Paulo: Universidade Metodista de São Paulo).

Gramsci, A. (1994) *Letters from Prison* (New York: Columbia University Press).

Grey, D. and Sadoff, C. (2007) 'Sink or Swim? Water Security for Growth and Development', *Water Policy* 9(6), pp. 545–571.

Habermas, J. (1989) *The Structural Transformation of the Public Sphere: An Inquiry into a Category of Bourgeois Society* (Cambridge, Mass: MIT Press).

Hardt, M. and Negri, A. (2009) *Commonwealth* (Cambridge, Mass: Harvard University Press).

Hoijer, B. (2011) 'Social Representations Theory: A New Theory for Media Research', *Nordicom Review* 32(2), pp. 3–16.

Levy, P. (2001) *Cyberculture* (Minneapolis: University of Minnesota Press).

Moscovici, S. (2000) *Social Representations. Explorations in Social Psychology* (Cambridge, UK: Polity Press).

Odugbemi, A. (2008) 'Public Opinion, the Public Sphere and Quality of Governance: An Exploration' in S. Odugbemi and T. Jacobson (eds), *Governance Reform Under Real-world Conditions: Citizens, Stakeholders and Voice* (Washington, DC: World Bank).

Pellegrino, A. (2004) *Migration from Latin America to Europe: Trends and Policy Challenges* (Gêneve: International Organization for Migration).

Piaget, J. (2012) *La equilibración de las estructuras cognitivas: Problema central del desarrollo* (México: Siglo XXI).

Piscitelli, A. (2002) *Ciberculturas 2.0: En la era de las máquinas inteligentes* (Buenos Aires: Editorial Paidós).

Proctor, R. N. and Schiebinger, L. (eds) (2008) *Agnotology: The Making and Unmaking of Ignorance* (Stanford: Stanford University Press).

Schachtner, C. (2012) 'Social Movements and Digital Media: Trans-territorial Online Public Spheres in the Middle East and North Africa', paper presented to the International Sociological Association Research Committee Futures Research (RC07), Buenos Aires.

Sullivan, S. and Tuana, N. (eds) (2007) *Race and Epistemologies of Ignorance* (Albany: State University of New York Press).

Taylor, P. (1986) *Modernities: A Geohistorical Interpretation* (London: Polity Press).

Thompson, John B. (2005) 'The New Visibility', *Theory, Culture & Society* 22(6), pp. 31–51.

Wallerstein, I. (2001) *Geopolítics and Geoculture: Essays on the Modern World-System* (Cambridge/Paris: Cambridge University Press and Maisson des Sciences dell' Homme).

Wallerstein, I. (2011) 'The Fantastic Success of Occupy Wall Street', http://www.iwallerstein.com/fantastic-success-occupy-wall-street/, accessed 1 February 2013.

White, L. (1964) *Medieval Technology and Social Change* (Oxford: Oxford University Press).

Wildermuth, N. (2011) 'Digital empowerment beyond ICT4D', paper presented at *Ørecomm Festival, 2011*, 9–13 September, Malmö, Copenhagen, Roskilde.

3
Advocacy Communication for and about Women

Karin Gwinn Wilkins

Advocacy communication builds on a critical understanding of the public sphere, not as an idealized pluralistic space, but as a site for struggle and resistance. Based on the understanding that power dynamics facilitate different potentials for domination and resistance, strategic advocacy builds on multiple sources of capital, including human, social and cultural, as well as financial and political resources. Academic work on development and social change is beginning to incorporate the need to pay attention to social and political movements as they compete for attention and work to change leadership and policies and to motivate people. At the heart of this approach to intervention is recognition that social justice is central to development work. This chapter connects advocacy communication in development and social change to emerging frameworks in the public sphere. After a theoretical exposition, I explore how this approach works in relation to advocating both for and about women's rights in the global development industry.

Advocacy communication in development

Advocacy communication builds on a critical history of approaches in the fields of development, social change and social movements, using strategic communication to offer alternative discourses to a dominant position, to mobilize action against dominant agencies, and to promote structural and normative change. Historically, development communication can be seen as using communication *for* development, by developing messages and building media infrastructure, as well as understanding communication *about* development, with the emergence of more critical considerations of discourse and praxis (Escobar, 1995; Wilkins, 2008a; Wilkins and Mody, 2001).

Most work in the field of development focuses on using communication for development (Gumucio-Dagron and Tufte, 2006; McAnany, 2012). Evaluations of social marketing and entertainment-education projects, for example, have drawn attention to the potential for media to change the knowledge, attitudes and practices (KAP) of individuals, when sufficiently motivated to do so. These projects have been somewhat varied in terms of their effects, depending on the resonance of the issue with the target community, the quality of the project, the political commitment of agencies and communities, and the funding levels from donors (Hornik, 1988; Snyder, 2002). However, these approaches have maintained their focus on individuals as a central locus for social change, at the expense of understanding the cultural, political, and economic contexts that guide and constrain individual action (Wilkins, 2000).

Advocacy communication balances an interest in participatory communication with recognition that political and economic conditions are constraints on engaging in dialogue and activating resistance (Wilkins, 2011). Concerned with a dialogic approach (Freire, 1983), collective engagement is a central part of a mobilization process in which communities consider how best to position their arguments against competing rhetoric. Dominant groups may be able to build ideological consent, in part through their control of finances, media industries and political elites (Herman and Chomsky, 1988), against which social movements must work.

Communication is not isolated as an individual response or a dyadic exchange, but understood as a social and political act. As a collective enterprise, communication becomes a strategic effort to engage in structural and normative change to benefit marginalized and oppressed communities. Normative change involves creating a climate conducive to shifting the specific attitudes relevant to the strategic intervention, as well as ideas about potential self- and collective efficacy. Attitudes might need to change gradually in ways that support the intended goals and reduce the constraints on meeting them. Moreover, people need to believe that there is the potential to create change in existing policies in order to activate the energy and resources to motivate participation in their struggle. Structural change means creating beneficial policies and decisions within the organizations and governments that structure actions. Changing the rules of the game at these levels of power is critical in order to create more equitable and just playing fields (Wilkins, 2000).

These goals serve a social justice orientation (Melkote, 2012), conceptualizing communication as a dialogic process, facilitating praxis and combining thoughtful reflection with informed action (Freire, 1983). Communication is not perceived as limited to a hierarchical diffusion of information, or within horizontal connections across communities, but instead as facilitating activist strategies. Communication therefore represents a social and political process of creating and asserting meaning in a particular historical context, in which access to resources affords some groups more power than others to assert their voices (Enghel and Wilkins, 2012).

Communication promotes advocacy in support of a particular political cause. Advocacy focuses our attention on strategic programmes that attempt to change policies, by mobilizing direct support as well as shifting indirect normative social support. Servaes and Malikhao (2012) describe advocacy as a 'key term in development discourse', aiming 'to foster public policies that are supportive to the solution of an issue or programme' (Servaes and Malikhao, 2012, p. 229). Focusing on entertainment-education, Tufte (2012, p. 92) calls for these strategies to supplement individual behaviour change approaches 'to advocate for social change…in order to find solutions'. Advocacy communication engages in strategic intervention with clear political positions, having no pretence to neutrality, but valuing social justice.

While advocacy communication engages with politics explicitly, the history of the field demonstrates that communication about development often attempts to 'depoliticize' the work of development institutions (Dutta, 2011; Sparks, 2011) in order to justify limited approaches to social change that do little to question the underlying processes that perpetuate inequities. Critical scholars connect these inequities to global capitalism, as a comprehensive system that dominates economic exchange and supplies ideological narratives that glorify individual consumption and imply benign free markets (Mattelart, 2011). In US-based development approaches, capitalism becomes conflated with approaches to democracy in ways that guide quests for modernization (Shah, 2011).

Global development is perpetuating global capitalism by relying on a neoliberal logic (Richey and Ponte, 2011). As Dutta explains, neoliberalism serves as

> an economic principle that constitutes the opening up of global markets to corporations that operate across the boundaries of nation states, the minimization of state interventions in the operation of the market, and the increasing privatization of public sectors that are brought under the framework of the free market logic. Markets and privatization are assumed to be the natural order. (2011, p. 86)

Neoliberalism flows through development support for the privatization of systems and partnerships with corporate donors. Bilateral and multilateral development agencies, funded by governments increasingly affected by economic crisis, applaud these corporate partnerships, promoting the idea that private aid can substitute for the state's responsibility to address collective needs, even though Official Development Assistance from donor countries still funds proportionately more global development work (Kremer et al., 2010). Privatization is supported when bilateral programmes, such as USAID, work to open up markets for investment (Dutta, 2011, p. 47) or multilateral agencies, such as the World Bank, push for structural adjustment programmes that marginalize those with fewer resources (Dutta, 2011, pp. 59, 119). Farmers' suicides in India, for example, have been traced to the commercialization of agriculture making it difficult for smaller producers to repay bank loans (Sainath, 2012). The agricultural industry is ripe with examples of rhetorical positions that assert corporate control over the Earth as an inevitable manifestation of a market economy (Murphy, 2011).

Within a hegemonic model of social change, there is room for resistance against dominant agencies and rhetorical positions. Working for social justice builds on the recognition of differences in power (Willis et al., 2008). While elite groups may attempt to control communication as a way to maintain their dominance in a global capitalist context, the dialectics of communicative practices allow the possibility of advocacy.

There are several ways in which communication might facilitate advocacy. Communication can be used to encourage recognition of problems and potential solutions by those engaged in the collective effort, as well as those being targeted, such as public constituencies or policymakers. In addition to educating and mobilizing, communication sites can serve as a venue in which groups contest interpretations of problems and proposed solutions. In contrast to a pluralist approach to communication, advocacy communication recognizes that differences in access to resources create spaces in which some groups have more power than others to assert their perspectives. Working within a hegemonic process, advocacy communication provides the potential to negotiate and work towards changing conditions for the public good. This understanding of social change is predicated on a critical framework of the public sphere.

Advocacy communication in the public sphere

Advocacy communication privileges political issues as central to collective engagement in social change. As a political enterprise, this framework cannot rely on an overly idealized and pluralist vision of a public sphere in which all agents have equal access and ability to voice their perspectives. To consider how best to work within a public sphere model, advocacy for and about development builds on critical approaches.

Although classic Habermasian descriptions of the public sphere emphasize dialogue, the assumption that rational discussion is made possible by being inclusive and free from coercion is overly idealistic. Realistically, we recognize that not all are able to participate and those who do are not all conversing freely or on equal terms (Dutta, 2011). Sparks (2011) agrees, raising an additional concern – that Habermas's model of public sphere engagement makes unrealistic claims to universality of rationality. Many scholars of communication and politics have criticized these idealized public sphere visions for their simplistic assumptions about pluralism and universal rationality.

A critical vision of the public sphere recognizes the importance of structure in creating possibilities and challenges for civic engagement. Within political and economic structures, we need to understand the social and cultural contexts in which people actively voice their perspectives (Williams and Delli Carpini, 2011). Couldry, Livingstone and Markham (2010) illustrate how public connection is necessary to enable thoughtful and active participation in the public sphere, but – depending on social and structural conditions – not always present.

Civic engagement need not only refer to formal structures that perpetuate political systems – it can attempt to change these structures or work separately from them. Engaging in the politics of our communities may not work within a formal governance structure, particularly when the leadership has lost its legitimacy with citizens. Including social and political movements as part of the public sphere therefore means that we are talking not just about voting, but about more broadly based acts of strategic engagement (Downing, 2011; Huesca, 2001; Stein et al., 2009).

Advocacy communication contributes to communication for social change by building on an emerging framework of the public sphere that recognizes conflict as part of political negotiation. Recognizing the value of dialogue in fostering a sense of collective responsibility, highlighted in the Habermasian public sphere, our critical approach also understands the potential for this idealized sphere to be limited to an elite group. Dialogue can be understood as not confined to the conversations of this group, but facilitated through the labour of those who service the coffeehouses, digital websites and other communicative spaces, with the volume and translation of these discussions contingent on the relative power of those articulating their agendas (Maxwell and Miller, 2012). An emerging sense of public sphere must understand the context in which people are enabled to participate, including issues such as labour to create public venues in mediated space and geographical territories, and to access dialogic venues.

Instead of seeing political participation as limited to individual acts of voting within a defined system of governance, political expression and action are engaged in the particular contexts in which groups struggle to advance their agendas. In keeping with the approach of this volume, instead of focusing on strategic communication interventions funded through Western development institutions, advocacy communication extends its attention to broader forms of participation, such as protest and resistance.

To illustrate how communication can work for and around advocacy through a critical understanding of the public sphere, I focus on development programmes working to promote women's rights. The programmes focused on below attempt to engage in structural and normative change, which are central to advocacy, and recognize that the contexts of engagement do not begin with equality among participants. These programmes resonate more closely with approaches in Gender and Development and the concerns raised through feminist analyses of development work. Historically, development programmes concerned with Women in Development have privileged individual women as the locus for social change, emphasizing strategic interventions to promote family planning, nutrition and health (Wilkins, 1997). While these efforts are important for promoting healthy decisions that affect the well-being of families, other programmes attempt to raise standards of living through the development of technical skills and economic resources, and to promote political rights and recognize gender inequities. Feminist critiques of post-colonial work (Mohanty, 1991) highlight the problematic assumption that all women's issues are the same across cultural and economic positions: a concern similar to the assumed universal rationality of the Habermasian public sphere. Recognizing the cultural contexts of gender dynamics draws us to those programmes that promote changes in policies and attitudes through advocacy communication.

Advocacy communication for and about women's rights

Advocacy communication engages with strategic programmes that work to promote women's rights as human rights, as well as alternative discourses that see gender inequity as a matter of social justice.

Communication can be used for social justice by engaging in strategic intervention, and recognizing challenges in an existing discourse about gender. This section explores the ways in which organizations attempt to advocate on behalf of women's rights.

The development industry has tackled women's and gender issues in quite disparate ways over time, after ignoring women's contributions as active agents in communities for decades before the Decade for Women in the 1970s (Cardinal et al., 1994; Dagenais and Piché, 1994; Wilkins, 1997; Wilkins, 2005). Attention to women's issues and gender concerns is currently integral to the global discourse promoted by dominant development institutions, through their articulation of the global Millennium Development Goals (UN, 2010). Among other concerns, these goals focus on reducing maternal mortality, achieving universal access to reproductive health services, and improving rates of female participation in formal education, paid employment and elected office. While attention to women in development is valuable, concerns about gender highlight the ways in which programmes articulate problematic assumptions about women and men in society.

Feminist critiques of mainstream development enterprises highlight the patriarchal nature of a discourse that privileges men's roles over those of women (Wilkins, 2007). Part of the problem lies in development approaches that subjugate women as passive targets of strategic communication campaigns, constructed as participants only when contributions are valued in the service of imperialism, patriarchy and capitalism. For imperialism, women become prominently part of the justification for military intervention in their role as victims in need of a saviour. For patriarchy, women are targeted in population and nutrition programmes as conduits for reproducing and feeding new generations. For capitalism, women are relegated to small-scale entrepreneurial micro-lending schemes within the confines of the capitalist market. Critical discourse analysis highlights these problematic visions of gender, which harm both men and women in their articulation of narrow roles for civic engagement. Given this concern with communication about gender dynamics, programmes that attempt to shift the discourse on gendered roles in political participation are crucial to a comprehensive advocacy strategy.

Many different donors claim to be advocating on behalf of women, but do so with quite different understandings of gender and power. Donors involved in these efforts range from the better-funded bilateral and multilateral agencies to non-governmental organizations (NGOs), civil society organizations (CSOs) and other collective movements. Brief descriptions of some of these agencies help to illustrate the variety of ways in which organizations articulate their work promoting women's rights.

Funding bilateral development, the US Agency for International Development (USAID) highlights 'gender equity and women's empowerment' as 'core development objectives, fundamental for the realization of human rights, and key to effective and sustainable development outcomes' (USAID, 2011). Its central goals include reducing gender disparities by improving women's access to key resources, ending gender-based violence, and increasing women's and girls' capacities to control their rights and lives. Bilateral institutions elsewhere join this chorus towards gender equality, emphasizing different aspects of women's rights. While USAID's justifications tend to be articulated in terms of economic efficiency and individual rights, the Swedish International Development Cooperation Agency (SIDA) articulates a mission for gender equality that details 'fair distribution of power' as well as concerns with poverty, the environment and climate, and discrimination (Byron and Ornemark, 2011). Although nearly as large a donor as USAID, the Japan International Cooperation Agency (JICA, 2013) allocates less funding specifically for women, but does include 'gender and development' as one of its development themes, articulated in terms of 'gender mainstreaming' within existing national systems. Overall, however, JICA's rhetorical deference to women's issues does not command as many specific allocations of funding or active engagements with a variety of domains as other bilateral institutions (Wilkins, 2003). While most bilateral agencies recognize gender concerns as part of their missions, particularly since the 1995 Beijing Conference, their approaches differ widely.

Multilateral institutions within the United Nations system offer a set of development agencies that include those that pay specific attention to women's role in development. Although several UN agencies, such as UNFPA and UNICEF, address women's issues, the organization most directly related to these topics is the United Nations Entity for Gender Equality and the Empowerment of Women (formerly UNIFEM), which was created in 2010 (UN Women, 2011). Similar to bilateral development work, this multilateral agency focuses its coordination on and targets its grant giving to changing national policies, coordinating intergovernmental groups, and improving the accountability of the UN itself.

With no structural allegiance to governmental agencies, NGOs have some choice in the degree to which they accept funding from and collaborate with public donors, along with other types of funding mechanisms ranging from individual donations and private foundations to corporations. Some NGOs, such as the Global Fund for Women (2013), rely on a range of donations from individuals, foundations, corporations and governments. This large fund serves as an intermediary between these donors. With assets of more than USD 20 million, it allocates almost USD 9 million a year to about 600 global organizations in 172 countries in the areas of health and sexual rights, economic and environmental justice, civil and political participation and social change philanthropy. Although the fund accepts corporate donations, which represent about 2 per cent of its total budget compared to 37 per cent from individual donors, 30 per cent from foundations, and 29 per cent from government sources, others consciously avoid corporate collaboration. The Global Fund for Women highlights social justice rhetoric in its public mission statement, working for a 'just, compassionate and equitable world' and promoting 'human rights' where 'women have a voice, choices, and are able to realize their full potential' (Global Fund for Women, 2013). Advocacy targets include policy changes such as criminalizing domestic violence against women, ensuring women's right to inherit property, and creating laws to prohibit sex trafficking.

This attention to advocacy to protect marginalized groups from the consequences of injustice and inequity is echoed across several other NGOs in their work. ActionAid connects women's issues to their disproportionate probability of living in poverty, advocating on behalf of their inheritance rights, reproductive choices, access to education, services and employment, through grants to organizations in 45 countries across many regions (ActionAid, 2013). Although these efforts fulfil the criteria for advocacy efforts, one of its US branch's central initiatives, contributing to the work of the G20 Global Agriculture and Food Security Programme, focuses on investing in women who work as small-scale farmers in the wider arena of agricultural development. ActionAid differs from some organizations, however, by having a central administrative office in South Africa, rather than in North America or Europe.

Also headquartered in Africa is the African Women's Development Fund (2013). It restricts its contributions (about USD 3 million per year in recent years) to the continent, supporting over 800 women's organizations across 42 countries. The donors to this fund are quite diverse, ranging from the Global Fund described above to private foundations such as Ford and the Open Society Foundation, as well as Dutch, Danish and Norwegian bilateral agencies. The group sees itself as promoting advocacy through its grants as well as its support for feminist meetings and movements in the region, thereby working outside as well as within mainstream development.

The Open Society Institute (OSI) supports women's rights as human rights in several regions, most directly through its International Women's Health Coalition (2013). In 2010, this programme allocated 106 grants worth over USD 9.3 million to groups in Latin America, Africa, Asia, Eastern Europe and the Middle East. Its overarching goals are designed not only to change policies at the national level in order to reduce discrimination and violence and enhance access to justice, but also to promote policies within the UN that address sexual violence during conflict.

Changing the structures within the development industry is a worthy endeavour, recognizing that it is not just 'other' women but all women who deserve voice and opportunities. The Women's Environment and Development Organization (WEDO, 2013) integrates funding from UN agencies devoted to women, the UNDP and other NGOs such as Oxfam (GB). It works to include women in UN meetings and to promote leadership on the environment and sustainable development, recognizing the importance of gender equity. Agricultural development has been a critical sphere for gaining attention to women's contributions to development, but health remains an area that attracts considerable funding where women are explicitly recognized as critical participants.

Many NGOs focus on women's health issues in global development. The International Women's Health Coalition (2013) distributed almost USD 4 million in 2011 to 61 organizations in Africa, the Middle East and Latin America, given by their diverse donor base of bilateral (Netherlands) and multilateral (UNFP, UNAIDS and UNPF) agencies, private foundations (including Ford, MacArthur, Gates and OSI) and individuals. Not directly connected to USAID, this coalition is able to engage in critiques of US foreign policy, as well as of global and local health policies that restrict women's sexual and reproductive rights. This network brings together elites from different groups, including corporations, to change policies and to increase funding for women's health. Similarly, Care International (2013) brings together funding from governments, foundations and individuals to work in over 80 countries in Africa, Latin America, Asia and the Middle East. Positioning their mission as 'fighting poverty', Care International articulates its advocacy as working to promote women's health as a human right and to label gender-based violence as an abuse of human rights. While Care International works through its grants to other organizations, Development Alternatives with Women for a New Era (DAWN,

2013) mobilizes networks of feminist scholars, researchers and activists from the global South to promote women's rights, using their funding from the Global Fund – the UN Fund for women and private foundations, such as Ford and MacArthur.

These approaches to supporting women in development are not the only strategies being forged. Global attention to women's rights as human rights has inspired serious policy change in state governments, assisted by regional organizations. The Maputo Protocol, negotiated through the work of the African Union and during the period designated as the African Women's Decade (2010–2020), is a critical case in which clear advocacy efforts resulted in concrete policy change.

The Maputo Protocol (African Union, 2012; AWDF, 2013) represents a regional affirmation expanding and reinforcing women's rights as human rights. It has been ratified by about two-thirds of the African Union's member states. Botswana, Egypt, Eritrea and Tunisia, among others, have not signed (D'Almeida, 2011). This lengthy document highlights the conditions deemed relevant to women in the region, including sections on reproductive health and services in areas such as HIV/AIDs, inheritance laws, the prohibition of female genital mutilation (FGM), and the abusive representation of women in advertising and pornography.

Solidarity for African Women's Rights (SOAWR) was created to help implement national policies that facilitate this regional protocol, bringing together the work of 36 CSOs. SOAWR (2012) articulates its mandate as influencing public opinion in favour of the protocol, building regional networks, raising awareness of these issues, attracting media attention and strengthening women's organizations. In order to change national policies, it sees communication as helping to inform and mobilize constituents, and to shift norms about the importance of gender concerns. Like many of the NGOs described above, this coalition receives support from the Global Fund for Women as well as ActionAid International, the African Women's Development Fund, the Ford Foundation, OSI East Africa, Oxfam and other agencies. Among other projects, SOAWR developed the Crossroads radio drama, which is broadcast in the region in order to promote awareness of the Maputo Protocol. The radio drama uses an entertainment-education model, and is centred on the fictional life and travails of a middle-aged woman, highlighting gender inequities when she and a male police officer switch bodies after drinking a magic potion.

Promoting the Maputo Protocol has met with resistance from a variety of organizations. Opposing groups highlight specifically attempts to eradicate FGM and to secure women's reproductive rights (Human Life International, 2011). This political controversy raises issues that stem from religious and cultural groups over control of women's bodies and the implications for sexuality and fertility. These rhetorical challenges can have devastating consequences when enacted in policies that inhibit women's potential for decision-making. Attention to competing discourses is critical to understanding the broader contexts in which strategic advocacy must work.

Women's rights advocacy and the public sphere

Building on our emerging understanding of the public sphere as a dynamic space of contested communication, strategic advocacy for and about women's rights can take divergent approaches. Advocacy can be used to articulate political perspectives within an existing system, arguing for policies that do not change underlying power structures. For example, programmes that focus on changing individual behaviour, or on access to existing resources such as health services, serve to promote women's connections to an existing public sphere. Opportunities for more substantive voice or more control over resources are not addressed. More substantive change, along the lines of what Murdock refers to as allocative control (1988), would involve advocating for policies that shift the fundamental distribution of resources, in terms of either tangible goods and financial capital or social and human capital. Changing the rules of the game involves a greater degree of change than influencing an individual to take or resist an action under a pre-existing set of conditions. Programs that shift government policies to allow women to inherit property, for example, result in shifting resources over time towards more equity across gender. Control over resources helps women contribute to dialogue with men, necessary for equitable civic engagement. Within a critical model of the public sphere, advocacy would need to aim for more enduring and more comprehensive policy and structural changes (Wilkins, 2000).

These frameworks for political change inform our analysis of political movements. Some political advocacy strategies work within existing systems, while other strategies fight against them or create competing systems (Wilkins, 2008b). To illustrate, social movement organizations working against problematic gender stereotypes might support hiring more women in professional positions, such as writers and directors, or rewarding positive representations of gender, thus working within the media industry. Other organizations might organize boycotts of films, thereby standing outside of the industry in order to raise concerns about it. When changing dominant industries, from either within or the outside, seems intractable, another approach is to foster alternative venues, such as supporting alternative media production and distribution. Advocacy strategies can take divergent approaches, depending on the relationship of the agencies to the broader group of organizations and their designated agendas.

Advocacy for and about women's rights resonates with this potential for diverse strategies. Most development programmes work directly within political systems, allocating resources to change individuals or to improve access to services, such as on maternal and reproductive health. If we intend to change the structure within which public sphere dialogue might operate, programs need to change policies that structure rights and resources. Work to support the Maputo Protocol, for example, fits this broader approach. Working against the development industry, by definition, becomes engaged through social movements that attempt to argue against development programmes and to refute the dominant rhetoric. Political opposition to programmes offering family planning services or eradicating FGM would also fall into this category. Smaller development agencies as well as social movement organizations might attempt to work in parallel with the development industry, working on smaller-scale programmes more directly with communities on changing norms, for example, about gender roles in occupations. While specific agencies and communities can take these different strategic approaches, working to change a system, to fight against or in parallel with dominant approaches, their networks of funding and collaboration make such advocacy approaches more intertwined in practice than can be neatly categorized in theory.

Many of the issues raised in promoting women's rights call for integrated strategies that advocate on many levels. Addressing gender-based violence, for example, calls for structural change in creating and enforcing laws and providing access to health care and legal counsel, as well as normative change in shifting attitudes about the severity of these events (Usdin et al., 2000). Advocacy strategies to promote women's rights as human rights, whether broadly based or specifically focused on issues such as gendered violence, rely on the public sphere as a venue for civic engagement and collective resistance.

Our emerging sense of the public sphere begins with an assumption that our ability to engage is contingent on our connections with structures of power, limiting access to resources that enable the production of texts that permit voice as well as spaces for engagement. Although

---

conflict is central to civic engagement, seeing the public sphere as dynamic allows us to understand the value of mobilization, with all the complexity inherent in human collective action. Moreover, understanding public sphere dynamics, particularly in terms of potential to promote gender equity, must be historically and culturally contingent. We can see historically that our discourse on women, gender and feminism has changed dramatically, and that the development industry has promoted many different kinds of programmes with varying degrees of success. This more comprehensive and historical context allows us to consider advocacy communication as a more complex, yet hopeful, enterprise to improve the human condition.

References

Actionaid (2013) http://www.actionaid.org, date accessed 16 January 2013.
African Union (2012) Protocol to the African Charter on Human and Peoples' Rights on the Rights of Women in Africa, http://www.africa-union.org/root/au/Documents/Treaties/Text/Protocol%20on%20the%20Rights%20of%20Women.pdf, date accessed 29 December 2012.
African Women's Development Fund (AWDF) (2013) http://www.awdf.org, date accessed 16 January 2013.
Byron, G. and Ornemark, C. (2011) *Gender Equality in Swedish Development Cooperation* (Stockholm: SIDA).
Cardinal, L., Costigan, A. and Heffernan, T. (1994) 'Working towards a feminist vision of development' in H. Dagenais and D. Piché (eds), *Women, Feminism and Development* (Montreal: McGill-Queen's University Press), pp. 409–428.
CARE International (2013), http://www.careinternational.org, date accessed 16 January 2013.
Couldry, N., Livingstone, S. and Markham, T. (2010) *Media Consumption and Public Engagement: Beyond the Presumption of Attention*, revised and updated edition (Basingstoke: Palgrave Macmillan).
Dagenais, H. and D. Piché (eds) (1994) *Women, Feminism and Development* (Montreal: McGill-Queen's University Press).
D'Almeida, M. (2011) 'African Women Push for the Ratification and Implementation of the Maputo Protocol'. Civil Society Voices for Better Aid, http://betteraid.org/en/blog.html?view=entry&year=2011&month=11&day=13&id=15%3Aafrican-womens-organizing-for-the-ratification-and-implementation-of-the-maputo-protocol, date accessed 29 December 2012.
Development Alternatives with Women for a New Era (DAWN) (2013) http://www.dawnnet.org, date accessed 16 January 2013.
Downing, J. (ed.) (2011) *Encyclopaedia of Social Movement Media* (Thousand Oaks: Sage).
Dutta, M. (2011) *Communicating Social Change: Structure, Culture, Agency* (New York: Routledge).
Enghel, F. and Wilkins, K. (eds) (2012) 'Communication, Media and Development: Problems and Perspectives', *Nordicom. Special Issue*. Vol. 31.

Escobar, A. (1995) *Encountering Development: The Making and Unmaking of the Third World* (Princeton: Princeton University Press).

Freire, P. (1983) *Pedagogy of the Oppressed* (New York: Continuum).

Global Fund for Women (2013) www.globalfundforwomen.org, date accessed 16 January 2013.

Gumucio-Dagron, A. and T. Tufte (eds) (2006) *Communication for Social Change Anthology: Historical and Contemporary Readings* (South Orange, NJ: Communication for Social Change Consortium).

Herman, E. and Chomsky, N. (1988) *Manufacturing Consent: The Political Economy of the Mass Media* (New York: Pantheon).

Hornik, R. C. (1988) *Development Communication, Information, Agriculture and Nutrition in the Third World* (New York: Longman).

Huesca, R. (2001) 'Conceptual Contributions of New Social Movements to Development Communication Research', *Communication Theory* 11, pp. 415–433.

Human Life International (2011) 'The Maputo Protocol: A Clear and Present Danger', http://www.maputoprotocol.com/about-the-protocol, date accessed 29 December 2012.

International Women's Health Coalition (2013) http://www.iwhc.org, date accessed 16 January 2013.

Kremer, M., van Lieshout, P. and Went, R. (2010) *Doing Good or Doing Better: Development Policies in a Globalizing World* (Amsterdam: Amsterdam University Press).

Japan International Cooperation Agency (JICA) (2013) *Gender and Development*, http://www.jica.go.jp/english/our_work/thematic_issues/gender/index.html, date accessed 24 January 2013.

Mattelart, A. (2011) *The Globalization of Surveillance* (Cambridge: Polity Press).

Maxwell, R. and Miller, T. (2012) *Greening the Media* (New York: Oxford University Press).

McAnany, E. (2012) *Saving the World: A Brief History of Communication for Development and Social Change* (Urbana: University of Illinois Press).

Melkote. S. (2012) 'Development Support Communication for Social Justice: An Analysis of The Role of Media and Communication in Directed Social Change' in S. Melkote (ed.), *Development Communication in Directed Social Change: A Reappraisal of Theory and Practice* (Singapore: AMIC), pp. 15–38.

Mohanty, C. T. (1991) 'Cartographies of Struggle: Third World Women and the Politics of Feminism' in C. T. Mohanty, A. Russo and L. Torres (eds), *Third World Women and the Politics of Feminism* (Bloomington: Indiana University Press), pp. 1–50.

Murdock, G. (1988) 'Large Corporations and the Control of Communications Industries' in M. Gurevitch, T. Bennett, J. Curran and J. Woollacott (eds), *Culture, Society and Media* (London: Methuen), pp. 118–150.

Murphy, P. (2011) 'Putting the Earth into Global Media Studies', *Communication Theory* 21, pp. 217–238.

Open Society Foundation (2013) International Women's Program, http://www.opensocietyfoundations.org/about/programs/international-women-s-program, date accessed 16 January 2013.

Richey, L. and Ponte, S. (2011) *Brand Aid: Shopping Well to Save the World* (Minneapolis: University of Minnesota Press).

62   *Karin Gwinn Wilkins*

Sainath, P. (2012) *Farmer Suicides and the Way Forward.* http://actnaturallyblog.wordpress.com/2012/01/18/english-translation-of-p-sainaths-farmer-suicides-and-the-way-forward, date accessed 28 August 2012.

Servaes, J. and Malikhao, P. (2012) 'Advocacy Communication for Peace Building', *Development in Practice* 22(2), pp. 229–243.

Shah, H. (2011) *The Production of Modernization: Daniel Lerner, Mass Media and the Passing of Traditional Society* (Philadelphia: Temple University Press).

Snyder, L. (2002) 'Development Communication Campaigns' in W. B. Gudykunst and B. Mody (eds), *Handbook of International and Intercultural Communication* (Thousand Oaks: Sage), pp. 457–478.

Solidarity for African Women's Rights (SOWAR) (2012) 'Solidarity for African Women's Rights', http://www.soawr.org/en, date accessed 29 December 2012.

Sparks, C. (2007, reprinted 2011) *Globalization, Development and the Mass Media* (London: Sage).

Stein, L., Kidd, D. and Rodriguez, C. (eds) (2009) *Making Our Media: Global Initiatives Toward a Democratic Public Sphere* (New York: Hampton Press).

Tufte, T. (2012) 'Facing Violence and Conflict with Communication: Possibilities and Limitations of Storytelling and Entertainment-education' in S. Melkote (ed.), *Development Communication in Directed Social Change: A Reappraisal of Theory and Practice* (Singapore: AMIC), pp. 80–94.

UN Women (2011) United Nations Entity for Global Equality and the Empowerment of Women, http://www.unwomen.org, date accessed 12 October 2011.

United Nations (2010) *Millennium Development Goals: At a Glance* (New York: UN Department of Public Information).

US Agency for International Development (USAID) (2011) USAID Gender equality and women's empowerment, http://www.usaid.gov/our_work/cross-cutting_programs/wid/about.html, date accessed 12 October 2011.

Usdin, S., Christofides, N., Malepe, L. and Maker, A. (2000) 'The Value of Advocacy in Promoting Social Change: Implementing the New Domestic Violence Act in South Africa', *Reproductive Health Matters* 8(16), pp. 55–65.

Wilkins, K. (1997) 'Gender, Power and Development', *Journal of International Communication* 4(2), pp. 102–120.

Wilkins, K. (ed.) (2000) *Redeveloping Communication for Social Change: Theory, Practice and Power* (Boulder, CO: Rowman & Littlefield).

Wilkins, K. (2003) 'Japanese Approaches to Development Communication', *Keio Communication Review* 25, pp. 3–21.

Wilkins, K. (2005) 'Out of Focus: Gender Visibilies in Development' in O. Hemer and T. Tufte (eds), *Media and Glocal Change: Rethinking Communication for Development* (Göteborg, Sweden: University of Göteborg, NORDICOM), pp. 261–270.

Wilkins, K. (2007) 'Confronting the Missionary Position: The Mission of Development/The Position of Women', *Communication for Development and Social Change: A Global Journal* 1(2), pp. 111–125.

Wilkins, K. (2008a) 'Development Communication' in W. Donsbach (ed.), *International Encyclopedia of Communication* (Oxford, UK and Malden, MA: Blackwell Press), pp. 1229–1238.

Wilkins, K. (2008b) *Home/Land/Security: What We Learn about Arab Communities from Action-Adventure Film* (Lanham, MD: Lexington Books).

Wilkins, K. (2011) 'Advocacy Communication' in S. Melkote (ed.), *Development Communication in Directed Social Change: A Reappraisal of Theories and Approaches* (Singapore: AMIC), pp. 39–52.

Wilkins, K. and Mody, B. (2001) 'Reshaping Development Communication: Developing Communication and Communicating Development', *Communication Theory Special Issue* 11(4), pp. 1–11.

Williams, B. and Delli Carpini, M. (2011) *After Broadcast News: Media Regimes, Democracy and the New Information Environment* (Cambridge: Cambridge University Press).

Willis, K., Smith, A. and Stenning, A. (2008) 'Introduction: Social justice and Neoliberalism' in A. Smith, A. Stenning and K. Willis (eds), *Social Justice and Neoliberalism: Global Perspectives* (London: Zed Books), pp. 1–15.

Women's Environment and Development Organization (WEDO) (2013) http://www.wedo.org, date accessed 16 January 2013.

4
The Public Sphere and the Dialectics of Globalization

Thomas Hylland Eriksen

Globalization is a term that came into fashion around 1990. It generally refers to the processes that lead to the increased density, speed and reach of transnational connections, associated with the global spread of capitalism and new information and communication technologies. Globalization can be studied in its economic, political, ecological or cultural aspects, and there is a rich scholarly literature, much of it interdisciplinary, dealing with the subject (see Eriksen, 2013; Ritzer, 2011 for overviews). Moreover, globalization can be studied as a macrophenomenon, with a focus on the global economy, transnational companies, and so on, or as a micro-phenomenon, by focusing instead on relationships between people and small groups. It is not going away. The financial crisis of 2008 led some commentators and analysts to conclude that globalization had suffered a severe setback (see Rodrik, 2011). While this was doubtless true, at least temporarily, of global financial capitalism, other processes of economic globalization continued unimpeded in realms such as communication and migration, commodity trading and climate change prevention, although the growth rate has slowed in many parts of the world following the financial meltdown and subsequent uncertainty surrounding the euro, the fiscal deficit in the United States, and political volatility around the Mediterranean.

This chapter does not delve into the economics of globalization. Instead, it outlines some of the economic parameters of globalization in order to highlight its implications for the transnational public sphere. The public sphere has been intimately linked with the nation state and to the consolidation of national identities, democratic values, language communities and civil society, by theorists as diverse as Habermas (1989 [1962]), writing about the structural transformation of the public sphere since the 18th century, Sennett (1976), analysing the collapse of the distinction between public and private, and Anderson (1983), who argues that print capitalism, the standardization of languages and mass communication were crucial preconditions for the development of national identities in the early modern world (see also Castells, 2009). Given this background, it is highly pertinent to ask what becomes of the public sphere in an era of transnational mobility and communication, porous boundaries and destabilized national identities. I draw on examples from various life-world realms to show that the same patterns and mechanisms witnessed elsewhere are characteristic of public debate and the public sphere more generally.

Parameters of globalization

The period since the Second World War, and especially since around 1990, has been one of strongly intensified global interconnectedness. In the first post-war decades, the number of transnational companies grew, as did the number of transnational non-governmental organizations (NGOs). The United Nations rapidly became a conglomerate of sub-organizations with offices in most countries. International travel became easier and more common. In the 1960s, the Canadian media theorist, Marshall McLuhan, used the term 'global village' to describe the new situation in the mass media, in which television in particular could create shared frames of reference and mutual knowledge between people across the globe (McLuhan, 1994 [1964]). In this period, global change – economic, environmental, political and cultural – became the subject of many scholarly books. Some used the term 'development', intimating that the poor countries would eventually 'catch up' with the rich ones. Others preferred the term 'imperialism', suggesting that the rich countries were actively exploiting the poor ones and preventing them from developing.

Various parts of the world had already become interconnected, and there was considerable awareness of this long before the term 'globalization' was coined. Yet, it is possible to argue that something new about the world arose roughly at the end of the Cold War in 1989–1990, which goes a long way to explain the rise of public interest in globalization and transnational phenomena more generally. Three factors, roughly coincident, can be mentioned.

First, the end of the Cold War entailed more and closer global integration. The two-bloc system, which dated from the mid-1940s, made it difficult to think of geopolitics, transnational communication and international trade in terms not dictated by the opposition between the

United States and the Soviet Union and their respective satellites. With the end of this conflict, the world appeared to have become a single marketplace.

Second, the Internet, which had existed in embryonic form since the late 1960s, began to grow exponentially around 1990. Throughout the 1990s, media buzzwords were about bandwidths, websites, portals, and 'the new economy' and its business opportunities. The World Wide Web was introduced in 1992–1993, around the same time as many academics and business people became accustomed to using e-mail for their daily correspondence. Mobile phones became ubiquitous in the rich countries and eventually in poorer ones. The impact of this double de-localization – the physical letter replaced by e-mail, the fixed telephone line replaced by the wireless mobile – on the everyday life of millions of people has been considerable.

Finally, identity politics – nationalist, ethnic, religious and territorial – were at the forefront of the international agenda: from above, through states demanding homogeneity or engaging in ethnic cleansing, and below, with minorities demanding rights or secession. The Salman Rushdie affair, itself an excellent example of the globalization of ideas, began with the issuance of a fatwa by Iran's Ayatollah Khomeini following the publication of Rushdie's allegedly blasphemous novel *The Satanic Verses* in 1988. It soon became apparent that Rushdie could move nowhere in the world freely, since the fatwa had global implications. Two years later, Yugoslavia dissolved, leading to civil wars based on ethnic differences. In the same period, debates about immigration and multiculturalism came to dominate political discourse in several Western countries, and the Hindu nationalists of the BJP came to power in India.

These three dimensions of globalization – increased trade and transnational economic activity, faster and denser communication networks, and increased tensions between and within cultural groups due to intensified mutual exposure – suggest not that the world has been fundamentally transformed since the late 1980s, but that the driving forces of economic, political and cultural dynamics are transnational – and that this is now widely acknowledged. As Robertson (1992, p. 8) puts it: 'Globalization as a concept refers both to the compression of the world and the intensification of consciousness about the world as a whole.'

Not everybody who writes about the contemporary world agrees that it has recently entered a distinctively 'global' era (see e.g., Hirst and Thompson, 1999). Some argue that the extent of global integration was just as comprehensive, and in some ways more all-encompassing, in the *belle époque* of 1890–1914, and that the origins of fully fledged global capitalism in that era could be traced back to the early modern world of European conquests, colonialism and slavery (Chanda, 2007). Others, such as Giddens (1985), claim that the nation state remains 'the pre-eminent power container of our era', although he later revised his position. Yet others point out that a large number of people, and huge areas of social and cultural life, remain relatively untouched by transnational processes.

Interconnectedness

In spite of these counterarguments, it would be difficult to argue against the view that the world is more interconnected today than at any earlier historical period, and this is nowhere more evident than in the world of communication – through satellite television, the Internet and mobile telephony, migration and tourism, trade and an intensified traffic in signs and meanings, we are each other's contemporaries and aware of one another – however vaguely. The culinary capital of India might be London, and that of China San Francisco. In order to carry out anthropological fieldwork in a village in the Dominican Republic, one has to spend at least a few months in New York City, since half the villagers are at any one time working and living in the Big Apple. The little trolls, 'Scream' t-shirts, and expensive knitted sweaters sold as souvenirs of Norway to tourists visiting Oslo are made in Taiwan, Pakistan and Sri Lanka, respectively. The largest city in the English-speaking Caribbean is London. Finally, if the classical patriarchal kinship system of the Taiwanese had been able to withstand the pressures of individualism and modernization, several shop owners in the Silicon Valley might still be in business: The patri-clan is an efficient economic unit where interest-free loans and free services are available, and when shops in California (and elsewhere) have to close down because their customers have lost their jobs, this is partly a result of competition from East Asia. Such is the extent of global interconnectedness. I could go on to describe satellite television, the Internet, cheap flights and mobile phones. The implications for the public sphere are evident but not predictable.

In some realms, people remain unexpectedly resilient to change, while other areas change much faster than might have been expected. For example, when cable and satellite television became widespread in Europe in the 1980s, many predicted that it would be detrimental to national cohesion since people could now watch television programmes from any country in the world. Domestic programming remains the most popular in every country, however, including the smallest ones, in spite of the huge selection of channels. Globalization has affected the public sphere and put pressure on notions of national culture, but it has not obliterated them.

Food habits, on the other hand, have changed faster than predicted in many parts of the world – especially the rich countries. In the UK, chicken tikka masala has been declared the national dish. (It is likely that the dish was first made in a Glasgow restaurant in the late 1960s.) The boiled potato, a staple with virtually any hot meal in Norway in the 1970s, has become a rare sight in that country – beyond the tourist circuit, where it remains popular. Coffee bars and fast food restaurants have become a familiar sight in every European city.

The differences between regions are not obliterated due to increased interconnectedness. The global village is a community of communication and exchange, not of homogeneity. However, the cultural differences between regions, peoples and nations are much less clear-cut in the globalized era than they were before, since similar goods and services are available worldwide. However, they are articulated through local contexts, which remain different (Eriksen, 2007). This has implications for the public sphere, to which I return below.

Forms of mixing and demands for purity

Globalization is often associated with 'cultural hybridity' or, put simply, mixing. Perhaps especially visible in popular culture, new cultural forms emerge out of diverse materials in a situation of increased intercultural contact. Musical subgenres such as bhangra, which has South Asian and British elements, literary forms such as Nigerian literature in English, culinary innovations such as salmon paté (North European and French), and mixed personal identities ranging from Black British to Ukrainian-Canadian emerge in a world of heightened mobility.

Commonly seen as 'Westernization', processes of mutual cultural influence and mixing – the cultural dynamics of globalization – must in fact be understood as a multidirectional and truly complex process (Amselle, 2001; Appadurai, 1996; Hannerz, 1996). Moreover, it must be kept in mind that there is no such thing as a 'pure' culture. Mixing has always occurred, although its speed and intensity are greater than before. A number of terms are used to describe cultural mixing, and it may be useful to distinguish between the main forms (see Eriksen, 2007 for a fuller treatment).

Cultural pluralism directs attention to the relative boundedness of the constituent groups or categories that make up a society. It is a close relative of multiculturalism. In the realm of consumption, pluralism would imply that different groups consume different kinds of goods systematically because of cultural differences.

Hybridity directs attention to individuals or cultural forms that are reflexively – self-consciously – mixed: that is, syntheses of cultural forms or fragments of diverse origins. It is thus distinctive from either pluralism or multiculturalism, where boundaries between groups remain intact. Hybrid consumption entails the creative mixing of products and services of diverse origin.

Syncretism directs attention to an amalgamation of formerly discrete world views, cultural meanings and, in particular, religions.

Diasporic identity is an essentially social category consisting of people whose primary subjective belonging is in another country.

Transnationalism directs attention instead to a social existence that attaches individuals and groups not primarily to one particular place, but to several or none.

Diffusion directs attention to the flow of substances and meanings between societies, regardless of whether it is accompanied by actual social encounters.

Creolization, finally, directs attention to the cultural phenomena that result from displacement and the ensuing social encounter and mutual influence between two or several groups, creating an ongoing dynamic interchange of symbols and practices, and eventually leading to new forms with varying degrees of stability.

Hybridity is the most generally used concept, and it can refer to any obviously mixed cultural form. World music, various forms of contemporary 'crossover' cuisine and urban youth cultures that borrow elements from a variety of sources, including minority cultures and television, are typical examples of phenomena explored under the heading hybridity. Hybrid cultural forms are often counteracted by quests for purity and 'authenticity', which may be, but are not necessarily, politicized in situations of increased ethnic diversity due to immigration. What is nonetheless clear is that one main effect on the public sphere of the forms of mixing engendered by globalization is a heightened polarization and strengthened potential for conflict around group identities. Although few in the West today subscribe to the fiction of cultural purity, neo-nationalist movements react to the unpredictable changes taking place by insisting, often in militant ways, on the authenticity and moral superiority of that which is rooted and local. Neo-nationalism often targets immigrants, and especially Muslims, as the unwanted 'other'. It is paralleled by identity politics among Muslims who attempt to draw a clear boundary between 'us' and 'them', purifying Islam and positing the Western world as 'the other'.

One main form of ideological polarization, therefore, seems to emerge between two forms of identity politics: nationalism and Islamism. The two share the same underlying logic, trying to stem the tide of global hybridization by withdrawing into something rooted, old and clearly bounded. It may thus be more accurate to speak of a polarization between various forms of antagonistic localism – nationalism, Islamism, and so on – on the one hand, and celebrations – or at least acceptance – of hybridity and 'impurity', on the other.

Homogenization and heterogenization

I have argued that neo-nationalism and Islamism are two sides of the same coin. Apparently starkly different from each other, they conform to the same grammar and represent similar reactions to the turmoil of globalization.

Let us tentatively ask whether globalization leads to homogenization or heterogenization: Do we become more similar or more different owing to the increase in transnational mobility and communication? In one sense, people arguably become more similar. Individualism – the belief that individuals have rights and responsibilities regardless of their place in wider social configurations – is a central feature of global modernity. It is also easy to argue that similarities in consumer preferences indicate a certain 'flattening' or homogenization. At the same time, however, local adaptations of universal or near-universal phenomena show that global modernities will always have local expressions, and that assumed similarities may either conceal real differences in meaning or be superficial with no deep bearing on people's existential condition. Although neo-nationalism and Islamism share the same formal features, their content varies not only mutually, but also from locality to locality.

In a recent book about what I call the dialectics of globalization, Ritzer (2004) contrasts what he sees as two pervasive tendencies in the contemporary world: the *grobalization of nothing* and the *glocalization of something*. He defines glocalization as that which is 'locally conceived and controlled and rich in distinctive substance' (2004, p. 8), while grobalization is defined as 'generally centrally conceived, controlled, and comparatively devoid of distinctive substantive content' (2004, p. 3). In other words, standardized, mass-produced goods catering to an assumed common denominator of disembedded market tastes are the outcome of grobalization, while anything that could not have been produced anywhere but in a particular location is defined as glocalization.

Ritzer argues that there 'is a gulf between those who emphasize the increasing grobal influence of capitalistic, Americanized, and McDonaldized interests and those who see the world growing increasingly pluralistic and indeterminate' (2004, p. 80). Moreover, he distinguishes between the grobalization-glocalization of places, things, persons and services. The more personalized, place-bound and unique something is, the more glocalized. For example, while a craft barn represents the glocalization of something, Disney World stands for the grobalization of nothing. A bar frequented because of its skilful bartender or because it is where one's friends hang out is a 'something', whereas hotel bars with new customers every evening and a standardized, transnational selection of cocktails is a 'nothing'. In Ritzer's account, the big and standardized stands for nothing, while the small and locally fashioned stands for something.

Ritzer concedes that things are more complicated. He admits that 'grobalization can, at times, involve something (e.g., art exhibits that move among art galleries throughout the world, Italian exports of food like Parmiagiano Reggiano and Culatella ham)' (2004, p. 99) and, conversely, that the glocal can also produce 'nothings', such as tourist trinkets. He even concedes that there are 'people today, perhaps a majority, who prefer nothing to something and who have good reason for that preference' (2004, p. 16): thinking about those – hundreds of millions – who scarcely have the opportunity to participate in the consumption of nothing. People in poorer countries produce much of the richer world's nothingness, but can scarcely afford any of it for themselves.

Inspired by the anthropologist Augé's concept of *non-places* (Augé, 1991), but also by Weber's classic theory of disenchantment and rationalization, Ritzer establishes a series of simple contrasts where everything mass-produced, ready-made and instant appears dehumanized, and everything which is one-of-a-kind (be it a product or an employee) is 'enchanted' and authentic.

Many writers on globalization would be inclined to see this analysis as simplistic. Amselle (2001, p. 22) points out that even McDonald's restaurants 'do not sell the same products everywhere'. In India, where the majority of the population does not eat beef, for example, the Big Mac is a lamb burger. In addition, apparently identical products and services are perceived in distinctly local ways. Coca-Cola, an everyday product in most of the Western world, is associated with weddings and other rituals by many people, not least in Africa. The Macintosh computer, according to Amselle (2001), became a symbol of identity among French intellectuals resisting the global dominance of Microsoft in spite of the fact that it was a US product. In other words, against the grobalization of nothing, locals can invest a 'nothing' with something in discriminating, critical ways. It is nonetheless a significant fact that the transnational standardization of commodities and services is one important dimension of globalization, even if the meanings of the products and services thus disseminated vary locally.

The relevance of this perspective for the public sphere is twofold. First, there is almost everywhere a vibrant public discourse concerning the relationship between the local and the global in matters concerning consumption. Everybody, it seems, wants to have it both ways, but there is no broad consensus concerning what is the appropriate mix between local and global. Second, the contrast suggested by Ritzer, somewhat facetiously, between 'something' and 'nothing', can be found in a whole range of public discourses across the world concerning politics, identity and culture in a broad sense.

Three brief examples illustrate the point, but keep in mind that we are now looking at the McDonalds versus the Culatella ham of identity politics, but in contexts where it is by no means obvious that the local should gain precedence over the global. The local is not necessarily more virtuous than the global. Universalism can sometimes be good, as in human rights.

The first example concerns the Danish cartoons of Muhammad in 2005 (for analyses see Larsen and Seidenfaden, 2006; Eide et al., 2009). This example is especially interesting in so far as the local and the global are difficult to disentangle. Briefly, many Danes and others argued that publishing the cartoons, although they were perceived as blasphemous and offensive by many Muslims, represented a defence of universal values, that is, the freedom of expression. However, the Danish value that open, explicit disagreement is a positive thing was also mentioned. On the other side, those attacking the cartoons also sought to mobilize universalist arguments, concerning both the sanctity of religious belief and the universal truth of Islam, and localist ones – it should be accepted that not all cultures share the Danes' enthusiasm for satire and disagreement.

In other words, universalist arguments could be invoked regardless of whether one defended the publication of the cartoons, as could localist arguments, whether they invoked the peculiarities of Danish civil society or the multiculturalist virtues of tolerating specific cultural values in a complex society.

The so-called Arab Spring and its aftermath also lends strength to this view. This is not the place to summarize the events, which began in early 2011 and have ended, thus far, in a protracted and terrible war in Syria. Nonetheless, the uprisings in Tunisia, Egypt, Libya and elsewhere, which led to regime changes in the three North African countries, were inspired by democratic ideas of 'global' origin. In addition, the mobile telephones and computers used to organize demonstrations, spread information and rumours, and discuss politics are similarly universalistic and 'global' in character, confirming the point that there is a shared global grammar underlying contemporary public discourse. However, the social realities in the three countries were different not only from Western European societies, but also from each other. The articulation of discontent and unrest with political authorities therefore functioned in very different ways in the three countries – and in a fourth, tragic way in Syria. Moreover, the substantial demands of the rebels differed, and were – again – internally diverse, ranging from secular republicanism to Islamism. These ideological orientations drew on universalist claims but were necessarily locally articulated, and finally led to an ideological polarization within that mirrored the controversy around the Danish cartoons. What is at stake is an authoritative definition of the appropriate balance between the local and the global, the particular and the universal.

The third example further strengthens the argument about the dialectics of globalization and its ensuing polarization. The terrorist attack on Norway on 22 July 2011, when a right-wing extremist killed 77 people, was fuelled by the conviction that impurity, multiculturalism and migration were destroying the country, and the terrorist Breivik expressed sympathy on numerous occasions for a cultural conservatism that shares important formal traits with militant Islamism. The terrorist attack served as a reminder that Norway, like many other societies, is a divided society where militant particularism – neo-nationalism – strongly opposes tendencies towards mixing, cultural pluralism and fuzzy boundaries.

To sum up, the effects of globalization on public spheres 'across the world' have not led to the dissolution or even fragmentation of public spheres, but to polarization along new lines. Whereas the focuses of debate and controversy in earlier periods have been the role of the church, or the contradiction of labour and capital, the main template for ideological polarization now concerns the relationship between the global and the local. It is often expressed in paradoxical ways, as when defenders of universalist values invoke local, cultural traditions of disagreement, as in the cartoon controversy; or when champions of ancient tradition use the Internet and mobile phones to get their message across, and when Islamists epitomize modernity, through their ways of communicating with each other, their often cunning dealings with the media, and the transnational and standardized form of their ideology.

Dialectics of globalization

In spite of the phenomenal growth of global interconnectedness since the Second World War, not everything is in sync with everything else. First, as Mittelman (2001, p. 7) points out, 'the [global] system affects its components in very different ways. Globalization is a partial, not a totalizing phenomenon. Countries and regions are tethered to some aspects of globalization, but sizeable pockets remain removed from it.' Although there is an information technology (IT) 'boom' in India, and the country is emerging as a major power in the production of IT, more than half the Indian population have never made a phone call.

As many writers on globalization have noted, one particularly visible feature is the emergence of strong localist and traditionalist identities. The contrast between a borderless global network society, on the one hand, and fervent isolationism, on the other, is like flypaper for journalists and scholars, and book titles such as *The Lexus and the Olive Tree* (Friedman, 1999) and *Jihad vs. McWorld* (Barber, 1995) are irresistible when the browsing customer in an airport bookshop stumbles across them. There is a simple dialectic to be grasped here: The transnational network economy and its cultural correlates create opportunities for some and powerlessness for others.

French filmmakers are unhappy about Hollywood's global dominance; pious Muslims are unhappy about images on cable television, and from the London and Paris streets they walked as students; Scandinavians worry about the future of their welfare state in a situation of global economic competition; and indigenous leaders worldwide are concerned about retaining a way of life and a culture that are at least semi-traditional. Global capitalism, it is often said, produces both losers and winners, both poverty and wealth. It could be added that even in the cases where it provides increased (measurable) wealth, it can also produce poverty at the cultural or spiritual level.

Counter-movements against the limitless standardization and homogenization that seemingly result from globalization can thus be founded from a variety of motivations, but all of them are linked to autonomy at the personal or community level. Globalization, even when met with little or no resistance, can usually be described as *glocalization*: the pre-existing local is fused with global influence. The particular merges with the universal to create something true to the universal grammar of global modernity, but at the same time locally embedded.

Herein lies much of its conflict potential as well. It has become something of a cliché to state that people's identities are threatened by globalization but, like many clichés, there is considerable truth in it. Everywhere in the world, there are people who feel that they are no longer allowed to define who they are, or to influence their own destiny or their own society in effective ways. They may become Islamists or neo-nationalists, or they may support less politicized phenomena such as slow food or local history groups, but it is clear that the ideological tensions characterizing the public sphere of the early 21st century are fundamentally framed by the tension between the global and the local, the universal and the particular, and the differing subject positions taken in this regard. In this way, the public sphere can be read as a dramatization of the dialectics of globalization, playing itself out on stages that are nationally delineated but underpinned by a global grammar. In several countries, both in Western Europe and elsewhere, the public sphere is being polarized along such lines. The democratization of the right to free expression, a direct result of technological change, has enabled new groups to express themselves effectively, and a distinctly xenophobic, anti-universalist public sphere has evolved on the Internet along parallel lines with the more equivocal 'old' media spheres. This discourse, which targets multiculturalists, immigrants and cultural relativists, but most of all treacherous politicians, tends to insinuate that democracy has failed and that the elites are deceiving the people by nurturing destructive multiculturalism. This kind of discourse, although it purports to be national, has many shared characteristics in different countries and illustrates – albeit in a somewhat unpalatable way – a central tension in globalization – that between the universal and the particular. This tension sets the stage for the main battles of the public sphere in the coming years – between the universalism of the brain and the particularism of the heart.

Concluding remarks

Truly global processes affect the conditions of people living in particular localities, creating new opportunities and new forms of vulnerability.

Risks are globally shared in the era of the nuclear bomb, transnational terrorism and potential ecological disasters. On the same note, economic conditions in particular localities frequently (some would say always) depend on events taking place elsewhere in the global system. If there is an industrial boom in Taiwan, towns in the English Midlands will be affected. If oil prices rise, it means salvation for the oil-exporting Trinidadian economy and disaster for its oil-importing neighbour, Barbados. In the same way, and by the same token, however, the publication of 12 blasphemous cartoons in Denmark can lead to riots in Nigeria. Everything is being globalized, including the insult.

The values and dreams that guide people's lives seem to merge in certain respects. People nearly everywhere desire similar goods, from mobile phones to readymade garments. A precondition for this to happen is the more or less successful implementation of certain institutional dimensions of modernity, most notably that of a monetized economy – if not necessarily evenly distributed waged work and literacy. The ever-increasing transnational flow of commodities, be they material or immaterial, creates a set of common cultural denominators that appear to eradicate local distinctions. The hot dog halal or, as the case may be, the pizza and the hamburger – or, in India, the lamb burger – are truly parts of world cuisine. Identical songs are played in identical night spots in Costa Rica and Thailand. The same Coca-Cola commercials are shown with minimal local variation in cinemas all over the world. Jo Nesbø's books are ubiquitous wherever books are sold, and so on. Investment capital, military power, and world literature are being disembedded from the constraints of space – they no longer belong to a particular locality. With the development of the jet aircraft, the satellite dish and, more recently, the Internet, distance no longer seems a limiting factor for the flow of influence, investments and cultural meaning.

Millions of people – indeed hundreds of millions – will never have access to wealth because they are simply ignored and squeezed into increasingly marginal areas, like hunter-gatherers encountering armed, well-organized agriculturalists in an earlier period. The suffering of slum dwellers, dispossessed peasants, unemployed men and women in cities, victims of war and economic exploitation, and their occasionally well-orchestrated rebellions or alternative projects seeking autonomy from globalized capitalism, are the trueborn children of globalization, just as the mobile phone and the Internet, the proliferation of international NGOs, cheap tropical holidays and the growth of transnational soccer fandom are results of globalization. The global village is not a place devoid of tensions or diversity, but a site, or a network of networks if you prefer, where people are brought into intensified contact with each other, leading to confrontations and friction, enrichment and opportunities in the world of consumption, as elsewhere.

In the global village, everyone is a neighbour of everyone else. It is worth noting that one activity that neighbours are universally known for indulging in is looking over the fence to compare their lives, in a spirit of envy, admiration, spite or condescension. Wives ask their husbands for a new kitchen like the one the people across the street have just installed, and husbands compare cars and mobile phones. In the global – or glocal – comparisons can be made across vast distances and between otherwise different, that is, incomparable groups. This is evident not only in the realm of consumption, but also in politics and public discourse. Contemporary identity politics are based on some globally shared presumptions about what it takes to be a proper group – leadership, symbols, myths of origin, enemy images of the other, and so on – and their leaders look across towards each other, in a genuinely glocal endeavour, for new ideas. As a result, indigenous groups in Siberia employ many of the same methods as indigenous groups in Northern Europe; the terrorists of al Qaeda are inspired, at the level of methodology, by the insurgent Zapatistas of Mexico; South African Zulus market themselves using the same methods as natives of the Pacific; and ethnic and religious identity politics are remarkably similar everywhere. With a global grammar and local content, they are truly glocal and deeply contentious.

References

Amselle, J. L. (2001) *Branchements: Anthropologie de l'universalité des cultures* (Paris: Flammarion).
Anderson, B. (1983) *Imagined Communities: Reflections on the Origins and Spread of Nationalism* (London: Verso).
Appadurai, A. (1996) *Modernity at Large* (Minneapolis: University of Minnesota Press).
Augé, M. (1991) *Non-lieux: Introduction à une anthropologie de la surmodernité* (Paris: Seuil).
Barber, B. (1995) *Jihad versus McWorld: How Globalism and Tribalism are Reshaping the World* (New York: Ballantine).
Castells, M. (2009) *Information Power* (Oxford: Oxford University Press).
Chanda, N. (2007) *Bound Together: How Traders, Preachers, Adventurers, and Warriors Shaped Globalization* (New Haven: Yale University Press).
Eide, E., Kunelius, R. and Phillips, A. (eds) (2008) *Transnational Media Events: The Mohammed Cartoons and the Imagined Clash of Civilizations* (Göteborg: Nordicom).

Eriksen, T. H. (2007) 'Creolisation in Anthropological Theory and in Mauritius' in C. Stewart (ed.), *Creolization: History, Ethnography, Theory* (Walnut Creek, CA: Left Coast Press), pp. 153–177.

Eriksen, T. H. (2013) *Globalization: The Key Concepts*, 2nd edn (London: Bloomsbury).

Friedman, T. L. (1999) *The Lexus and the Olive Tree* (New York: Farrar, Straus and Giroux).

Giddens, A. (1985) *The Nation-State and Violence* (Cambridge: Polity).

Habermas, J. (1989 [1962]) *The Structural Transformation of the Public Sphere: An Inquiry into a Category of Bourgeois Society* (Cambridge, MA: MIT Press).

Hannerz, U. (1996) *Transnational Connections* (London: Routledge).

Hirst, P. and Thompson, G. (1999) *Globalization in Question*, 2nd edn (Cambridge: Polity).

Larsen, R. and Seidenfaden, T. (2006) *Karikaturkrisen: En undersøgelse af baggrund og ansvar* (Copenhagen: Gyldendal).

McLuhan, M. (1994 [1964]) *Understanding Media* (London: Routledge).

Mittelman, J. (2001) 'Globalization: Captors and Captives' in J.H. Mittelman and N. Othman (eds), *Capturing Globalization* (London: Routledge), pp. 1–17.

Ritzer, G. (1993) *The McDonaldization of Society: An Investigation into the Changing Character of Contemporary Social Life* (Newbury Park: Pine Forge Press).

Ritzer, G. (2004) *The Globalization of Nothing* (London: Sage).

Ritzer, G. (2011) *Globalization: The Essentials* (Oxford: Wiley-Blackwell).

Robertson, R. (1992) *Globalization: Social Theory and Global Culture* (London: Sage).

Rodrik, D. (2011) *The Globalization Paradox* (New York: W. W. Norton).

Sennett, R. (1976) *The Fall of Public Man* (New York: W. W. Norton).

Part II

Contemporary Drivers of Social Change: Art, Technology and Public Pedagogy

5

What Is an Intellectual, Anyway?

Ingrid Elam

There is an intellectual, if not for all times, then at least for every time. In the late 1940s, the French author Jean Paul Sartre emerged as the moral conscience of his age, speaking out about the social and political situation not only in France, but in the world at large. However, what is often forgotten is that Sartre related himself to the current issues of the times: the German occupation in the 1940s and the liberation war in Algeria in the 1950s.

Since then, new names have dominated the public sphere, and the role of the intellectual has been shaped by a variety of new contingencies. My argument is that the role of the intellectual is constantly changing, not only in its focus but also in its scope. The role changes with the political and social situation, and with the transformation of the public sphere.

I was asked to contribute to a discussion on the role of the intellectual in the public sphere, and was amazed at the confident affirmativeness of the title, since I am not so sure about how to define an intellectual, or if there is such a thing as a single public sphere. However, I then received a new title, which narrowed it down, and all the answers were already there: 'from public man to niche intellectual'. It is a man in a corner, which makes everything so much easier.

Back in the upbeat decade of the 1960s, it was easy to define what an intellectual was. An intellectual was somebody who was not only informed and professional, but also deeply engaged in critical thinking and reflection. What is more, he had a name: Noam Chomsky. In 1967, Chomsky wrote an article, *The Responsibility of Intellectuals*, in which he discussed the role of the intellectual in relation to the Vietnam War. The main target of his article was media intellectuals, journalists and critics, especially in television. According to Chomsky, they only served the ruling ideology. He advocated another kind of intellectual who had the integrity and the audacity to tell the truth when governments lie. Those most able to carry out this mission were academics like Chomsky himself, who combined deep knowledge of a specific field with the ability to step outside this field into other areas of moral debate. A leading expert on Shakespeare is not necessarily an intellectual, but an expert on Shakespeare who will contest the violation of human rights in Cambodia is. 'For a privileged minority', Chomsky (1967) argued, 'western democracy provides the leisure, the facilities and the training to seek the truth lying hidden behind the veil of distortion and misrepresentation, ideology and class interest, through which the events of current history are presented to us'. The responsibilities of intellectuals were therefore much deeper than the responsibility of, say, an industrial worker or a farmer, given the unique privileges that intellectuals enjoy.

Chomsky started out as a researcher in linguistics and became famous for his universal grammar theory. He worked all his professional life in academia but played an important critical role in the public sphere when few other scholars did. In the late 1960s and throughout the 1970s, he became a role model for many young students who were involved in political movements that opposed the Vietnam War and supported liberation movements all over the world.

The moral dilemma that confronted the supporters of liberation struggles could be expressed in Chomskyan terms as a choice between backing party politics – that is, the ideology governing the liberation movement in question – or supporting groups within the population in distant countries that struggled against oppression not only from Western imperialism, but also from the local liberation movements themselves. Towards whom should our solidarity be directed? The question ought to concern anyone who calls herself an intellectual. Do we adhere to an ideology, or do we cultivate doubt and critical questions, even towards our own standpoints?

In the 1990s, Chomsky's model became more problematic, not only because it was more difficult to have a clear standpoint on the Balkans than on Vietnam, but also because the 'Chomskyists' always tended to choose ideology before doubt. Furthermore, in the 1990s, Chomsky was not the only intellectual on the stage. A new hero had emerged: a Palestinian in exile in the United States, Edward Said. In 1993 Said gave six lectures on the role of the intellectual that illustrated the shift in public debate from ideologies – and ideology critique – to identity politics (Said, 1993). Said leaned heavily on Gramsci's notion of the *organic intellectual*,[1] that is, an intellectual rooted in and produced by capitalism, and who serves the fundamental classes of that system. Intellectuals may not organize the class relations of production, but they certainly organize class consciousness. Gramsci's intellectual organizing of class-consciousness can easily be transformed into Said's organizer of identity politics.

Whereas Chomsky relied on the professional – the academic intellectual who could unravel all the lies of governments – Said underlined the importance of the intellectual being an amateur. Said's intellectual has to be an outsider, exiled and alienated from power. He saw four dangers in professionalism: specialization, the cult of the expert, the attraction of power in government, and dependence on financial support.

Looking at the public debate today, it is easy to conclude that none of these dangers has been eliminated or even limited. Truly independent intellectuals are hard to find. They emerge in times of war and major crisis, but even then they are as rare as tall trees in a low grown Icelandic wood. Most of today's 'niche intellectuals' are financially dependent: they think for their supper. Similarly, specialization and professionalization are ongoing processes in the public sphere, or rather in various public spheres.

Now, where Chomsky criticized media intellectuals for serving the ruling ideology, and Said saw professionalization as the biggest danger facing the intellectual, today's public cultural debate seems to have lost contact with the bigger issues. The cultural pages in Sweden's largest morning newspaper, *Dagens Nyheter*, seldom contain articles on ongoing wars, widening economic gaps, environmental threats or other contentious matters. Last year's two main debates, which ran for several months, focused on the representation of political issues rather than the issues as such. In other words, the discussion concerned the *form* rather than the *content* of politics.

One of the debates, launched by the writer and columnist Bengt Olsson, claimed that there is a leftist conspiracy among Sweden's middle-aged middle class, acting as one voice to negate any initiative from anybody outside the large group of old leftists among the intellectuals who have access to the public media. It is not what is said that matters but who is saying it, Olsson claimed, and the debate went on for months without venturing outside the narrow frame of 'who is who in the media'. In this way, Olsson unwittingly confirmed his own thesis: it is the fact that he has access to and can publish his texts in the pages of *Dagens Nyheter* that gives his opinion weight, not what he actually is saying.

The second debate in *Dagens Nyheter* last year concerned a film directed by the young Gothenburg director, Ruben Östlund. The film, *Play*, follows three black suburban youngsters who are pursuing three white city boys. The question raised was whether the film was racist. Again, nobody discussed topics such as urban segregation or widening social gaps. Instead the disagreement concerned how these problems, which were taken for granted, can be represented artistically. For instance, whether racism can be treated in and transformed into art.

Thus, one could argue that the ideological debate of the 1960s and 1970s was replaced by identity politics in the 1980s and 1990s, but that there is a growing interest in form and format today. The empirical basis for such an argument might seem brittle, but mediation and forms of representation have become key concerns for anyone who wants to get a message across.

Some things, however, have not changed. Women are still more or less invisible in public debates. This is not because they are not asked to participate: women just do not seem comfortable with such debates. This does not mean that they are unintellectual; they just use different arenas to men. In recent years, young women authors in Sweden have published a series of novels that deal in fiction with political and social issues. Karolina Ramqvist, Maria Sveland and Maja Lundgren are authors who write about women in their thirties who live the freedom their feminist mothers fought for in the 1970s, but experience this freedom as a new form of constraint.

Today's young intellectuals do not use newspapers, popular media or even the Internet when they want to engage in serious debate. Facebook is for friends and feel-good messages, newspapers are for news, but if you want reflections on inequalities, global warming or emerging fascism you are well advised to turn to art. As a matter of fact, art schools in Europe today are deeply concerned with the public, or rather the absence of a truly public sphere. A couple of years ago, the University College of Arts, Craft and Design in Stockholm had all their masters students do their exam work under the heading of the 'public sphere'. Some of the results became media news due to their drastic intervention into the public domain. One graffiti artist was arrested for painting a subway car, another for building a three-story cardboard house for the homeless, without planning consent, of course. A third student faked a mental breakdown in order to expose violence in psychiatric wards.

At about the same time in Dublin, at the National College of Art and Design, a group of students initiated an art project to expose the fact that Ireland is a society where there is no trust whatsoever in the public sphere. Nobody debates anything in public anymore. The art project was an attempt to reinvent the public sphere. Students transformed an empty shop into a stage, and moved their school onto that stage, where all lectures and art seminars took place behind a huge shop window. The public, known intellectuals, and anonymous passers-by were invited in to take part in the literal reconstruction of the public sphere, in the process 'deconstructing' notions such as 'public health' or 'public access' and confronting people with concepts such as class, access and human rights. Just as theatre has for many hundreds of years been locked up in a black box, fine art has been exposed in white cubes. Today, however, artists take their art out on to the streets, into the public sphere where niche intellectuals have left open spaces for serious discussion.

In sum, there is no such thing as 'the public sphere' anymore: an arena from where intellectuals can reach out to a large audience and involve this audience in critical debate on commonly shared social and political issues. The public sphere has been fragmented. There are many different channels for information, entertainment and debate, but their combinations and these channels seldom interconnect. This leaves the intellectual, as we knew him in the recent past, with a smaller, often already consenting audience. The shift from wartime intellectuals like Sartre and Chomsky to identity politicians like Said is a step away from the universalist public man towards the niche intellectual.

Furthermore, when the public debate tends to focus on form and format rather than social and political issues, intellectuals move away from the traditional arenas and look for other spheres where they can reinvent public critical exchange: hence, the focus in contemporary art on interactivity and public intervention. There will always be intellectuals – you just have to look for them in new places.

Note

1. The notion of the organic intellectual is developed by Gramsci in his book *Prison Notebooks*, published in various editions after his death in 1937.

References

Chomsky, N. (1967) 'A Special Supplement: The Responsibility of Intellectuals', *New York Review of Books* 8(3).
Said, E. (1994) *Representations of the Intellectual: The 1993 Reith Lectures* (London: Vintage).

6
What I Think about When I Think about Being an Intellectual

Carsten Jensen

I will start with a confession that should probably immediately bar me from contributing to a discussion about the role of the intellectual in the public sphere: I do not know what an intellectual is. I will take it a step further. Despite being invited to give this address because I am considered to *be* an intellectual, I do not really care what the word means.

I used to swear by the definition given in the foreword to the 1258-page *Dictionnaire des Intellectuels Francais* by its editors, Jacques Juillard and Michel Winock: 'The scientist who works on a nuclear bomb is not an intellectual,' they write. 'When he starts considering the danger to which he exposes humanity and he persuades his colleagues to sign a petition against the bomb, he becomes an intellectual'. They elaborate by saying that an intellectual is somebody who, with an expertise acquired elsewhere, interferes in the political debate by proposing an analysis, a direction or a moral. They quote Jean-Paul Sartre's dictum that the intellectual is somebody who gets himself involved in matters that are none of his business – the implication being that authority prefers to conduct its affairs without interference. To me, the first part of Juillard and Winock's definition sounds more like the description of a whistle blower than of an intellectual.

I can understand what is meant when we talk about the expertise of the scientist, but is it possible to talk about the expertise of a writer? Here I am not so sure. I do not personally feel I have expertise in anything apart from the use of language – but we are all users of language. What expertise do humanities students graduating in post-structuralism or deconstructivism have to offer? None that I can see. The only thing they are qualified to do is lobotomize new generations of students with nonsense theories. Nobody needs them. The only petition they will ever sign is one protesting against university cuts.

What about the writer? Writers have a curiosity about the human condition, and that is what drives their creativity. Do they have any special expertise that qualifies them to confront the powers that be? In totalitarian states where lies are disseminated on a grotesque scale and language undergoes constant pollution, yes they do. Or at least they should feel that they do. When they wield their expertise in the name of truth, intellectualism sees its finest hours. In a well-established, well-functioning democracy in which freedom of expression is a given, however, who on earth needs writers in the role of intellectuals?

Even though most totalitarian states have evaporated, the noun 'intellectual' still exists, and it quite often pops up in the media, although it is not a service you can look up in the Yellow Pages. Intellectuals tend to be referred to in the plural, as though they were a uniform, homogenous group, and they are almost always mentioned in a negative sense. They are usually deemed to have failed, and to have done so in a wide variety of ways. In the now bygone rhetoric of the Cold War, their most frequent crime was siding with the totalitarian oppressor or failing to denounce the enemies of democracy. In the now popular clash-of-civilizations debate, Western intellectuals betray democracy by not distancing themselves thoroughly enough from Islam or multiculturalism. Mostly, the accusation is that you stayed silent when you should have spoken out, the underlying premise being that a writer should have an opinion on everything and a constant willingness to perform in the mass-media circus.

I sometimes perform in that circus myself. I try to do it on my own terms, but it is always a difficult balance. I cannot really explain why I bother. Maybe it is a case of temperament. I certainly have no ambition to be considered a respected intellectual – and I can assure you that I am not. I sometimes do it out of a feeling of duty. Having privileged access to the mass media, I do feel an obligation to speak out when nobody else does. If 'sensitivity to injustice' sounds too pathetic as a motivation, call it 'sensitivity to the abuse of language' instead. In politics and the mass media, dishonesty abounds. Usually the closest you will get to a truth is a half-truth, and a half-truth is just a lie with a bit of whipped cream on top.

Language was invented for the purpose of communication, and I think lying is a bad way of communicating. This applies everywhere and all the times – but especially in a democracy because democracies are based on the notion that all citizens should be able to participate in crucial decisions based on knowledge.

Know your enemies, goes an old proverb. 'Don't hate your enemies', adds the last remaining head of the Corleone family, played by Al

Pacino, in *Godfather 3*: 'It clouds your judgment'. This is good advice that I have always followed, but maybe it should go a step further. Do not just know your enemy: get to know yourself better by listening to what he says about you.

This summer I was invited by the publicly funded radio channel Radio24-syv to host four programmes about the war in Afghanistan. The directors of the channel were ambitious. They wanted to build the whole series around an interview with the former Danish Foreign Minister, Per Stig Møller, who over the course of nine years presided over the two wars in which Denmark participated in the first decade of the new millennium: Iraq and Afghanistan. Møller was not only a first-hand witness to the decision-making process, but an active participant. Sadly, the producers had to drop the idea because as soon as Møller learned I was to host the programme, he declined to go on air. The reason I understand he gave when the producer of the program Søren Steen Jespersen called him was that I was 'undemocratic, full of hatred and "un-Danish"'.

What can I learn from this? First, let us take a closer look at Mr Møller. He is not just a politician but a prominent intellectual. He has written as many books as I have. If you asked him about his public role, he would probably say that he was an intellectual first and a politician second. So here you have an intellectual cast in the privileged role of decision maker. When he was foreign minister, Møller was not – as many intellectuals are – seeking dialogue with the powerful, because he *was* the powerful. When asked about the positive outcomes of those two tragic wars, his answer was that whenever he went to Washington, doors opened for him. Finally, small and insignificant Denmark had become part of world history. In his eyes, the opening of doors in the corridors of Washington justified the untold suffering of the people of Iraq and Afghanistan.

At the same time, another foreign minister who was – like Møller – an intellectual was urged by the US to support the Iraq war. He was Germany's Josckha Fischer. When Møller was presented with the lie about the existence of weapons of mass destruction, which served to legitimize the invasion, he not only embraced it with enthusiasm, but gave the Danish Parliament a long list specifying the many kinds of deadly weapons that could be found in the arsenal of Saddam Hussein. When Josckha Fischer was presented with the same 'information', he did not use it as a libretto with which to serenade the German *Bundestag*. Instead he uttered the four words which proved him to be, beneath the mantle of foreign minister, the true intellectual he is: 'Ich bin nicht überzeugt'. [I am not convinced.] (Bernstein, 2004)

As you have already noticed, I am not particularly interested in defining the word 'intellectual', but I am very interested in noting the minefields that people who consider themselves to be intellectuals should avoid. Each in their own way, Møller and Fischer teach us a valuable lesson about the price a person should or should not be prepared to pay when invited to participate in the making of history. Ich bin nicht überzeugt: I am not convinced. These four words are as close as you can get to the credo of an independent-minded citizen, which is basically what an intellectual is. You can even boil it down to: 'Convince me!' That is the demand we should make of those in power. Do not force me, do not threaten me, do not seduce me, do not bribe me or attempt to buy me. Just convince me. In the basic language of democracy: argument based on rationalism.

Revisiting the Mohammed cartoons

Six years ago, I attended a reception at my Danish publishing house, Gyldendal. As I stood there with the mandatory glass of wine in my hand, I suddenly heard myself being denounced as an enemy of freedom of expression. The accusation came from my editor, the literary director of the publishing house, Johannes Riis. In his ritual speech at the opening of the book-season, he declared it ironic that the very writers who had benefited from freedom of expression had now turned against it. I was not the only one being accused. Together with 11 other writers, I had recently published an open letter to the citizens of Denmark protesting at the increasingly discriminatory laws directed against ethnic minorities, the obvious intention of which was to make their lives as unbearable as possible. We also protested against the right wing's hateful demonization of immigrants and their descendants, especially those with a Muslim background. This protest was immediately interpreted as an attempt to limit free speech.

Even though we did not mention the Mohammed cartoons in our letter, the heated reaction that followed had everything to do with that cartoon crisis, which during those months was in the process of going global, with Danish embassies in the Middle East being set on fire. It was presented as a black-and-white conflict. Either you stood your ground in the most uncompromising way, or you were on the side of those attacking the very foundations of democracy. There was no third way. To my own surprise, I found myself denounced for being on the wrong side.

I will forgive you if you now give a deep sigh and think: 'Oh no, not *that* again.' Can we not move on? Do we have to keep hearing about these blasted cartoons? The reason I mention them, however, is that they will not go away. The issue they raised keeps popping up. It takes on new guises, but basically it remains the same. In September 2012, the US ambassador in Libya and three of his colleagues were murdered in Benghazi. The parallels with the fall-out from the cartoon crisis were striking. The trigger was that a fundamentalist Christian right-wing group had posted an amateur film mocking the Prophet Mohammed on YouTube. When the video was dubbed into Arabic and an Egyptian television station broadcast it, a mob went on the rampage. Only a couple of years previously, one of the men behind it, a US pastor, Terry Jones, apparently determined to provoke Muslims into a murderous rage, had burned a copy of the Koran, prompting a mob to run amok in Mazar-el Sharif in northern Afghanistan. They attacked a United Nations compound, killing seven employees, among them two Norwegians.

In contrast to the reaction of the Danish Prime Minister, Anders Fogh Rasmussen, to the publication of the Mohammed cartoons, President Obama immediately condemned the video on YouTube. He did not, however, do what the Muslim protesters would probably have urged him to do, which was to imprison and punish the pastor. This brings us back to the issue at the heart of the cartoon crisis: freedom of expression, for or against.

I regard Denmark as a kind of laboratory for the future. Until recently, a populist right wing party, the Danish People's Party, regularly penetrated public discourse with abusive rhetoric on all fronts, from street talk to the mass media, and from parliamentary and ministerial debate to discussion in significant parts of the centre-left-wing opposition. In the wake of the Mohammed crisis, the verbal abuse of minorities in Denmark took on tsunami-like proportions, while those advocating a more civilized tone – such as 'the twelve writers', of which I was proud to be one – were denounced as enemies of free speech. The debate was never about what was being said, but always about the extremists' right to say it. Every new verbal attack became 'a blow for free speech' and, as time went on, the extremists grew cockier. By the time the regime was voted out, it seemed that anything could be voiced aloud in public, and nobody spoke out in protest because nobody wanted to be accused of being against freedom of expression or fostering taboos. This was an era in which free speech in Denmark became the primal scream of the frustrated, cheered on by manipulative populist demagogues nobody dared contradict.

The real victim of this era was of course freedom of expression itself. Public discourse found itself in a state of deadlock, estranged from its original function of promoting the competition of well-reasoned arguments in open debate. The British say that the proof of the pudding is in the eating. In the case of the Danes, the pudding was left untouched. All you had to do was to swear that you believed in the principle of free speech and then button your lip while the extremists screamed away at the top of their voices. Who benefited from the whole debacle? The right-wing populists.

How does one emerge from such a stranglehold? In Denmark it all simply ground to a halt when the right wing government lost the election. The populists fell silent, as if shocked by the unthinkable. For the first time, their abusive rhetoric had not ensured victory. I do not champion laws against so-called 'hate speech'. Nor do I campaign for blasphemy paragraphs. I am in favour of the community taking another kind of action. It is your human right to scream out your innermost hatred and prejudice as long as you do not accompany it with physical violence, but it is not your human right to be respected for it. It is not your human right to have every one of your abusive utterances echoed in the mass media. It is not your human right to be invited into government coalitions and be handed a degree of power totally out of proportion to the number of your votes. We need to meet the extremists not with subdued silence but with open contempt and a firmly expressed distance.

As of late 2012 the Danish People's Party is marginalized and has remained remarkably silent. The Dutch populist, Gert Wilders, suffered a humiliating defeat in the 2012 elections. What looked like an unstoppable trend has been reversed, but it is not over. Not everywhere. In Norway, the largest centre party, *Høyre*, which has so far kept its distance from the populist *Fremskridtspartiet*, is now ready to stretch out its hand. If it does, you can be sure of one thing: the Danish disaster will repeat itself in Norway.

In the decade that I do not hesitate to call Denmark's darkest in post-war history, I learned a lot, not least about freedom of expression and about my fellow intellectuals. What I learned is summarized in the bitter wisdom of the Swedish writer Anders Ehnmark, expressed 30 years ago: 'To the intellectuals it is not of any great relevance whether they find themselves on the left wing or the right wing. What really matters to them is whether they are on the winning side or the losing side. They are the bounty hunters of the class struggle.' If the term 'class struggle' feels a bit obsolete to you, feel free to replace it with any phrase of your liking – as long as it reflects the deep ongoing conflict that lies at the heart of our societies.

So what exactly did I learn about freedom of speech during that hellish decade? I learned its limits. Free speech is usually regarded as the foundation of democracy, and I agree unless the loudspeakers of freedom of expression transmit nothing but the howling of the wolves. Free speech is usually associated with everybody's right to their own opinion, and I am in accordance with that, too – unless your opinion is based on nothing but prejudice or the total absence of any relevant knowledge about the subject on which you have so strong a need to communicate. To be a good citizen in a democracy, is it enough to have an opinion rooted in nothing but your own precious personality? Are the uninformed masses democracy's best champions?

A walk on the dark side

What about the Internet? What about Google, the most ambitious universal encyclopaedia the world has ever seen? Does it not, by representing the total sum of human knowledge and making it available to everybody for free, become the true inheritor of the Enlightenment? Well, yes and no. Surf the Internet and you are taking a walk not just on the wild side, but the dark side. You may hear the silver trumpets of truth and clarity, but just as often you will hear the jungle drums of the subconscious. The Internet is two things: a unique source of human knowledge and a breeding ground for those dark desires that most societies prefer to keep at bay for fear of collapse. On the net, people can express themselves with all the uncensored brutality of raw desire.

I am not on Facebook. I consider it a waste of time. Maybe I am too old, maybe I already have enough friends, or maybe it is simply that my narcissism finds other mirrors in which I can enjoy my reflection. I do not blog and I never have. Once in a while I read one, but mostly it is an experience I do not feel the need to repeat. There is a rawness and an absence of filtration, which some might see as censorship, others as self-censorship. My point is: What is so wrong with that modicum of professionalism that reveals an editing hand? The ambition to communicate with those who might disagree with you, rather than just listening to your own voice screaming away at its shrillest, is what I would call civilization. That is what I do not find in most blogs, and that is why I do not bother reading them.

I have had my own negative experiences of the net. Whenever my comments are published in a newspaper, they also appear on the paper's website where, within the space of a few hours, they provoke hundreds of comments, many conveying the same message as Mr Møller when he refused to appear on the radio with me. On one occasion, when I received the Olof Palme Prize, named after the murdered Swedish prime minister, I was denounced in 600 comments as a traitor to my country. One bright spark even asked: 'Where is Christer Pettersson when we need him?' For those of you unfamiliar with Swedish history, Christer Pettersson was the presumed murderer of Olof Palme.

Such comments are invariably written by people hiding behind the mask of anonymity, the go-to headgear of freedom of expression's Internet boom. I personally find such anonymity completely incompatible with democracy. What kind of free speech is it when the speaker dares not show his face? The editors of newspaper websites finally seem to have realized this. As of late, you can no longer post your comments without giving your full name and a verifiable address. This seems to have put a sharp brake on readers' need to share their innermost thoughts. Where there were once 100 comments, there are now only five; where there were 500, there are now at most only 50. Even the right-wing newspaper, *Berlingske Tidende*, which used to defend the abusive tone of the debate about immigrants, now advises its readers to keep their language polite. So what has happened? Has freedom of expression suffered yet another blow or has civilization won?

The Internet favours anonymity. It even promotes it. Its freedom is the freedom to speak from behind a mask, a freedom that operates by breaking the link between a person and his words. Where a message has no sender, no one takes responsibility. Every act is permitted, but only because its perpetrator can never be found or punished. You will never be held accountable for what you say. Your words are free, in that it costs you nothing to speak them. Being weightless, you will never have to weigh them.

The Internet acquired a reputation for being a genuine instrument for the promotion of democracy because of the way Facebook and Twitter were used in the so-called green protest movement in Iran and the Arab Spring in Egypt. In both cases, the popular protest movements were celebrated as Twitter revolutions. Once again the social medium was mistaken for the message, in the naive belief that new technology is automatically a useful tool for social change. In an uprising against an authoritarian state, the anonymity of the sender is an advantage, and you might even say a precondition, of the whole rebellion, but the green revolution in Iran was defeated and the Arab Spring took an unexpected turn when the Muslim Brotherhood took power. Only 4 per cent of the Egyptian population has access to Facebook and Twitter, which of course explains a great deal, including our fascination with it. We saw the Arab Spring as a mirror of ourselves – a young Westernized elite ready to turn its politics in the same direction as ours. Once again, however, the medium was not the message. In Egypt, the mosque proved a stronger force of change than Twitter.

Why is the idea of anonymous protest received so uncritically by Western proponents of democracy and social change? Or rather, why does it appear so attractive to certain activists? We live in societies that are increasingly under surveillance. There are security cameras everywhere, and if the state so desires, it can easily gain access to our computers and read our most intimate secrets. New anti-terror laws give us less and less protection, but we do not seem to mind this development. Big Brother is no longer a threat to our privacy. On the contrary, he has become a cherished member of the family. The state turns its camera lenses on us, but who directs the cameras towards the state? Who watches the watchers? The media is the normal answer – the press, the Fourth Estate – but this is no longer as true as it used to be. Freedom of expression might come under occasional pressure from violent semi-totalitarian or extremist groups opposed to democracy in general, but its stronger and brighter big sister, freedom of information, is under threat from much more powerful forces. States have a tendency to become more and more secretive about their own doings. Decisions with huge implications for people's lives and futures tend to be taken at an ever-increasing distance from the citizens they concern. Crucially, the media seem to care less and less. Where we should find facts and information, we find a gaping black hole. At the heart of democracy, we find a vacuum.

Mass media and the absence of information

There are many reasons for this absence of information at the core of our societies. One is the media itself. Fewer and fewer resources are set aside for investigative journalism. The same citizens who have learned to love Big Brother tend not to fret about the doings of the decisions makers as long as they feel safe from potential danger. We tend to see ourselves not as citizens with the right to influence but as consumers, including consumers of politics. What we want from politicians is a flattering bargain, not raw reality.

For the past decade, most Western countries have been involved in two wars in the Middle East and Central Asia. It is an elementary lesson that the first victim of any war is truth, but this seems to have been forgotten by the media, which willingly turn themselves into a propaganda arm of government: That black hole once again. What does such a vacuum mean when it comes to public debate about the purpose and methods of war? You cannot base a debate on the gaps in your knowledge. It is not enough to have an attitude to the war, to give it a thumbs-up or a thumbs-down, denoting in the universal sign language of Facebook your like or dislike. Defining yourself as a pacifist or a hawk does not accord your opinions with any relevance. The practically non-existent debate about the current war in Afghanistan shows the limits of freedom of speech. It is not enough to have an opinion. You have to have a minimum level of knowledge, too. If you do not have access to that knowledge, what then?

It is possible that my criticism of the media is too primitive. Journalists do not just lie down and allow themselves to become vehicles for propaganda. Incompetence plays a part, too. Many journalists arrived in the complex societies of Iraq and Afghanistan with little or no prior knowledge of the cultural labyrinths-cum-war zones they had entered. The same went for the invading armies. How can you question a blindfolded person about what they see in their self-imposed darkness? It is now recognized that this arrogant lack of advance knowledge was a major factor in the disastrous outcome of both wars, but this realization dawned way too late.

The intellectual is not a journalist. He is not a fact-finder. His genre is the essay. The Danish writer, Per Lange, once gave a very good definition of the essay: 'If you have a gap in your knowledge – and of course you have a gap in your knowledge – it is this gap that you explore' (Lange, 1964, p. 147). What he meant was that not everything can be reduced to facts. There are truths that we will never grasp fully but can only approach through interpretation. The intellectual is an interpreter, and this is what makes the essay his natural habitat. The intellectual, however, must also ask himself: What is the use of interpreting a war and saying wise and humane things about violence, suffering and sudden death when you have no idea what is going on?

I have visited Afghanistan on four occasions, but it was not until my fourth visit that I became a critic of the war. I was embedded with Danish soldiers in Helmand for two weeks. I stayed with them in their outposts and joined them on patrol. I saw the landscape, and I met local people. Although I did not witness any battles, I learned enough about how the war was being conducted to realize that everything I had hitherto read or heard about the conflict was a shameful lie.

Instead of this realization becoming my conclusion, it became my starting point. I did not for a moment see myself in the role as an intellectual at that point. I saw myself as a collector and collator of facts: journalism was my genre. It was only at a later stage, when I wanted to widen my scope, that I returned to the essay form.

When I came back from my trip, I started consulting historians and other journalists – because independent-minded people stubbornly pursuing the truth are always out there somewhere. You might not see them on television or on the front pages, but they are there, scattered all over the world, doing the often thankless job of defending the citizens' right to know what is being done in their name. I realized that if I was to enter the debate I needed to have a better grasp of the facts than the politicians and even the military officers themselves.

It is at moments like this that the Internet comes into its own. Most notably in the form of sites like Wikileaks, whose volcanic outpourings of raw facts have embarrassed and infuriated governments worldwide – and many media moguls, too. In Denmark, the editors-in-chief of the leading newspapers, with two honourable exceptions, distanced themselves from Wikileaks. Even the President of Danish PEN stepped back. With friends like these, freedom of expression clearly needs no enemies.

Whatever one may think of Julian Assange and his political ideas, with their strange mixture of conspiracy theories and paranoia, his uncertain future clearly shows that he is at the frontline of the fight for democracy – and that there is a real war going on about freedom of information. The appalling fate of the young soldier, Bradley Manning, who set too much store by what his school history lessons said about human rights in a democracy, is another case in point. The fallout from his act of idealism in leaking reams of sensitive military information bears comparison with the fate of any dissident in a totalitarian state. Although his legal status as a prisoner remains unclear at the time of writing, there are indications that he has been physically abused and tortured. One thing is certain: this young man will not walk free in daylight again.

The website Wikileaks no longer exists. Not because it has been banned by any existing law, but because it has simply been sabotaged out of existence. Other sites have sprung up, however, and this is where the Internet is at the forefront of the struggle for democracy. Even though I do not condone Internet activists hiding behind the mask of anonymity, I do increasingly understand them. They are not always on the right side of the law, but they are mostly on the right side of democracy. The two states need not be mutually exclusive, especially not in times of turbulence and crisis such as these. We do not want to live in a society subsumed to anarchy, but sometimes it takes an anarchic impulse to change the world for the better.

When anonymous activists take to the streets in their Guy Fawkes masks, I do not cheer them. I believe the struggle for democracy can only truly be fought barefaced. Bare faces are democracy's most powerful weapon and symbol, and a man behind a mask can never be a source of inspiration or a role model. The movie, 'V for Vendetta', in which the Guy Fawkes mask is first introduced as a symbol of resistance, describes a United Kingdom sunk into an Orwellian state, but we are not there yet. We need the net activists, and they need the established media – as the case of Wikileaks clearly showed when Julian Assange cleverly established intensive cooperation with selected magazines and newspapers across the world. The enormous quantity of raw data required professional editors to process it, and that collaboration resulted in a glorious moment in the otherwise deplorable recent history of the media. Cooperation of this kind constitutes a tightrope walk between illegal and legal activities, but it is a necessary tightrope walk.

The truth be told

Let me end with an anecdote. Recently, I found myself in a cemetery in Copenhagen standing in front of a grave where a fallen soldier from the war in Afghanistan was buried. Next to me stood a comrade of his, a captain in the Danish army, who had invited me to join him. The captain had recently gone public with a devastating criticism of the Danish presence in Afghanistan, in which he confronted – among others – the generals. He was the first to do so publicly. By this I mean that he used his own name and showed his own face. He had been stationed at the army outpost Armadillo, made famous in the Janus Metz's documentary. His team suffered heavy losses: of 110 soldiers, 2 were killed, 75 were wounded and 12 suffered mental breakdowns. It was not al-Qaida or the soldiers of the Taliban who constantly attacked the Danish soldiers and planted deadly IEDs; it was the locals – the very farmers they were supposed to be helping. There was only one conclusion to be drawn from this debacle. The Afghans did not want foreign troops on their land. This was the plain, simple, devastating message the captain had gone public with.

I had interviewed him on the radio programme I hosted. He had also been interviewed in the Danish daily, *Politiken*, and written an article of his own. We had been emailing intensely during this period. He had been feeling raw and vulnerable due to the media exposure and uncertainties over his future career. After having described to me in gruesome detail what an exploding roadside bomb had done to his dead comrade, he told me why he went to visit his tomb so often: 'Whenever I doubt whether I have done the right thing, I come here to think', he said, 'and I always leave convinced that going public was right. Because he deserves the truth to be told.'

Whether Juillard and Winock would have judged that the captain's words warrant him a place in their encyclopaedia of intellectuals is neither here nor there. What matters is the captain's message: we all deserve that the truth be told.

References

Bernstein, R. (2004) 'The German Question', *The New York Times*, 2 May 2004.
Julliard, J. and Winock, M. (2009) *Dictionnaire des Intellectuels Francais* (Paris: SEUIL).
Lange, P. (1964) *Samlede Essays* (København: Gyldendals Forlag).

7
Round-table Discussion Led by Thomas Hylland Eriksen: The Flattening of the Public Sphere and the Loss of Respect for Knowledge

Oscar Hemer

Thomas Hylland Eriksen: It would be fun to compare notes with Carsten Jensen regarding how one is perceived as a cosmopolitan intellectual in Norway and Denmark, respectively. There are some striking similarities, and I could subscribe to several of the points made.

In Norway, we had a right-wing terrorist attack in the summer of 2011. Since then, it has become more difficult – not easier – to defend cosmopolitan values. When you begin to defend cosmopolitan values in this context, the people on the other side – and they are the majority – will say that you are paving the way for the terrorists. People who talk about genetically inferior Pakistanis and low-IQ Somalis are blackmailing newspapers. Unless you publish our articles every day', they say, 'something similar will happen again'. There will be a new attack because the people are not going to put up with this anymore.

The accusations have shifted from 'naive multiculturalists' to 'traitors' over the past few years, and the number of death threats has increased. So what Ingrid Elam said about the shift from ideology to identity is extremely interesting, because we are now seeing a major polarization in many Western societies. Denmark and the Netherlands have gone before the rest of us, but we are getting there as well, to a conflict that you could vaguely describe as nationalism vs. cosmopolitanism, and which does not follow a left-right divide. There is a Maoist newspaper in Norway, the editor of which comes across every second day as a reactionary nationalist – in fact as a *national socialist* not in the old sense, but in a new sense. The only think tank or intellectual body of any size in

Norway that is positive towards minorities today is a liberal think tank associated with the conservative party called 'Civita', which is very optimistic – too optimistic in fact – about how well everything is going.

Regarding the necessity of speaking the truth, well, yes: But is everybody entitled to say anything at all about anybody at any time? That is also the issue regarding WikiLeaks, because one of the objections to WikiLeaks is similar to the objections to the Mohammed cartoons – that everybody does not have the right to say anything and everything about anybody at any time. We have the right to some privacy. The problem somehow with WikiLeaks is how it mixed information about public lies, which the public clearly has the right to know about, with gossip about ambassadors and politicians – the kind of thing we tell each other over a beer – which was never intended for the wider public. So where should we draw the line? I think one of the things we need to consider when we think about the role of the intellectual, and the fact that we are all now wandering around in this small Icelandic forest, is the role of new media and how they have somehow erased the boundary between private and public. Wikileaks is a clear example of this. Where is the boundary between secrets of state, a lie by the foreign ministry, and gossip about common acquaintances? Should we be able to gossip about people we do not like without it being published on the Internet? I think we should – and that is one of the difficulties with drawing this boundary.

Only last week, a controversy erupted in Norway because a historian published a few lines on his Facebook wall about 'genetically inferior Punjabis'. 'Why should we import these genetically inferior Punjabis to the country?' he asked. And he ranted about 'cultural Marxist bicycle networks' in Oslo West. He had probably had a few beers too many, and forgot that he was not just talking with his mates over a beer, but actually posting things on Facebook. It was immediately picked up by someone who copied the thread and spread it. The historian immediately erased his thread, but by then it was too late. Within minutes, hundreds of people knew about it, and it was an item on the national news. Some of his enemies were interviewed by the newspapers, and he was invited to debate the whole affair on the radio. He defended himself by saying that he might just as well have made his remark about Swedes. Of course that is not the case. The point is, however, that he thought he was communicating in private, but he wasn't – he was speaking in a public sphere.

So Facebook is an interesting case. Why am I saying this? Because I think the reason why there are no tall trees is the fragmentation of the public sphere largely due to new media. It is democratization. So let us say that this is a general issue. I think both Carsten and Ingrid touched on it – the fact that we no longer produce towering figures like Jean Paul Sartre, Chomsky and Solzhenitsyn, for that matter, while he was still in the Soviet Union. These people were trusted and listened to, people who spoke with authority and could tell the truth to the powers that be. People whose statements had consequences.

Now that everybody is talking at the same time, in a world that is too full and overheated, it is hard to identify statements that are worth taking seriously. There is an element of democratization. Everybody agrees that it seems that the Internet is a good thing because it allows everybody to have a voice, such as the historian I mentioned and various others, extreme right-wing groups who can spread their poison as they like, incite hatred, and inspire terrorism as they have done and continue to do. Of course it is a good thing that everybody is allowed to say what he or she wants, but one outcome of this is a form of nihilism –where everyone's utterances have the same value:

'Don't tell us that your statement has more authority than everybody else's'.
'Well, I am just a professor at the University'.
'Exactly, you are nobody, my statements are just as worthy as yours!'

Such are the comments after Carsten's articles. Their authors see themselves as just as authoritative and claim that their statements should have the same weight. If you disagree, you are an elitist – and you do not want to be an elitist. This egalitarianism leads to a general flattening, and it also entails a loss of respect for knowledge. The public sphere no longer respects people who know more than anybody else about a certain subject, because that makes them elitist – and usually subversive traitors and multiculturalists as well, but that is another matter.

That is one thing. In addition, and Ingrid touched on this as well, there is expert positivism: that is, the idea of the expert as someone who has privileged knowledge, as opposed to that of the intellectual who speaks from the basis of general knowledge and general intelligence and who should represent a form of recognizable reasoning, common sense. This is an instrumentalist view of knowledge, which is also bad news for the essayists and the novelists. It is good news for people who have a specialist field of knowledge, but bad news for the generalists. It is the generalists, of course, who have a better sense of judgment. So that is another dimension of this egalitarianism and democratization: a general loss of interest in *complex* knowledge. There is an immense demand out there right now for simple answers to complex questions. Think about the rise of so-called evolutionary psychology, which is a kind of fancy version of socio-biology. There are lots of complex questions that we ask, and there are simple answers to all of them. The answer is Darwinian natural selection, amen. It is a form of evangelical religion, where people pray to St Dawkins and St Pinker, and they thank them every evening before going to bed for bringing some simplicity into a hopelessly complex world. As a result, real, deep intellectual thinking suffers.

To sum up, the main reason why we no longer produce these towering figures and the main reason why intellectuals no longer have the position they used to have is the loss of respect for knowledge, partly due to new media. In the old hierarchical world, people who had authority could speak with authority and, for better or worse, that hierarchy no longer exists.

Panel debate: democracy is to agree to disagree

Oscar Hemer: Before handing over the floor, I would like to throw in two comments. The first is about the lack of controversy on this panel. We do not have a representative of the nationalist position that could accuse the others of 'multiculturalism' or of being 'traitors'. Another thing that just struck me, with regard to what Thomas said about egalitarianism and the flattening of debate, is that when talking or thinking about the public intellectual here in Scandinavia, it is inevitable to think about the *public enemy*, which somehow applies to the position of both Carsten and Thomas in the public spheres of Denmark and Norway, respectively. I assumed that the kind of comments that Carsten receives in the threads after his articles is the kind of reaction you find all over the world, but it strikes me now that this is to some extent a typically Scandinavian phenomenon, which may have to do with our egalitarian tradition.

Ingrid Elam: It might be somewhat Scandinavian because there is this drive for consensus in Scandinavia. Everybody loves consensus, so if you are not in it, you are against it – you are an enemy, so to speak. I would like to comment on two things. First, the Mohammed caricatures. I was on the wrong side, too, in Sweden, because I thought that it was a really stupid thing to do. I debated with people who I respect immensely who were, I would say, freedom of expression fundamentalists. The problem is that people were talking about the right to heresy, and I think that heretical movements have had an immense importance in European history. Heresy is important, but in my experience, the true heretic commits heresy towards his own gods, not those of other people. What happened in Denmark was not heresy, but defamation of other people's values. You would think that intellectuals and artists, of all people, should know that everything is context-dependent. In what context did these caricatures appear? Not one where these cartoonists were under any form of threat, but a context in which immigrants in Denmark, as Carsten explained, were the losers. The reason why I repeat this is that it is a sign of intellectual dishonesty. You do not sort out the arguments.

Regarding flatness and expertise: I think they can be combined. Democracy can be combined with knowledge. I have been spending some time this summer reading Montaigne. He talks about himself as somebody who is really not learned. He lived in a medieval society where the learned were inside the Church, and he sees himself as an amateur. Yet he is really an intellectual in the way we have defined it – somebody who doubts all the time and questions everything. The thing is that he discusses all the time. He is alone in his castle with his books, and he discusses all the time with ancient writers. He tries to live in the contemporary world, but is discussing with Epameinondas and others. So he is really learned, and there is not one fact but a tonne of facts that he tries to put into context. So that is why I was saying that it is a fact that the world is getting better, but it is also a fact that it is getting worse. I think we can agree that we do not have to agree.

Carsten Jensen: I was surprised to hear that Thomas was an optimistic intellectual because that was not the impression I got from what he just said. My own natural inclination is not to be just pessimistic, but almost apocalyptic, and I have actually learned a lot from some of Thomas' books. He wrote a book about happiness in which he talks about climate change and the need to present arguments not by invoking apocalyptic visions but by encouraging positive action. I felt that was a correction to my own inherent pessimism, to which I all too often happily surrender. I think the premise of these discussions, at least concerning Western democracies, is that we are finding ourselves at a point in world history where life has never been better. I think that is why I am on the alert because I can envisage us losing it all. It is as if all progress can lead in one of two directions: to an even better society or to disaster. I do think that this fragmentation of the public sphere is embodied by the Internet in a very deep sense. Because, if you take somebody like Anders Breivik, he was able to use information from the Internet to construct a totally private world that was never corrected by any outsiders, and which he actually shared with quite a large group of people. Normally, if you move into the public sphere – if you read a newspaper or watch the news on television – you are unavoidably confronted with somebody who thinks differently from you, who interprets things differently. I think that this is the essence of democracy – not to agree but to disagree. It is a way of channelling conflict in a peaceful way. I think Thomas invented a word for this in the wake of Breivik, when he talked about democracy as a community where you agree to disagree: *Uenighedsfællesskab* [Disagreement Community]. I think that is a brilliant way of describing it. A community does not work if it does not include the right to disagree. Nor does it work without empathy – by trying to imagine how the other half lives, those who are not like you. This does not mean that you uncritically accept their way of life, but at least you try to understand it from within.

Thomas Hylland Eriksen: Regarding optimism vs. pessimism, the glass is always half full or half empty, and you can sometimes choose whether to be an optimist or a pessimist. When I grew up in the 1960s, 1970s and 1980s, everybody told us that things were going really badly, and that we were sailing over the edge of a cliff ecologically, and so on. Here we are, many years later, and things are still going reasonably well. So that is why I think we should take the more apocalyptic visions with a pinch of salt. I see the most serious challenge confronting us today as having to do with identity and human rights vs. nationalism. A few people can do a lot of harm, on both sides.

Regarding what Ingrid said about Montaigne, I think the problem with the new and fragmented media is that people do not seem to have the time. You never have five minutes to listen to an argument. For example, the Mohammed cartoons: I think we have been saying pretty much the same things in our different countries. You cannot ban them, but you can say that it was bloody stupid to publish them and disrespectful because of the defamation. It takes five or ten minutes to go over the argument and to understand it, whereas it takes a much shorter time to say: 'Are you in favour of freedom of expression: yes or no?' So simple answers to complex questions save a lot of time for people who have a stressful everyday life. I joined Facebook half a year ago partly for ethnographic reasons – I think it is interesting because it is a bit like life itself, but much more fragmented. You can view maybe 10 or 20 news items in a couple of minutes, but how much complexity do you get out of that? It is like headline news on CNN – you feel twice as stupid after a programme than you were before it started.

Questions and answers

Carsten, you have an article in *Politiken* today in which you criticize the opposition, the government and journalists. You have only 35 comments under your article and almost all of them are positive. This is a new development.

Carsten Jensen: I think it has a lot to do with the fact that you cannot make comments anonymously anymore. You have to stand up and show your face. In my opinion, you should not try to control freedom of expression with laws, but there is nonetheless a question of civilized behaviour – what it means for strangers to live together. This is a lesson we learn every day when we take the train or walk the streets. There is an expression, 'white lies', which means that you do not always say out loud what you think. This is essential for living with other people, even living in a family. If you always speak your mind, your life will be a battleground from the moment you get out of bed. I am a great fan of white lies – I think they are the basis of civilization.

Ingrid, you talked about creating discussion through the art scene instead of in the media. I was thinking that if you raise a question through an art project in the public sphere, then it might be discussed in media, and that maybe they would discuss the case and not what the project was really about: for example, the project where an artist jumped from a bridge to try to discuss psychiatry and the health system in Sweden. The discussion was not about that, but whether the event was art. You said that maybe an intellectual could step out of the white box. Do you think that the issues fine arts bring to the public sphere can be discussed in the media?

Ingrid Elam: I do not think it is a question of whether you should step out of the white box. You are already out of the white box, but not everybody has realized that. There are so many communities around. I was in a discussion this summer where somebody was talking about an article and suddenly a woman turned to me and said: 'What article are they talking about?' I said it was in *Dagens Nyheter*, and she said: 'Well, I live in Malmö. I don't read that paper.' It was just taken for granted that she would have seen it on the Internet. What I meant with art, especially fine arts and the performing arts, is that many young artists and art students have come to mistrust not only the public sphere, but also their own art material, so they try to experiment in public, and they try to reach out to the public. I think if you see new movements today, they are small crowds, and they are out on the streets. It is a romantic view, but I think it is really a question of reinventing a public sphere where you can talk directly to people, discuss and be there. I do not know whether it will be successful, and the mass media still have an enormous impact. The mass media are adjusting to the consumerism we are living through, however, and it bores me.

So you think that most of the interesting stuff is taking place outside the media spotlight?

Ingrid Elam: Yes, there are a lot of interesting projects going on; it is just not recorded in the newspapers. Where I am now, at the Faculty of Fine, Applied and Performing Arts, Gothenburg University, the region, its politicians and organizations are very interested in cooperation, how to reach out to the public audience, and so on. I think there is a lot of change going on, to speak Obama's language.

Given that Oscar writes fiction and is also an academic, and two of you on the panel are active novelists, my question is more about being an intellectual, writing novels, and the role this plays in your need to express yourself and your need to have an opinion.

Thomas Hylland Eriksen: I could answer for Carsten. His book *Vi de druknede* [*We the Drowned*] was highly successful, both commercially and critically, for the novel as a genre. By tracing the history of a seafaring community from a couple of centuries back to the present, he decentralizes the Danish identity. People enjoy it as a good story with recognizable people that go through a lot, and they unconsciously rethink their own identity as Danes. Denmark is portrayed as a result of contact with the outside world, and not as something that has sprung up from the ground. That is my reading of it in the context of a broader humanistic project, which has its polemical side but also its literary side.

Ingrid Elam: Could I just comment on that? Because women are reluctant to take part in official debate. If you see debates in the newspapers it is men, men, men. If you look at women's fiction in Sweden today, all the problems of backlash and so on, are in novels, not the newspapers. So they use fiction in a way they would never use the public sphere.

Carsten Jensen: I would like to thank Thomas for his characterization of my book. We talked about identity, and in that way, fiction has something to do with identity. It is not like in politics where you deliver a ready-made identity; it is about questioning the very idea of identity and showing how complex we are. Before writing it, I did think about the change in the way Danes have viewed themselves over the past century. If you asked a Dane a couple of generations ago: 'What kind of nation is Denmark?' they would have said we are a seafaring nation. Today, they would say that historically we are a farming nation. I think that the current answer is testimony to a tragic loss of historical memory. Thinking about yourself as a seafaring nation makes you much better equipped for the challenge of globalization than thinking of yourself as a farming nation. Sailors and farmers have very different attitudes to strangers. We talked about nationalism, and I think that we should remember that the strongest anti-globalization movement that exists is nationalism, and that is why in recent years nationalism has been experiencing a renaissance. It is dressed up as nationalism, but it is also a protest against the kind of impotence you feel when you are faced with globalization: The feeling that every important decision is out of the hands of your own nation and your own politicians. As such, it must be taken seriously. I think it would be a mistake if we thought that present day nationalism is just a bad copy of the nationalism of the 1930s. That is not its real source of inspiration. It is not fascism all over again. It is not concerned with racial issues: it is concerned with cultural issues. It is not about *blut und boden*; it is about the welfare system, it is about hospitals, it is about the fear of losing the privilege of living in a welfare state.

Thomas Hylland Eriksen: Well, I think it is about a lot of things. When you look at all these statements that float around in the public sphere, you should try to find out what motivates them. We have a number of people back home who are motivated by resentment, hatred and suspicion. They never say what they are in favour of, they never have any good stories about immigrants, they only have bad stories about fanatical Muslims. If that is their motivation, you may wonder if it is love of hospitals that drives them and not hatred. As a citizen and an intellectual, I would ask: What kind of emotions drives this? Is it hatred? Will it make the world a better place if someone prints cartoons of Mohammed? Will there be more love, peace and solidarity in the world as a result?

Carsten Jensen: I do not think it is a question of whether they are motivated by love or hatred. A lot of people are not motivated by love or hatred, but by fear – and when you are fearful, you cannot think clearly. That is when you become an easy victim of populist demagogues.

8

Interview with Måns Adler: The Democratization of Live Streaming Tools

Liv Stubbe Østergaard

Giving everybody a broadcasting bus in their pocket

In 1985 – when Måns Adler, one of the founders of the live streaming tool Bambuser, was four years old – his best friend in Malmø had to move with his parents to Indonesia. The first conversation they had over the phone sounded something like this: '... "Hallo" ... (break) .... "Hi" ... (break).... "How are you?" ... (break) .... "I'm good" ... (break) –... "Mummy, I can't do this anymore – it takes too long!"'.

This was Adler's first understanding of what communication was all about. That kind of conversation could not remain spontaneous because of the delay – for a four-year old, in particular, ten seconds is a lifetime. However, the boys managed to find a way to communicate during their time apart. The Swedish postal service had a special service called Sound Letters. It was a simple cassette tape that you could put into your cassette player. You pressed record, recorded for ten minutes, took it out and put it back in a yellow envelope. Three weeks later, his friend in Indonesia could pick it up, put it in his tape recorder, listen, then turn the tape around and record an answer. Six weeks later, it would arrive back in Malmø, and it was like Christmas.

This story illustrates how far we have come in one lifetime with regard to communication, and the story has been an integral part of the development of Bambuser in regard to what it takes to keep a conversation going.

Bambuser was developed in 2007. The idea behind the application was to give everybody a 'broadcasting bus' in their back pocket as a way to democratize the technology of live broadcasting and the tool of live video streaming. At that time, live video broadcasting was something that only a lucky few had the opportunity to do: that is, CNN, the BBC, and so on. There were only a few organizations that could afford broadcasting buses or owned a channel that could broadcast live video material. The founders of Bambuser wanted to see what would happen if that technology was democratized and put into everyone's hands. According to Adler,

> When looking at this from a democratization perspective, for me this is all about one thing: lowering the extremely high production costs there were back in 2007 to a marginal cost, which means that you actually have a broadcasting bus in your pocket and do not pay the EUR 30–40 per second for distribution that traditional broadcasters do; you can take it as part of your existing flat rate data plan.

The high production costs of the traditional broadcasting system also meant that it was forced to air shows that many people would watch, or to aim for the lowest common denominator. By providing an application that gives people access to technology previously unavailable to them, the developers were keen to find out what people would choose to broadcast, and what people would choose to watch. Adler notes:

> By marginalizing the production costs, all of a sudden it becomes interesting to see what people choose to broadcast. You will not end up with a scenario where you only shoot a premier league soccer game – a father can watch his 11-year old daughter playing the same game, and you can watch it live on your television or on your computer screen. So it disrupts the traditional pattern to a more distributed model where people choose to watch the things that actually are meaningful.

Bambuser was developed as part of Måns' final project at the KaosPilot program.[1]

It is an interactive mobile video streaming platform that enables users to effortlessly stream and share live video using a smartphone or a computer equipped with a webcam. In addition to being accessible on the Bambuser website, broadcasts can be shared on various social media websites such as Facebook, Twitter, tumblr and Blogger. The interesting thing about Bambuser is that it changes the way video is recorded by letting people share their videos at the same instant as they are being created. Instead of recording it on your device, uploading it somewhere, and then getting access, the video is uploaded as it is being produced – enabling people to broadcast live in real time.

From set arrangements to revolutions: watching the watchers

In the initial development phase of Bambuser, the developers wrote about three use scenarios: (a) an elderly person who could not travel to her granddaughter's graduation, but by using Bambuser would be able to view the event in real time; (b) the 11-year old girl playing soccer, where someone in the crowd could pick up their phone and live stream it to her father who could not make it to the game; and (c) the young man in the streets of Baghdad, at the time of the height of the post-Iraq war violence, who would be able to stream live footage of US soldiers shooting at civilians – footage that CNN and the BBC might choose not to broadcast under pressure from the US Army.

At the beginning, there were a lot of weird examples of how people would use it. People would tape their mobile to a radio-controlled aircraft or stream parachute jumps live. Someone wanted to find out if his fridge really turned out the light when he closed the door. The main uses, however, were lectures and press conferences – set arrangements in date and time for which the audience was booked in advance. As Adler explains, if you just pick up your mobile phone and start broadcasting something you see on the street, it is harder to get people to watch.

However, one specific event and use of Bambuser would come to highlight the real advantage of the tool, and the gains of switching from recording videos on a mobile phone in order to upload them onto YouTube to stream live. In June 2010, at a demonstration outside a police station in Cairo after the police had beaten the famous blogger, Khalid Said, more than 200 people were arrested and all their mobile phones were confiscated. The police stated that they had not used excessive violence, but all the pictures and video of the event had been erased. One of the protesters had used Bambuser, however, so even though the police had confiscated his phone, the video had already been streamed live and recorded on Bambuser's servers on the cloud. It was therefore already accessible on the web. The police could not confiscate or suppress the material. The protesters were able to use it in court and to tell the rest of the world about the police violence: 'The police thought they had control over the information landscape. But they didn't really,' Adler continues. 'From that point on, I think people understood the importance of having somewhere where the video is uploaded and leaves the phone in the same instant that it is created.' After this event, a lot of activists, especially in the human rights movement in Egypt, began to train each other to use Bambuser.

The practices of using electronic equipment to watch over authorities has been dubbed 'sousveillance' by Steve Mann, a pioneer in wearable computing at the University of Toronto. In his research, Mann outlines the difference between surveillance and sousveillance – 'sur' coming from an authority from above and 'sous' from a crowd below and manifesting itself in a form of inverse surveillance (Mann, 1998). Bambuser has distributed a way for people to keep track of their own governments.

Leading up to the Egyptian election in November 2010, Bambuser experienced a peak in the amount of videos arriving on its servers. On the day of the election, more than 10 000 of the videos that arrived on the servers were from Egypt. This mass movement in Egypt had started to use Bambuser's services to observe and document what was going on. Since no international election observers were allowed in the country, people took it into their own hands to share what was going on in Egypt right there and right now.

Two months later, on 25 January 2011, Bambuser again started to receive a lot of videos – the kind of broadcasts that were being shown in the mass media, but also other kinds. One of the streams from Egypt that demonstrated the potential of the tool was of an activist who was being beaten by the military during the demonstrations after Mubarak stepped down. The activist managed to stream this for nine minutes through the phone in his pocket, before his phone was confiscated. The video was shared on Facebook and Twitter, and was one of the first to show that the army was also suppressing the people, nuancing the story of the military being solely on the side of the people during the demonstrations and protests. The video made it all the way to Al Jazeera as well as other networks broadcasting inside Egypt, and when the activist was brought to a police station later that day, the chief inspector was too afraid to take him into custody.

During 2011, Bambuser started to receive a lot of streams from Syria. The influx of streams was consistent. Every day, Bambuser would receive hundreds of videos of user-generated content from citizen journalists. The streams were typically low frame rate, shot from a rooftop, of people shouting out and chanting on the street in big parades and protests. After three or four months, the footage from Syria started to get some interest from the rest of the world. Streams from other countries, such as Bahrain, did not receive as much attention – and they were not able to keep their revolution 'in the air' in the same way as in Syria.

While some videos depicted the bombing of cities, others showed different kinds of stories that might not otherwise have come out. One example is a video of a gas light and a solar panel revealing that the Syrian government was shutting off the electricity for several hours a day. This made it hard for people to use media to get their message out because the batteries on their electronic devices would not last as long as the power cuts. In addition, when the electricity came back on, it was at 400 volts, which blows the chargers. If you cannot power your electronic equipment, access to the Internet is irrelevant. The video shows the use of alternative sources of energy to charge the batteries of electronic devises.

According to Adler, the main reason why Bambuser has been embraced by activists around the world, especially in relation to the Arab Spring, is that it has faster delivery and better technology than other live streaming tools. The delay or time difference between what the camera sees and what you as a viewer see at the other end of the Internet is very small. Bambuser is also able to adapt to very low bandwidths, and covers more platforms than similar tools such as Ustream and Justin. Bambuser covers all Nokia phones and Windows mobile phones, which are more popular in the Middle East than iPhones and Androids. A final factor is that when a community starts building around a certain tool, this simply becomes the tool to use.

Broadcasting on traditional media outlets

Interest in streams from Bambuser has grown tremendously, especially since the Arab Spring, and the more traditional media outlets have started to use material from Bambuser's platform to a greater extent. Towards the end of 2012, the Associated Press, which cooperates with Bambuser, distributed more than 4000 Bambuser videos. Some 3000 were live from Syria, and the rest were local videos from South America, Asia and the United States. The videos from Syria in particular went out live, rather than on demand, through CNN, the BBC, Sky News and Al Jazeera.

Asked about mechanisms for the verification of material on Bambuser's servers, Adler explains that it is really hard to fake something when it is live because everything would need to be organized like theatre. If you are going to fake it, you need to organize everybody to do exactly the right thing in the right order at the right time. Therefore, the verification that a lot of journalists and news outlets try to undertake is to try to communicate with the person who is broadcasting, for example, by typing or saying: 'film to the right'. If the camera moves to the right, you can be sure that the event is happening there and now. Sometimes, more established media outlets also get the user's Skype address so they can talk before or after the clip in order to seek more verification.

People can upload directly to Bambuser, and there is no filter on the content, since it is difficult to filter live broadcasts because you cannot predict or know what will happen in the next second. 'So you might imagine a video making it all the way through to CNN and then someone stepping out and dropping his pants, but is hasn't happened yet,' Adler remarks.

Disruptions of the network and security risks

As a controversial tool in the eyes of authoritarian governments, Bambuser is blocked in several countries, such as Syria, Bahrain and Turkey. As the protests began to erupt in Egypt in 2011, Bambuser was the second service to be shut down after Twitter, followed by Facebook, Blackberry and BBM services.

There are different levels of censorship. In some countries, you can stream from your phone, but you cannot watch on Bambuser.com. Thus, you cannot access videos in the country, but you can still stream videos out of the country. However, the fact that there are now several services similar to Bambuser means that when one service is shut down or blocked in a country, its users can quickly move on to other services, such as Quick, which is now owned by Skype, Justin.tv or Ustream. The fact that Bambuser is on the radar of authoritarian regimes around the world is a clear signal to its founders that their project of democratizing video broadcasting is of significance and poses a real threat to authoritarian regimes.

The use of tools like Bambuser entails security risks for the activists. There are examples of activists in Syria being arrested just for having the Bambuser application on their phone. Furthermore, there have been a number of cases, especially in Syria, where people have been streaming from rooftops, and the army has been able find out where the camera is – possibly by triangulation using a mosque tower or another building they know the exact location of. If they identify where the camera is, they can start shooting at it. According to Adler, 'One problem with streaming live is that when people see the broadcast, they can quickly figure out where you are, and you are there right then, so they can go and get you'.

What will the future bring?

Since the initiation of the tool, Bambuser has been developed in several ways. The design and concept are constantly being adjusted at the request of its users. However, the users are often better at expressing what they dislike about the product than giving advice about what they would like instead. It is therefore up to the designers to make developments that fit the needs of users. One way to do this is to put themselves in the situation of the users:

> Me and my co-founder Jonas (*sic*) went to Egypt to be close to the users during the first free elections they had in 2011, to meet the users and see how it is to use Bambuser. It is one thing to use it in a safe environment with a good Internet connection in Sweden, but a completely different story if you are on the frontline of a protest where the police are shooting rubber bullets and throwing gas.

During their trip to Egypt, the founders discovered the importance of making their tool simple. For example, if the Internet connection goes down, or the police turn off the 3G connection around Tahrir Square, the videos need to be recorded so they can be uploaded later. In such a scenario, you just need to get the video out, Adler says: 'It is a lot about making it simple. Making sure there is just one button you can hit, and it is easy to press. A lot of different features doesn't make sense in that scenario'.

The founders are now focusing on democratizing the technology on which Bambuser is based. They are making it easier for others who want to develop applications for live streaming.

> We are seeing a huge demand from different kinds of businesses in the ecology around live video wanting to have the same features as Bambuser. It can be a phone manufacturer, or it could be a news outlet that would like to release an app, so if you open it up, there will be a camera in there. At the moment, we are making it easy for others who want to develop applications for live streaming.

Currently, Bambuser has more than two million downloads of the application and 12 employees at the company. They receive a little over 10,000 broadcasts per day and have several million views each month. Bambuser is still growing rapidly. Adler calls Bambuser's business model a 'Robin Hood business model', referring to the fact that it is built around two different models. If you use it for commercial use, you have to pay for the service, but if you are a private person or use if for a non-profit use, it is free.

In the long run, Adler hopes that tools like Bambuser will open up a more democratic society where people can take part in things they normally have no access to, such as watching a press conference by a labour union that is trying to raise awareness of a specific cause: 'It isn't only the big, international democracy movements,' Adler says, 'but also within existing democracies where we could get access to events we might not normally have. So it is a tool for getting information out and a way to fight back.'

Note

1. The KaosPilots is a 3-year long alternative business school located in Denmark. The KaosPilot program teaches in the fields of leadership, new business design, process design and project design for challenges in business, society and organizations. The program focuses on personal development, value-based entrepreneurship, creativity and social innovation.

References

Mann, S. (1998) '"Reflectionism" and "Diffusionism": New Tactics for Deconstructing the Video Surveillance Superhighway', *Leonardo* 31(2), pp. 93–102.

9

Beyond Polemical Practice: A Tribute to Henry Gireoux

Geetanjali Sachdev

This chapter addresses the theme of the public sphere, communication and social change in the context of art and design pedagogy. It presents two perspectives adopted as part of a teaching approach that is built on Henry Giroux's concept of public pedagogy. The first perspective is described as polemical, and serves as a frame to design teaching and learning experiences that elicit resistance and contestation. According to this perspective, course learning outcomes enable students to protest against dominant hierarchies, social arrangements or imposed ideals. Based on research through teaching practice, the chapter discusses a second perspective, which explores the decorative arts for their pedagogic potential in serving as a frame of reference in the art and design curriculum. The case studies described in this chapter provide insights into the broader area of public pedagogy, offering these two perspectives, which could be adopted as part of a learning framework for teachers and practitioners in the field.

In 2010, I proposed a set of instructional strategies for formulating a pedagogical approach, based on research through my teaching practice (Sachdev, forthcoming 2014). It is a way to think about planning learning that includes the provision of certain types of experience as an instructional strategy. These strategies offer opportunities for students to engage with social and critical issues such as gender, health, class, caste and labour, to interrogate existing social arrangements and to question the values transmitted through various media. The approach also uses a specific perspective from which to view the power of education as a means to make interventions in the public realm: that of a critique of the ideas circulated by a dominant neoliberal consumer culture. This is the perspective offered by Henry Giroux, one of the founding theorists of critical pedagogy, to whom the genesis of the term 'public pedagogy' is credited.

Giroux uses public pedagogy as a theoretical construct to describe the processes of and sites for education beyond formal schooling. His concern is that the prevailing neoliberal consumer culture has a larger educational impact on students than that which is taught in the classroom:

> Within neo-liberalism's market-driven discourse, corporate power marks the space of a new kind of public pedagogy, one in which the production, dissemination, and circulation of ideas emerge from the educational force of the larger culture. Public pedagogy in this sense refers to a powerful ensemble of ideological and institutional forces whose aim is to produce competitive, self-interested individuals vying for their own material and ideological gain. (2005)

Giroux asks for a new understanding of how culture operates as a public pedagogy, how pedagogy works as a moral and a political practice and how agency can be evoked and organized through pedagogical relations (Giroux, 2010).

Based on research carried out through teaching, this chapter offers an alternative perspective from which to explore the pedagogical potential of the public realm. From this perspective, I propose that the ideologies espoused through the decorative arts exist alongside those of neoliberal culture as a powerful source of learning. They can be drawn on to counter the force of the ideas circulated by the prevailing neoliberal culture, as described by Giroux.

Section 1 briefly introduces the pedagogical approach and explains how Giroux's idea of public pedagogy provides the rationale for this approach in the context of art and design education. Section 2 offers a critique of the initial perspective adopted and the details of two learning endeavours that helped to form this critique. Section 3 examines how an exploration of the adornment of public spaces by the decorative arts could offer another frame with which to investigate the implicit instructional and educational forces within these spaces. Another four endeavours are described to demonstrate the development of this perspective. They are not discussed sequentially, in order to demonstrate the order in which they occurred, but instead to show the progression of ideas in the search for an alternative perspective. The chapter discusses the possible relationship between ornamentation, affect and agency and concludes with points to consider when designing a curriculum for public pedagogy.

According to Bob Gill, 'You cannot hold a design in your hand. It is not a thing. It is a process. A system, a way of thinking' (Ambrose and Harris, 2009). This definition of design offers an approach to design pedagogy that focuses on the process of creating, rather than the artefact as its object of expression. I see design as a way of thinking about the world and our sense of agency within that world, in order to act on it, and teaching as a way of evoking this agency in students.

The work of Howard Gardener and his colleagues on the concept of 'good work' influenced much of my early thinking on educational practices that can contribute to creating conditions for student agency, and for learning that is self-affirming. Good work refers to work of high quality that benefits wider society (Gardner et al., 2001). Gardener believes that there are conditions under which individuals are motivated to do socially responsible work that optimizes our contribution to society. I have found that locating students' creative expression within a wider sphere of concern through pedagogical interventions can contribute to creating such conditions.

Design pedagogy is in one way an institutionalized mode of intervention – it is about inculcating a way of thinking through the educational curriculum, providing a frame through which students can think when they encounter different environments. This chapter is an attempt to articulate such a frame. The pedagogical framework discussed below proposes ways in which students can think about the world in order to intervene in it, be it through their actions or their material creations. It takes forward the question asked by Giroux (2010): How can agency be evoked and sustained through pedagogical relations?

Developing an approach to design pedagogy

Srishti School of Art, Design & Technology is an educational institution that offers undergraduate and graduate courses in these three core areas. The school has an active artist-in-residence programme, through which artists can bring their practice to a range of pedagogical projects as part of the curriculum. Many of the teaching and learning experiences at the school draw on artistic practices to engage with designing in and for the public realm. Artistic practices offer ways in which a range of critical and social issues can be addressed.

Artistic practices could refer to the techniques or range of media that artists use, their conceptual approaches, or the creative processes through which they give expression and develop into ideas. Through their work, artists reflect, contest, imagine and reframe experiences and encounters, often through subjective explorations across a variety of contexts. They also use various modes of research, documentation and objective information, and engage in interactions that are collaborative, participatory, and have the potential to be transformative experiences. Artistic ways of knowing and expression offer us ways in which to start conversations about the nature of existing social arrangements and imagine alternative ones. They also offer methods for us to express the realm of possibilities through our imagination.

In designing courses, I have drawn on many facets of artistic practice in both planned and intuitive ways, and have over the years developed an identifiable pedagogical approach. This approach articulates planning strategies to incorporate the processes, media, techniques and modes of working and exploring that artists engage with in the process of expression. The approach is thus drawn from observations of working with various artists on projects. It proposes the provision of five experiences as elements: subjective experience, objective experience, participative experience, contesting experience and reflective experience. For example, as a starting point, artists often locate issues that originate in students' subjective interests. I found that the corresponding actions that emerge from the pedagogic intervention have the force of students' personal motivation, and that students have been able to drive their own learning within a frame. Thus, drawing on students' subjective experiences is put forward as an instructional strategy. The development of all five elements as instructional strategies and the use of experience as the basis for designing pedagogy are explained in detail in Sachdev (forthcoming 2014).

Within the Srishti art and design curriculum, artists Deepak Srinivasan, Ravindra Gutta, Smriti Mehra and I have been attempting to articulate what we call a 'public practice' approach to design pedagogy. We have collaborated on several pedagogical endeavours that work with social issues or use contexts in the public space as a basis for design enquiries. By drawing on our individual teaching experiences and repertoire of methods as artists-pedagogues, we have tried to identify some characteristic ways to describe how we design and engage with learning. Public practice is an area of practice in art and design that is synonymous with a range of terms, such as participatory art, community-based art, public art, situational art, social sculpture, relational aesthetics and social art practice. These terms describe a range of artistic practices and activities that engage with communities. Public practice: 'uses participation, reciprocal relationships and collaborations in community contexts to promote civic dialogue and investigate pressing issues of our time' (Herberger Institute for Design and the Arts, 2011). This chapter builds on many of the projects on which the four of us have collaborated since 2009.

Public pedagogy as a rationale

According to Brady (2006), cited in Burdick et al. (2010, p. 4),

> Public pedagogy... is an activism embedded in collective action, situated not only in institutionalized structures, but in multiple spaces, including grassroots organizations, neighbourhood projects, art collectives, and town meetings – spaces that provide a site for compassion, outrage, humour and action. Such pedagogy disrupts processes of injustice and creates opportunities for the expression of complex, contesting, and subaltern perspectives.

According to Henry Giroux (2005), the dominant neoliberal corporate culture operates through multiple sites that have a larger educational impact than the classroom. He argues fervently for a radical shift in the way knowledge is produced, received and consumed. Giroux's critique of neoliberalism operating as a public pedagogy provides the rationale for most of the courses and projects that I facilitate.

Since 2009, all the projects I have designed have been consciously located within a broader enquiry that aims to facilitate an understanding that public spaces are pedagogical sites where individuals learn to construct knowledge, values and identities. The instructional strategies that I use to teach design exhibit a pattern: students participate in an activity within a public space with various artists; they question the values and images transmitted in this space; they then find a message transmitted through the space that resonates with them personally. In the end, they counter these messages using their design skills through visible, embodied and overt contestations. Four examples are provided below.

First, in the course 'Aesthetics of Protest' (2009), the students designed a project they entitled 'Dark & Lovely'. They worked with graffiti on streets and public signage to make statements about imposed ideals of beauty that they received from various media. Second, in 'Street Signs' (2009), students worked with signs made by the elderly and other members of the public, generated through a public participation event. They put these signs up in different locations to explore public spaces as venues for personal and private expression, and to question the right to author and voice messages intended for public consumption.

Third, in 'Bengaluru Pride' (2010), students explored their own positions on gender and sexuality. At the end of the module, they created a series of posters to be used by local NGOs in Bangalore for the upcoming pride parade in the city. Even though the parade was a few months later, the students, many of whom were newly resident in Bangalore, walked in the parade and observed how the wider public received their designs. Through this experience, they saw the parade as a city event in which their designed artefacts were being used.

Fourth, in 'Happy Maids Day' (2010), students worked with the playwright and poet, Annie Zaidi, to explore gender and labour within their homes and in the local domestic labour market. They proposed and designed a Domestic Workers' Contract, after discussion and consultation with domestic workers they knew as well as the workers' employers. The intention was to send the contract to a group working on domestic labour issues in the city.

More details on the above projects is provided in Appendix 1. Analysis of the instructional strategies used to elicit the above contestations is provided in 'New Ways of Educating, Articulating Experience' (Sachdev, forthcoming 2014). By drawing from artistic practices and the construct of public pedagogy, learning experiences can use a diverse range of instructional strategies across multiple contexts – strategies that encourage students to critique and seek a reconceptualization of the relations between individuals and their environment through creative and contesting expression.

Facilitating learning endeavours based on Giroux's ideas has given me the insight that enabling human expression to be located in a wider sphere of social or public concern can help to create conditions that provide students with a sense of agency. Students are able to take values of social and public concern and reformulate them as individual enquiries within the classroom. They are motivated when they can draw on literacies they are confident with, or media they want to experiment with, in order to design expressions that interrogate the way in which public culture is experienced by them and others. By starting any project with their personal concerns surrounding any issue, the students begin to think about and question existing relations between institutions and individuals in a qualitatively different way. They are also motivated to express their inclinations in a public and visible way.

While artistic practices offer ways to problematize critical and social issues, Giroux's construct enables public contexts, needs and social spaces to be offered as a locus for the expressive inclinations of design students. Building a curriculum on the construct of public pedagogy in the context of art and design education can serve as a starting point for crafting pedagogy that can broaden and deepen students' engagement beyond classroom contexts.

Searching for an alternative perspective

My lens into public pedagogy so far had been filtered through the views of Giroux and work with a similar perspective. Kurt Hunker (2012) adopts an identical position when he describes how architecture and the design of the built environment has become subservient to the demands of the capitalist economy. Hunker critiques the presence of spectacle in contemporary architecture as a form of cultural production in support of consumerism, and sees it as a form of symbolic communication giving material shape to the desire for entertainment, sensation and affect (Hunker, 2012). The work of J. M. Francombe concerns public pedagogies of normalcy, which contribute to the construction of the norms of girlhood, and raise questions of how the bio-pedagogies of health the body and normality are constituted through their embodiment in the discourse of physical cultural technologies such as video games and television. These norms are no longer embedded only in the longstanding educational traditions and formal knowledge acquiring processes. She claims that discursive technologies offer theoretical constructs capable of monitoring the body for ends 'deemed normal by a heteronormative rhetoric', and thus need to be critiqued for their pedagogic potential (Francombe, 2010).

Be it pedagogy, identity construction or architecture, the perspective remains the same – that of a critique of neoliberalism and the dominant capitalist discourse. In each of the issues addressed through pedagogical endeavours that I facilitated – gender, beauty or forms of exchange – students might have designed and put forward other visions. However, through their designs against the homogenizing imagery of normality or the lifestyles that profit-driven corporations educate the public to aspire to, they always contested the existing use of public space. It seems to have become an antagonistic pedagogy. I felt that I was preparing students for visual combat when they encountered public space.

As a way of thinking about the wider realm in which to locate students' design capabilities, the pedagogical approach being developed inculcated an adversarial position as a starting point. Two pedagogical endeavours in particular, 'Persuading Mr Khan' and 'Crowds, Chaos and Trash', indicated that my approach needed rethinking. Both courses demanded that students engage in overt contestations through the teaching experience and exposed a learning strategy that was feeding off consciously evoked student resistance. They are described below.

a)   Persuading Mr Khan

'Persuading Mr Khan' was offered as a three-week course for first-year art and design undergraduate students in February 2011. The course explored grading as a widely used educational practice and argued for a public dialogue on grading reform. It critiqued the current system of grading students as an educational mechanism for sorting and ranking individuals in order to create categories and establish hierarchies. The course took the form of persuading a popular figure, Mr Khan, to open a public dialogue on educational assessment and grading reform. It was co-facilitated by Danika Cooper, Arathi Krishnappa, Raghavendra Rao and Nupur Sista.

During the course, the students designed a range of projects intended to persuade Aamir Khan, a famous Indian Bollywood actor, to start a conversation on assessment reform in the public sphere. The objective of the course was to design a persuasion. The 110 students participating in the course were allowed free reign to use any media they were comfortable with. A range of outcomes emerged – online, virtual and physical, as well as visual, sonic and performative. Students designed videos, websites, songs, animations, discussion forums, online polls, street theatre, interviews, and interactive sessions with the public and installations. A range of other interventions questioned the grading system and highlighted assessment practices they considered problematic.

Even though the title of the final assignment was 'My Gentle Persuasion', most responses had a strong emotive force and students adopted aggressive stances. Two assignments in particular were disturbing in their portrayal of student suicides. One was a graphic video in which a student, posing as the protagonist of the story, felt compelled to cut their wrists with a razor due to poor grades. The other was a street play that unfolded along similar lines. In inducing these visualizations, it was discomfiting to have provided the context for creating such dystopic imagery. The pedagogy was not motivating students in the way intended – to search for better alternatives while being provocative.

b)   Crowds, Chaos and Trash

'Crowds, Chaos and Trash' was a three-day workshop, co-facilitated with designer Danika Cooper, held in January 2012. It explored the relationship between crowds and chaos, and how they relate to ideas about trash. A concept note rooted the series of activities within the workshop:

> Imagine your entire class to be TRASH. Each person is a piece of trash that you see piled up on the street. Each person lends herself to the

composition of a pile of trash. On encountering this whole body of trash, envisage a series of photos that are titled 'Sorting Trash'. How would you organize your class? What categories would you create to 'sort' the trash? How would you compose your first photo with your entire class, to show your entire pile of trash as the first frame in your photo series? How would the series proceed as you sort your friends out, as trash gets sorted?

Among other views, the ideas of an anthropologist at Srishti, Dr Vandana Goswami, on the concepts of promiscuity, trash and sexuality were presented to students to help them respond to the idea of trash in different ways.

The students were required to create a collaborative piece of work in any public space. During the facilitation of this activity, there was a moment where 75 students could have been led into designing a public protest in the context of sustainability, where the rhetoric of anger and dissent could easily have been used as an entry point to urge the students to take a contentious stance and design a collective intervention. Instead, we asked students to design a public installation where all students used their bodies on the street to represent a pile of trash.

The teacher-student relationship is an easy one from within which to evoke dissent and protest. As an educator invested with the power to evoke and provoke, perhaps there are ways of drawing on resistance that are gentler, or other perspectives that offer students a way of looking at public space less a combat zone and more as a space where a plurality of positions can have an opportunity for voice and presence.

Another way of looking

'Persuading Mr Khan' and 'Chaos, Crowds and Trash' were turning points in my search for another perspective or rationale by which to reframe the ideas being presented to students. 'All human beings endeavor to understand what is happening around us, to make sense of our experiences. All human beings also have the capacity to frame experiences in certain ways – to construe them in a way that either motivates or paralyzes actions' (Gardner et al., p. 12). Could the public sphere be explored for its potential to provide meaningful contexts that evoke agency by acknowledging Giroux's notion of public pedagogy while going beyond his position that the dominant pedagogical force of the public sphere was that of consumerism and spectacle? Is there another position or reformulation of the way in which design students can conceptualize transformations in the public sphere?

This section addresses the above questions. It describes three pedagogical endeavours through which another way of looking at public culture was developed using research carried out through teaching practice. These three experiences offer another possibility for approaching the design of curricular experiences within the field of public pedagogy.

Smriti Mehra is an artist-in-residence at Srishti and works in the area of experimental video art. Since 2009, we have worked on several projects centred on her artistic practice with the Flower Project, through which she is researching the local flower economy in Bangalore. Collaborations with her and two other artists, Deepak Srinivasan and Gabriel Harp, have involved the decorative arts in different ways. The endeavours and projects described below could serve as an inspiration for thinking in new ways about public space pedagogy.

a)   Interactions in Public Space with the Flower Project

In this half-day workshop held in February 2010, students had to use flowers to decorate 'Rangoli' patterns on a residential street near the college campus. Rangoli is ancient folk art practiced in India. Decorative geometric and curvilinear designs are drawn on the ground in living rooms or courtyards, usually with chalk or coloured powder. The patterns are often embellished with flower petals, rice or sand. Rangoli patterns, also known as Kolam, are traditionally made in or outside the home during auspicious occasions, and the ritual is practiced widely as a daily activity in southern India. New patterns are made every day. It is an ephemeral art form: the designs are either blown away by the wind or trodden on in the course of the day. They are generally washed off every morning, and a new design is made.

Students began the workshop by buying flowers at the city flower market early in the morning. They returned to one of the Srishti campus buildings located on a residential street to separate the petals from the flowers. In a guerrilla-like activity, they decorated Rangoli and Kolam patterns, usually made by women just outside their houses, on the surrounding streets. Wherever possible, they sought permission from residents and asked them to join.

The Flower Project was thus a temporary public art project done on impulse to connect with local residents, rather than a conscious desire to resolve a problem. In the past, local residents had seen some Srishti students as a nuisance. However, although the workshop was not planned with the intention of creating amicable relations between the college and local residents, this was however one of the results. Most importantly, the idea of using Rangoli as a form of familiar local expression originated here. We had used a local art form that both the community and students found easy to connect to. It was also a form for which students could imagine aesthetic possibilities, drawing on their art and design skills.

b)   Calendar

'Calendar' is a video collaboratively designed by Smriti Mehra, Gabriel Harp (Gabe) and me. Gabe was an artist-in-residence at Srishti in 2008–2010. With a background in biology and an interest in patterns, he had been documenting several Rangoli patterns on Bangalore streets over the past year. Gabe documented the Rangoli event described above and images of the students' designs were added to his collection of patterns.

After the event, conversations between Gabe, Smriti and myself on Gabe's collection of images led to the conceptualization of a video, inspired by Allahu Akbar, and a film by the artist, Usama Alshaibi. Alshaibi's film is a continuous repetition of geometric patterns based on Islamic designs. The edited video was completed by Smriti in May 2010 and is a composition of moving images of Rangoli designs from the workshop, as well as others that Gabe had captured over time. The video was called 'Calendar' because it intended to mark each day of the year with an image of a Rangoli design.

'Calendar', as a form of output, has become an aesthetic text carrying documented evidence of the flower workshop for students. However, the video also showed that the decorative arts are as much a part of our everyday visual realm as Coke billboards. The video is a structural equivalent of the way we would encounter the street if we walked with our eyes cast down instead of up towards the billboards and neon signs.

The idea that these decorative forms could hold pedagogic value as a cultural resource for public space pedagogy arose after viewing the final edit of 'Calendar'. This insight led to the design of a pedagogical enquiry the following year: 'The Many Idealisms of the Decorative Arts: An Introduction to Public Aesthetics.' This endeavour sought to explore the different forms of self-expression encountered on a daily basis, to see whether they possessed the possibility to counter the ideological biases described by Giroux.

c)   The Many Idealisms of the Decorative Arts: An Introduction to Public Aesthetics

During this two-day workshop, held in July 2011, second-year students had to reflect on their encounters with public aesthetics. They were asked to explore and then document their daily encounters with the decorative arts and daily practices of self-expression. The workshop title drew on an essay by Christina Zetterland, a design and crafts theoretician and former curator of the Röhsska Museum of Design and Decorative Arts, Gothenburg. In her essay, the Many Idealisms of the Crafts, Zetterland (2011) refers to the ideals embedded in the crafts as 'faith in the value of investigations that take shape as something singular and solitary, about a form of expression that can be constant and settled, provisional or accidental, collective or something else' (Zetterland, 2011). Letterforms on different media in public spaces, especially those on transport vehicles, were used as a pedagogical resource to introduce students to vernacular typography. In particular, a comparison between the taxi cabs in New York and Calcutta was used to explain the idea of local aesthetics. In both cities, the taxis are yellow and black with the word 'Taxi' written on two sides of the vehicle. In New York, the letters are printed in a black sans-serif font, stencilled across the taxi's yellow body paint. In Calcutta, however, the word 'Taxi' is adorned with hand-painted circular designs of little florets and leaves. These floral patterns differ from taxi to taxi. On closer inspection, the designs reveal the locality in which the type was painted and the aesthetic preferences of the painter. During the workshop, practices in Rangoli and Pakistani truck art were used to introduce students to the idea of public aesthetics.

After reflecting on the idea of public aesthetics, the students listed the daily practices of self-expression they encountered. The list included garland shaped shop-front arrangements by local greengrocers, non-hierarchical and orderly, colourful jar arrangements on store shelves, the strings of white flowers which South Indian women use to adorn their hair, and bananas as decorations used on tea-stalls, as well as the shadow patterns of untrimmed trees, the way in which crows were sleeping, and the drapes of the 'dhoti' garment worn by men on a construction site. These were encounters that students described as 'daily practices of expression', every bit as much as the photographs of film stars painted on the backs of auto-rickshaws.

The 'Public Aesthetics' workshop showed that the practice of decorating objects of daily life is a mode of self-expression, a personal ideal, and that these expressions can influence us in the same way as any other aspect of our cultural surroundings. Taxi, rickshaw or truck art, as much as hair adornment, is a means of expressing the ideals of the community or individuals that practice the tradition or ritual. The ornamented surfaces of trucks reflect the values and ideas of the people who paint the vehicles as much as those who commission the works. Unique in their customizations, they are also huge, moving personal billboards, carrying and transmitting ideologies – in the same way as the landscape of signs and images owned by corporations does, and in the same way that a housewife expresses her aesthetic ideals in the colours she chooses to decorate her front door. We encounter the ideals of different communities through the decorative art we see every day. It reflects the ideals and aesthetic sensibilities embedded in expressions of everyday life.

d)   Learning Endeavour: Rangeen Rangoli

'Rangeen Rangoli: Mapping Courtship in Yelahanka' was a one-day workshop for postgraduate students held in November 2011, facilitated by Smriti Mehra, Deepak Srinivasan and me. Deepak Srinivasan is a performance and media artist with a background in neuroscience. The workshop was part of an art and design seminar conducted by the three of us in order to articulate the concept of 'public practice'. At this time, Deepak's interest lay in exploring how public spaces in a locality could be mapped to reveal locations where people were comfortable with displays of affection and intimacy. We chose Rangoli as a form to experiment with for this participatory public mapping activity. This choice was based on the insight from the earlier Rangoli intervention, 'Interactions in Public Space' with the 'Flower Project', which revealed that Rangoli was familiar and had a resonance with people in the locality. We chose a parking lot near the college campus for this activity, near the streets where 'Interactions in Public Space' had earlier been held.

During the workshop, members of the public in and around the parking lot were invited to map public spaces in Yelahanka using white rice powder. They were asked to draw on the ground in the parking lot itself. After drawing out a location with white rice powder, similar to the way a Rangoli design is drawn, people were asked to indicate affections that they felt comfortable expressing, such as a kiss or holding hands, within the particular location. They used freely provided flowers and coloured chalk to depict the actions and emotions requested. For example, holding hands was marked with white flowers, and a large pink flower was positioned within a drawing of a park where someone thought kissing was permissible. The same evening, the video 'Calendar' was shown as a free public screening event in the street where the 'Interactions in Public Space' intervention had been conducted earlier that year. Since this video was a translation of Gabe's document of the Rangoli patterns made by the residents of this street, the video was shared with the residents in a public event facilitated by students under the guidance of Smriti and Deepak.

Although the design expressions of the artists and students in the above endeavours were located in a social context, they did not originate from a need, problem or crisis. 'Rangeen Rangoli' and 'Calendar' were both forms of research that were modelled to students through Gabe's, Deepak's, and Smriti's artistic practice. The activities also drew on a daily decorating practice, a familiar mode of self-expression used generally only by women, in order to engage a wider public in a conversation by laying claim to public space in a different way.

The role of the decorative arts

Zetterland (2011) refers to craft as a 'decorative art' and, through her essay, investigates the arts and crafts to gain an understanding of the different ideals they express. She cites an observation by the Austrian art historian, Jacob von Falke, that the crafts, or decorative arts, play two roles: 'They should in part satisfy our longing for beauty, and in part fulfil a practical purpose'. In fulfilling a practical purpose, they are thus separate from the fine arts. However, in being able to give expression to striving for an ideal, they play a similar role to the fine arts.

The role of the crafts and the decorative arts can be explored beyond that of mere embellishment in the context of public pedagogy. Encounters with craft and decorative forms and practices are also rich resources, which can provide a counter or balance to the consumerist ideology that Giroux and Hunker refer to. As much as we encounter ideals of beauty, health, wealth and lifestyle choices espoused through contemporary consumerist culture, we also encounter the private expressions of different individuals and communities. The decorative arts are localized concepts of symbolism, of expressions that coexist with the billboards, neon signs, shop fronts and architectural spectacles that characterize many urban public spaces. They also operate as public pedagogies.

In concluding his article on the presence of spectacle in architecture design, Hunker (2012) observes that the rapid rise of Asian economics on a global scale could be heralding an interest in involving localized concepts of symbolism and iconography. It may well be that the received symbolism is that of 'the modern, post-industrialized society that has arrived' and that the homogenizing effects of globalism are clear to see, but 'if everyone has the same symbol, does it really mean anything significant anymore, at a cultural level?' Giroux, Hunker, Brady and others present one frame through which we can approach public pedagogy. It is one way to understand the organization of public culture, and to look into how this culture influences us to experience the world in a particular way.

The purpose of a Rangoli or Kolams is not solely to decorate. The myth is that ancient Kolams were drawn in coarse rice flour as an offering of food to ants so that the ants would not have to search too long to eat their meals. The ritual was an invitation to other beings to partake in what belonged to the personal and private, a gesture of harmony and peaceful coexistence. This myth lies within the form, and is embedded in our encounter with it.

Public spaces have their own subjectivity, and their own personal public aesthetic to counter homogenized private corporate templates of imposed normality. Decorative art forms and practices thus offer the possibility of another perspective through which public culture could be interrogated as part of the teaching and learning experience. They could lend another dimension to knowing how public spaces operate in local and implicit ways as a pedagogical force.

Affect and ornament: expanding frames of reference

In the approach to design pedagogy described above, students take values of social and public concern and reformulate them as individual enquiries in the classroom. They then draw on literacies with which they are confident or media with which they would like to experiment, in order to design expressions that interrogate the way public culture is organized and experienced. If protest and contention were removed from the pedagogical approach, the essence of this approach would be that the students' design skills are always used in a context that resonates with them at some level through affect or the experience of emotion or feelings. Finding a connection through the affect of anger and using protest is one way that has its own possibilities in terms of outcomes. However, the emotive value of experience can also catalyse us to act in other ways.

In *The Language of Ornament* (2001) James Trilling explores modernism in the context of forces that shape our way of seeing. He describes ornament as an art of intense and elaborately veiled emotion, and says that the emotional energies of ornament are implicit and marked by the discipline of pattern. In *The Function of Form* (2009) Farshid Moussavi discusses the function of ornament as an agent for specific affects, and dismantles the idea that ornament is applied to buildings as a non-essential entity. She proposes a theory of form that decomposes textural forms into their affects, and accords ornament with the capability of generating specific affects.

In *Touching Feeling: Affect, Pedagogy, Performativity* (2002) Eve Sedgwick considers the relationships between emotions and expressions. In discussing the work of the psychologist, Silvan Tomkins, she asks what motivates performativity and performance, and what the effects are that are mobilized in their execution, both at an individual level and collectively. In choosing the title 'Touching Feeling' for her book, Sedgwick explains that it records her intuition that a particular intimacy seems to subsist between textures and emotions (2002, p. 17).

Future learning endeavours in the field of public pedagogy could perhaps expand on the intuition expressed by Sedgwick and draw on Moussavi's research to explore the function of ornament within decorative forms for their ability to generate affect and evoke agency. What kind of affect does ornamental decoration achieve when we encounter its forms? Can decorative ornament evoke affects that generate a form of agency that sustains and is resilient, rather than that which is evoked through resistance and is often temporary?

Conclusion

This chapter describes public pedagogy as a set of teaching methods and strategies, which initially emerged in the context of teaching approaches that were polemical in nature. They were polemical in that they elicited overt contestation as an outcome, which took the form of interventions designed by students as protests against dominant hierarchies and social arrangements or imposed ideals. This also enabled the teaching to be understood as a public pedagogy. As Brady (2006) notes in Burdick et al. (2010, p. 4), this form of pedagogy creates opportunities for complex and contesting expressions to emerge.

However, in acknowledging that the use of cultural resources needs to be critiqued for the wider implications of the power to coerce, direct and educate, the pedagogy also needs to consider other templates of encounter that homogenize thought and behaviour through repetition. This chapter, in proposing a less polemical pedagogical practice, explores whether the decorative arts offer a way of thinking that is less adversarial, but still has the aim of evoking student agency and participation in civic, social and public life.

To create an artefact, resolve a problem or propose a system is to alter the context of a system of relationships between people, material and the environment. Design pedagogy is therefore a way by which students learn to intervene in an environment through their expressions – a way that includes thinking through a perspective, or many perspectives. As pedagogues, we can build nascent forms of students' cultural participation by looking at both 'big acts' and 'small acts' of design – the big billboards and the small taxicab swirls – not to privilege one or the other, but to allow a plurality of voices to coexist in the public realm through our ways of looking and designing.

We can find joy in our visual encounters with the highly decorative letterforms made by local street painters as much as we can find comfort in resting our eyes on the simplicity of a sans serif Helvetica typeface amid the typographic chaos. There is a delight in finding a Starbucks quietly tucked away in a corner of a noisy street in Phuket. We could call it two different ways of looking, or perhaps looking for two different things.

Acknowledgements

I would like to thank Avy Varghese, Colin Davies and Geetha Narayanan for their influence on my thoughts.

Appendices

Details of pedagogical endeavours designed based on the concept of public pedagogy

Appendix 1   Aesthetics of Protest (2009)

Type: Workshop

Month: November 2009

Duration: One week

Facilitators: Ravindra Gutta, Allison Kudla, Geetanjali Sachdev

Description: The workshop explored the nature and context of protest and was located within a broader pedagogical enquiry into the aesthetics of protest. It looked into the forms by which artists and designers engage with the notion of protest as a manifestation of dissent and resistance, expressed through visual forms, embodied action and performance. The workshop was intended to broaden learners' understanding of the aesthetics of protest. It introduced the idea that the aesthetics involved in protests lie beyond the creation of iconography and visual forms – the aesthetics of protest extend to the nature of the interaction of the protest as well its subsequent and residual impact on both the participants and the observers. Specifically, students looked at impositions of social ideals of beauty.

Appendix 2   Bengaluru Pride

Type: Course

Month: September–October 2010

Duration: 17 days

Facilitators: Ravindra Gutta, Ramesh Kalkur, Geetanjali Sachdev

Description: The aim of the Bengaluru Pride course was to conceive and develop a graphic interface for a specific context that involves the participation of a wider community. The graphic interface entailed addressing people of varied backgrounds and with differing levels of cultural awareness. The challenge in this course was to develop a set of visual tools that would enable the public to articulate their thoughts on a specific issue, in this case gender, in the context of the upcoming pride parade in Bangalore.

Appendix 3   Happy Maids Day! Name Place Animal Thing

Type: Course

Month: September–October 2010

Duration: 17 days

Facilitators: Annie Zaidi, Deepak Srinivasan, Jyothsna Belliappa, Anitha Santhanam, Sanjay Morlidhar, Tanya Khosla, Dharmang Prajapati, Geetanjali Sachdev

Description: The aim of this course was to explore issues surrounding gender and class. The course drew on the play, *Name Place Animal Thing,* by the poet and journalist, Annie Zaidi as its context. During the course, students looked at the household as a space that determines gender and power relations, the nature of housework as a source of inequality within relationships and the sexuality of female domestic workers and live-in maids as experienced at home. They also explored their own behavioural and moral patterns. The course had its origin in the concept of a 'Happy Maids Day', an idea mooted by Pragya Trivedi to encourage students to reflect on prevailing attitudes towards household help and domestic labour.

Appendix 4   Street Signs

Type: Workshop

Month: April 2009

Duration: 2 days contact

Facilitator: Geetanjali Sachdev

Description: In Street Signs, a two-day workshop, the first year Foundation students at Srishti were asked to put up hand-painted signs made by the elderly and other members of the public at a public park event in Indiranagar, Bangalore. The students were asked to put up these primarily typographic signs in a public space of their choice on the other side of the city. The intervention of hand-painted signs in public locations was intended to raise students' awareness about what kinds of signs are appropriate for public spaces, in terms of semantic content and visual form, and about who has the right to author and voice messages intended for public consumption. This workshop also discussed questions raised by the Sign the City project, which explored public spaces as venues of personal and private expression for members of the public.

References

Allahu A. (2006) *Usama Alshaibi. Resistance(s): Experimental Films from the Middle East and North Africa* (Paris: Lowave).

Ambrose, G. and Harris, P. (2009) *Design Thinking* (Singapore: AVA Publishing).

Burdick, J., O'Malley, M. and Sandlin J. (eds) (2010) *A Handbook of Public Pedagogy: Education and Learning Beyond Schooling* (New York: Routledge).

Burdick, J, O'Malley, M. and Sandlin J. (2011) 'Mapping the Complexity of Public Pedagogy Scholarship, 1894–2010', *Review of Educational Research* 81(3), pp. 338–375.

Gardner, H., Csikszentmihalyi, M. and Damon, W. (2001) *Good Work: When Excellence & Ethics Meet* (New York: Basic Books).

Francombe, J. (2010) 'I Cheer, You Cheer, We Cheer: Physical Technologies and the Normalized Body', *Television & New Media* 11(5), pp. 350–366.

Giroux, H. (2005) 'Cultural Studies in Dark Times: Public Pedagogy and the Challenge of Neoliberalism', *Fast Capitalism* 1.2, http://www.fastcapitalism.com.

Giroux, H. (2010) 'Neoliberalism as Public Pedagogy' in Burdick, O'Malley and Sandlin (eds), *Handbook of Public Pedagogy* (London: Routledge), pp. 486–499.

Herberger Institute for Design and the Arts (2011) 'Public Practice and Civic Engagement in Design and Arts', http://herbergerinstitute.asu.edu/institute/publicpractice/goals_initiative.php, date accessed 21 July 2011.

Hunker, K. (2012) 'The Tall Office Building Artistically Considered: Critical Events Since 9/11' in C. Aiello (ed.), *Evolo 04 (Summer 2012): Re-Imagining the Contemporary Museum, Exhibition and Performance Space: Cultural Architecture Ahead of Our Time*, San Diego, Calif. (PRWEB) 31 July 2012.

Moussavi, F. (2009) *The Function of Form* (Barcelona, Spain: Actar).

Sachdev, G. (forthcoming 2014) 'New Ways of Educating: Articulating Experience' in Vezzoli, C., Kohtala, C., Srinivasan, A. (eds), *Product-Service System Design for Sustainability* (Sheffield, UK: Greenleaf Publishing, in press).

Sedgwick, E. (2002) *Touching Feeling: Affect, Pedagogy, Performativity* (Durham, NC: Duke University Press).

Trilling, J. (2001) *The Language of Ornament* (London: Thames & Hudson).

Zetterland, C. (2008) 'The Many Idealisms of the Crafts' in L. Jönsson (ed.), *Idealism vs. Commercialism*, Graduation 08 HDK & HDK Steneby Master Programmes (Gothenburg, Sweden: University of Gothenburg).

Part III

Practitioners and Practices: New Communication for Social Change Perspectives and Initiatives

10
Public Discourses on Gender, Modernity, and Assaults on Women in India

Jyothsna Latha Belliappa

Introduction

A series of sexual and physical assaults on women in India throughout 2012, culminating in the brutal gang rape of a young woman in New Delhi, has given rise to vociferous debates across India on the issue of women's safety in the public sphere. Reactions to cases of sexual assault in India usually run along two lines. On the one hand, there are demands for stricter laws against sexual assault and for the creation of safe spaces for women. On the other hand, the victim's dress and behaviour are scrutinized, and women are cautioned to behave with greater decorum and discretion in public and encouraged to police their own behaviour. The second type of reaction is significant for the analysis in this chapter.

This chapter attempts to place these assaults in the context of some of the dominant discourses around modernity and gender evident in the Indian public sphere. At a time when national and international media and public discourses are focused on rape, it revisits an earlier case of sexual and physical assault, popularly known as the 'Mangalore home stay assault', of July 2012 to examine how the uneasy relationship between gender and modernity in a globalizing society creates a climate in which crimes on women are perpetrated. It suggests that the Mangalore assault and the responses to it help to clarify how discourses on gender and modernity – while ostensibly celebrating women's engagement in the public sphere – tend to circumscribe their participation in it. An analysis of the assault helps draw significant conclusions about the relationship between the public and the private sphere in the Indian context.

In the interests of specificity, it needs to be clarified that this chapter addresses assaults among university educated, urban women, that is, the middle classes. Although Indian women across the class and caste hierarchies are vulnerable to assault and violence, the case discussed below involves young, university educated urban women. The self-policing injunction is also arguably addressed to young urban women. When colleges and universities respond to incidents of violence by recommending dress codes for women, and right wing leaders respond with injunctions to women to act in accordance with cultural traditions to avoid inciting men, they are primarily addressing educated, urban women. The discourse on gender and modernity discussed in this chapter also concerns middle class women, although it tends to address middle class women as if they were a composite group representative of an 'average all-Indian woman'.

The Mangalore home stay case is fairly well known in India thanks to the extensive media coverage it received. On the evening of 28 July 2012, an assault was carried out in the coastal city of Mangalore in the southwestern state of Karnataka at a privately organized gathering of over 30 members of the *Hindu Jagran Vedike* (The Party for Awakening Hindus). Five women and eight men were beaten, and the women groped and molested – allegedly for having a rave party involving sex, drugs and alcohol. (Subsequent investigations found no evidence of drugs.) The party had been organized at a home stay, a type of bed and breakfast hotel common in southern India, which the perpetrators forcefully entered. Media personnel who had been previously alerted were present to film the assault, which was then repeatedly broadcast across the nation. The assailants claimed they were motivated by a desire to protect Indian values, which they argued were increasingly under threat in a culture where parties involving men and women, sex, drugs and alcohol were becoming the norm. However, there was also some suggestion, from the testimonies of the media personnel present and the men who were assaulted, that the attack was motivated by the impression that young Hindu women were partying with young Muslim men. I do not address here the public debate on the media's role in filming and broadcasting these assaults, or questions of whether they prioritized their journalistic goals over humanitarian ones – although these issues are important and could be the subject of another paper.

Reports of the assault gave rise not only to vigorous media debates around moral policing, but also to strong protests from students and citizens concerned about this type of violence. College students, social activists, academics and members of the public protested against the assault, and several state and national politicians condemned it. However, the responses of the chairperson of the Karnataka State Commission for Women, C. Manjula, and some other political leaders from the Hindu right, clearly indicated sympathy for *Hindu Jagaran Vedike*'s position that such gatherings lead to immorality and the exploitation of women, and that efforts should be made to prevent them.

Discourses on gender and modernity[1]

To understand the context for such incidents of violence against women, it is important to understand the discursive climate within which they occur. To do so, I briefly revisit India's globalization story and the relationship between gender, modernity and nationhood that came to be constructed in the 1990s and the early years of the 21st century. Since the deregulation of the Indian economy in 1991, which enabled the growth of private enterprise and allowed foreign direct investment in several industries that had hitherto been protected by the state, there has been a celebration of India's economic growth in the media, in particular the English language media, and in popular discourse. Throughout the 1990s, the state collaborated with the influential middle classes and the elites to promote India as an attractive investment destination with a relatively stable reform-oriented government, a large English-speaking workforce, and low production costs. Over time, a discourse emerged of India as a dominant economy and a resurgent nation. Although access to the job opportunities presented by globalization was highly skewed between the working class and the lower middle classes, on the one hand, and the upper middle class and the elites, on the other (Scrase and Ganguly Scrase, 2009), much of the discourse around globalization at the turn of the century was marked by a self-congratulatory optimism about the growth of the nation's economy and the purchasing power of the rapidly growing middle class.[2] Even though there was a discrepancy between the spending capacity of the middle class and its discursive constitution as a consuming class, consumption became a marker not only of the nation's prosperity and progress but also of middle class status. Alongside discourses of a resurgent nation that could rival the developed nations of Europe and North America, however, emerged the discourse of the 'new' Indian woman.

Since the 1990s, the emergence of the new Indian middle class woman as a discursive construct has saturated printed media, television, advertising and recurrent debates on morality and globalization. Indian women's magazines such as *Femina* and *Women's Era* might target middle class, urban, English-speaking women, but they address their readers as if they were representative of an all-Indian woman who crosses the barriers of caste, religion, language and class. Analysing this discourse through the deconstruction of commercial advertising and television in the 1990s, Rajeshwari Sunder Rajan highlights the construction of a 'new' Indian woman who is seen as 'intrinsically "modern" and "liberated"' (1993, p. 131). She is no longer located only in the domestic sphere, but also active in the professional and public domains. The international women's magazine, *Cosmopolitan*, was launched in India in the 1990s with the strap line: 'Honest, sexy, smart: Are you up to it?' It addressed its Indian readers as assertive, sexually aware and professionally compe-tent. The price of the magazine and its editorial line indicated that it was targeted at upper middle class, economically independent women, but it had an impact on the content of established English-language women's magazines in India which addressed wider audiences. *Femina, Women's Era* and *Savvy* relaunched themselves to compete with the foreign glossy. In addition to fashion and glamour, the women's magazines now devote space to professional and financial concerns, intimacy, lifestyle issues and travel.

Although the so-called newness of Indian women is repeatedly emphasized, in many respects the post-liberalization construction of Indian womanhood is a continuation of earlier nationalist repre-sentations of the middle class Indian woman, which recommended a selective modernization for Indian women that would enable them to participate in the public sphere without endangering their position as guardians of tradition within their homes and families (Chatterjee, 1989; Chakravarti, 1989). In the late 19th and early 20th centuries, there were fairly intense debates among Indian nationalists about the posi-tion of women in the emerging nation. Within these debates, women were often positioned as representative of a motherland that had been degraded by colonialism and imperialism. Indian women were thus to be shielded from corrupt Western influences while also being charged with the responsibility for guarding and upholding somewhat narrowly defined Indian traditions.

Such representations of Indian women arose partly in response to the colonial state's indictment of Indian culture as repressive of women, and partly out of a deeper sense of marginalization that arose from the colonial experience. Globally, such nationalist debates on the position of women have occurred with similar results in other colonized nations, including Egypt, Sri Lanka and Indonesia (see Pollard, 2005; Jayawardena, 2002; Ramusack and Sievers, 1999). In India, upper caste, middle class women were seen as both embodying and protecting a certain pristine spirituality within the private space of the home and family, while men engaged in the more material and morally challenging public work of serving or resisting the colonial authority.

Many dissenting voices could also be heard questioning this narrowly circumscribed role for women, but the traditionalist forces remained strong. The early 20th century saw these issues discussed and debated in the print media and in the speeches of nationalist leaders. Women's magazines were published in many regional languages.[3] They debated these issues in great detail, with some women writers encouraging women to prioritize their responsibilities to the home and family over public participation, while others questioned why a nation that aspired to Western style liberty and democracy expected its women to conform to tradition.

In many ways, the tensions within contemporary debates on modernity and gender mirror the nationalist debates of the early 20th century. The 'new' post-liberalization Indian woman represents the nation's modernity and its economic strength as well as its distinctive traditions. While she is less protected from the West than in the 20th century, she is expected to participate in the global economy and culture while adopting certain markers of Indianness in her identity: through her attire, her behaviour in public and her interactions with men.

In *Gender, Class and Reflexive Modernity in India* (Belliappa, 2013) argues that women often mobilize the support of their family members in order to succeed in the workplace within the framework of individualistic values, and that this support is offered only when they conform to the normative expectations associated with their positions as mothers, daughters or daughters-in-law. Their individualistic pursuit of personal and professional aspirations rarely challenges traditional authority structures based on age, gender and seniority.

Analysing the editorial message of *Femina*, which is targeted at upper middle class women, Meenakshi Thapan makes a similar argument. She suggests that Indian women are represented as glamorous, individualistic and globally aware, but also as family-orientated and thus embodying 'respectable modernity enshrined in tradition' (Thapan, 2004, p. 415). It is this respectability that is underlined in public discourse as the distinguishing characteristic of Indian women.

In spite of associations of glamour and beauty with the new Indian woman, there continues to be a certain tension and anxiety in the discourse regarding her sexuality. To an extent, this tension is resolved by suggesting that women should blend elements of tradition and modernity in creating an identity, but since both these categories are shifting and contextual, they can often be in conflict with each other. As the nation opens itself up to the influence of the global economy, women's bodies and sexualities are particularly vulnerable to the permissive cultural influences of the West. Rupal Oza (2006) argues that the relative loss of national sovereignty in the face of global capitalism is projected on to women's sexualities, which are more stringently controlled and regulated. She suggests that the anxiety around women's purity has been evident since the 1990s in the opposition to the Miss Universe contest being held in India, in recurrent public debates on women's clothing and, more recently, in the responses to violence against women in public.

The social and political context of the home stay assault

In response to the question of why the discourse of respectable modernity is particularly important in contemporary India, it is possible to argue that women are becoming more visible in the professional and public sphere, particularly in white collar jobs. Indian women's participation in the public sphere is not a contemporary phenomenon. As is suggested above, they played a significant role in the debates around their position during the nationalist period, and actively participated in the movement for independence throughout the first half of the 20th century.

Currently, women's participation in professional life is widely celebrated in popular media and public discourse. The media regularly profiles the small number of women in leadership positions in business and industry (see Mitra, 2013; Mukherjee, 2013; Unnikrishnan, 2013). The flagship industry of India's globalization story, the Information Technology (IT) industry, enjoys a reputation for being highly supportive of women employees, providing them with luxurious and high-tech working environments, maternity benefits, flextime and conveyance to and from work (Alexander, 2007). According to the industry's representative association, the National Association of Software and Services Companies (NASSCOM), the IT and ITES (information technology enabled services) industries employ a workforce which is about 30 per cent women (NASSCOM, 2012), offering them unprecedented incomes and a conducive work culture. Other service industries, such as biotechnology and banking, tend to model their human resource policies on the IT industry with the aim of recruiting and retaining women.

Economic analysis indicates that there has been a significant withdrawal of women from all levels of the workforce in India in recent years (NSSO, 2011). Although this phenomenon has been reported in the media (Thomas, 2013), it has enjoyed less coverage than women's participation – however limited – in white-collar jobs. The media's celebration of women's presence in white-collar employment would suggest that they are a highly visible minority in the corporate workplace and in urban spaces.

Women are becoming more visible in what might have hitherto been considered masculine spaces and time zones (many IT and ITES companies require women to work late at night to meet the needs of Western clients). They may also have disposable incomes that enable them to participate in leisure activities that tended previously to be the preserve of men. It is becoming increasingly common to see women visiting restaurants, pubs, bars and nightclubs, alone or in the company of men. These trends are celebrated in some sections of the media as signs of emancipation and gender equity, but are almost certainly seen as a threat by more traditionalist elements.

The home stay assault took place in Mangalore, in the Dakshina Karnataka region, which is known for the rise of right wing Hindu political parties, such as the *Bharatiya Janata Party* (BJP), and for an increasing number of assaults on women. Mangalore is some 350 kilometres from the state capital, Bangalore, which is the home of the IT industry. While Bangalore is known for its public and private sector industries, Mangalore is a university city that hosts a number of professional institutions and liberal arts colleges. It attracts students from all over India who are seeking an education that will enable them to take advantage of opportunities in the globalized economy in metropolitan cities such as Bangalore, New Delhi and Mumbai. These factors make Mangalore and its surrounding areas fertile ground for a clash of values between upwardly mobile, middle class, educated youth, who might wish to

experiment with the variety of lifestyle choices offered by globalization, and traditionalist forces that are threatened and marginalized by a
rapidly changing culture.

Globalization also tends to further strengthen and popularize right
wing ideologies that feed on society's insecurity about the erosion of
tradition and traditional identities. In Karnataka, the rise of Hindu major-
itarianism is evidenced by the steady rise of the BJP in the state. From
being part of a coalition government in 2006, it became the majority
ruling party in the 2008 elections. The regional elections of 2013 saw
the more secular Congress Party take over in Karnataka, but the BJP
remains one of the largest parties in the state opposition and is also a
strong contender for the national election to be held in 2014. In the
past five to six years, Mangalore and its surrounding areas, which were
a BJP stronghold until the 2013 elections, have seen a steady increase
in the number of acts of violence against religious minorities, such as
vandalized churches and attacks on the homes and shops of Muslim
families (see PUCL-K, 2009, 2012). Even if the BJP was not involved in
these attacks, there was a general apathy in the government's response
to and investigation of such acts, indicating its tacit acceptance of or
even support for the situation. The political parties perpetrating these
assaults, the *Ram Sene* (the Army of Lord Rama) and the *Hindu Jagaran
Vedike* are ideologically close to the BJP, although they tend to be more
extremist in their activities.

The *Hindu Jagaran Vedike's* assault on the home stay birthday party,
and an earlier assault by the *Ram Sene* on women in a bar in Mangalore
in January 2009, received national coverage, and several other assaults
and sustained attempts at harassment and intimidation have been
reported in the local press. An investigation by PUCL-Karnataka (2009)
found that in several of these incidents, the victims were young men
and women from different communities, often women from Hindu
backgrounds who are assaulted for fraternizing with Muslim or
Christian men. One such case involved a group from different religions having a drink at a roadside juice stand. In some cases, men of
one community may be assaulted by those of another community for
fraternizing with 'our women'. These assaults suggest both an attempt
to undermine the bonds between communities and a need to police
women's sexualities.

Right wing Hindu groups argue that young women are being lured
into romantic relationships by Muslim or Christian men who then
force them to convert either as a precondition for marriage or soon after
marriage, calling these practices Love Jihad – or the Holy War of Love

(see PUCL-K, 2009). They do not admit the possibility that individuals might choose such relationships or freely convert to another religion. Their statements indicate fears of the violation of religious boundaries as well as the particular vulnerability of women when these boundaries are policed by self-appointed guardians of the community. Young men take on a paternalistic role of teaching women appropriate behaviour and policing their social lives through the threat of violence and humiliation. The testimonies of the women involved in the home stay assault indicate that the perpetrators used morality to justify their molestation of the women, and media reports suggest that the state authorities and religious leaders condemned the violence of the perpetrators' methods but often supported discourses on morality and appropriate female behaviour (*Daijiworld Media Network, 2012; New Indian Express, 2012*). In the Mangalore home stay case, state-appointed investigators questioned the morality of the victims of the assault, arguing that young women need to be educated to avoid such gatherings (*Times of India*, 2012), in effect suggesting that women need to police their own behaviour.

The implications of the assaults

In the context of these debates around gender and modernity that regularly take place in the media and public discourse, the celebration of women's participation in public and professional life, economic and cultural globalization and the increasing power of Hindu majoritarian groups, we need to consider assaults on women such as the Mangalore home stay assault. Nira Yuval Davis (1997) argues that women are seen as the 'symbolic border guards' of community and nation. Not only are they expected to maintain collective honour by their dress and behaviour, they are also representative of that collective honour which can be violated by the 'other' – in this case by men from religious minorities. Therefore, not only do their bodies and sexualities need to be stringently policed, but they also need to be 'saved' from their own feelings of love or friendship towards the 'other', even at the cost of being brutally assaulted and publicly humiliated. In these incidents, gender-based violence is layered with communal violence and mistrust. It is difficult to tell where one ends and the other begins.

While a culture of harassment, intimidation and assaults on women is fairly entrenched in India, the home stay assault and the 2009 assault in Mangalore share some distinctive characteristics. The perpetrators of the pub assault claimed similar motivations – that they were upholding pristine Hindu culture, which was threatened by the women drinking and socializing with men. In both cases, the women were severely beaten, implying that the beating was meted out as a punishment for the transgression of normative behavioural standards. This 'policing' aspect of violence against women is a fairly new phenomenon. However, given that the women were also groped, there is a suggestion that, under the guise of 'punishing' the victims, the men were also indulging their own sexual desires.

Both the assaults took place in a somewhat liminal – that is, neither completely public and nor completely private – space. However, while the pub might be considered more public than private, a home stay assault is a more private space since it needs to be booked by a limited number of guests on payment of a fee. That information about a privately organized event could reach the ears of the perpetrators, and that they chose to enter a private space suggest that conventional dichotomies between public and private spaces are becoming increasingly blurred. Moreover, women are expected to place an invisible but tangible private boundary around themselves, even as they engage in public. By choosing to socialize with men and attend gatherings where alcohol is served, they are seen as suspending these boundaries and therefore not worthy of the honour and dignity that would be accorded to them if they had remained within a real or notional private space.

The perpetrators of the home stay incident violently challenged the behaviour, relationships and leisure practices of their victims, which might arguably be seen to stem from individual beliefs and values. By carrying out the assault, they opposed what might be considered to be private decisions about with whom to socialize, where and in what manner. The opposition to the so-called Love Jihad and the assaults on friendship groups also suggest that the perpetrators use force to undermine the personal decisions of the victims about love, romance, courtship and friendship. In so doing, young men unknown to the victims take on a parental role that might usually be reserved for their senior male family members.

The responses to the assaults that draw on the self-policing discourse also make similar comments on what might be considered private decisions. Questions are raised about why the victim chose to be in the place where the assault took place, who she was with, and how she dressed and behaved. These so-called private decisions are publicly debated and questioned. In her seminal response to Habermas's book *The Structural Transformation of the Public Sphere*, Nancy Frazer (1990) suggests that it is not productive to ignore private issues in the public sphere. Taking the example of domestic violence, she argues that viewing it as a private issue denies the opportunity to address a commonly held concern in the public sphere.

Conclusions

This chapter suggests that private issues of gender are addressed in the public sphere through both action, as in the home stay assault itself, and discourse, as in the responses of the authorities, which focused on women's responsibility for self-policing. Thus, while upholding Frazer's response to Habermas, one might also extend and modify it somewhat to suggest that the dichotomy of the public and the private is increasingly untenable, as privately held beliefs and values, and intimate relationships, are enacted in the public sphere, which could result in a public backlash from traditionalist forces. Right wing groups across the world choose to publicly condemn the private decisions and behaviour of women – and men – in relation to intimate issues of marriage, reproduction and sexuality.

A second conclusion that might be drawn from the assaults is that women's bodies become the sites on which tensions around gender and modernity play out. I suggest above that while the public and professional presence of Indian women is celebrated as a marker of modernity, it also causes concern about the erosion of tradition. These assaults are part of a larger tendency to control and circumscribe women's presence in public. Given that women are positioned as bearers of the collective honour of communities and nations, these assaults are part of an attempt to control the boundaries of religious communities and of the nation as a whole by policing women's bodies and sexualities.

Finally, we may conclude that while they may be viewed as part of a backlash against women's emancipation and individualization, these assaults are not only symptomatic of a gender backlash. They also need to be considered in the context of growing communal tensions in Karnataka and in other parts of India. Assaults on women cannot be viewed only in terms of gender. These incidents need to be understood through the multiple lenses of gender and communalism in addition to the threat of global capitalism. Thus, intersecting and often overlapping structures, including gender, caste, class, community and language, create subtle complexities in the Indian public sphere, which need to be accounted for in any discussion of it.

Individuals tend to participate in the public sphere not only by articulating their ideas but also through action. Women participate in and lay claim to the public sphere by challenging the boundaries of traditional gender positions through their dress, social and leisure choices, and life-styles, by experimenting with new ways of relating to men – through friendship and romance – and by taking professional roles in the new economy. Assaults such as those discussed above might be seen as part of a larger attempt to circumscribe and limit women's access to public space and their participation in the public sphere. However, the protests against the assaults, the continued presence and participation of women in public, and their vocal and visible defence of their right to socialize and fraternize as they wish indicate that extremist elements are unlikely to exclude women from the public sphere.

Notes

1. For a more detailed discussion of discourses on gender and modernity, see Belliappa (2013).
2. For a representative example of this type of self-congratulatory discourse, see Das (2000).
3. See Awaya (2003) on Malayalam magazines, and Talwar (1989) on Hindi and Bengali magazines.

References

Alexander, L. (2007) 'Women on Top!', *Hindu Metro Plus* (online edn), http://www.hindu.com/mp/2007/03/08/stories/2007030800730100.htm, accessed 22 September 2013.

Awaya, T. (2003) 'Becoming a Female Citizen in Colonial Kerala' in A. Tanabe and Y. Tokita-Tanabe (eds), *Perspectives from Asia and the Pacific* (Kyoto and Melbourne: Kyoto University Press and Trans Pacific Press).

Belliappa (2013) *Gender, Class and Reflexive Modernity in India* (London: Palgrave Macmillan).

Chatterjee, P. (1989) 'The Nationalist Resolution of the Women's Question' in K. Sangari and S. Vaid (eds), *Recasting Women: Essays on Colonial History* (New Delhi: Kali for Women).

Chakravarti, U. (1989) 'Whatever Happened to the Vedic Dasi? Orientalism, Nationalism and a Script for the Past' in K. Sangari and S. Vaid (eds), *Recasting Women: Essays on Colonial History* (New Delhi: Kali for Women).

Daijiworld Media Network (2012) 'Activists Wrong, But Immoral Behaviour Should Be Checked – Pejawar Swamiji', http://www.daijiworld.com/news/news_disp.asp?n_id=145620, accessed 22 September 2013.

Das, G. (2000) *India Unbound: From Independence to the Global Information Age* (New Delhi: Penguin).

Fraser, N. (1990) 'Rethinking the Public Sphere: A Contribution to the Critique of Actually Existing Democracy', *Social Text* 25/26, pp. 56–80.

Jayawardena, J. (2002) 'Cultural Construction of the "Sinhala Woman" and Women's Lives in Post-Independence Sri Lanka', unpublished PhD thesis, University of York, United Kingdom.

Mitra, S. (2013) 'Eight Women Leading the Indian Corporate Sphere', http://www.dsij.in/article-details/articleid/6827/8-women-leading-the-indian-corporate-sphere.aspx#sthash.0F2AQS23.dpuf, accessed 22 September 2013.

Mukherjee, A. (2013) 'Most Powerful Women in Indian Business Was an Occasion to Remember', *India Today*, http://indiatoday.intoday.in/story/business-today-businesswomen-the-most-powerful-women-in-indian-business – india-today/1/304730.html, accessed 22 September 2013.

NASSCOM (2012a) 'Nasscom Launches "New Leadership Program for Women in Technology"', Press release, http://www.nasscom.in/sites/default/files/Article_News/Press%20Release_TalentSprint%20Project%20LEAD%20docx%20doc%20doc.pdf, accessed 22 February 2013.

New Indian Express (2012) 'Alcohol blamed for Mangalore attack', http://ibnlive.in.com/news/alcohol-blamed-for-mangalore-attack/282273–62–132.html?utm_source=ref_article, accessed 22 September 2013.

NSSO (National Sample Survey Organization) (2011) *Employment and Unemployment Situation in India.* Vol. 537. Ministry of Statistics and Program Implementation, Government of India.

Thomas, J.J. (2013) 'A woman-shaped gap in the Indian workforce', *The Hindu*, http://www.thehindu.com/opinion/op-ed/a-womanshaped-gap-in-the-indian-workforce/article4287620.ece, accessed 22 September 2013.

Oza, R. (2006) *The Making of Neoliberal India: Nationalism, Gender and the Paradoxes of Globalization* (New York and London: Routledge).

Pollard, L. (2005) *Nurturing the Nation: The Family Politics of Modernizing, Colonizing and Liberating Egypt, 1805–1923* (Berkeley: University of California Press).

PUCL-K (People's Union for Civil Liberties, Karnataka) (2009) *Cultural Policing in Dakshina Kannada: Vigilante Attacks on Women and Minorities, 2008–2009* (PUCL-K: Karnataka).

PUCL-K and Forum Against Atrocities on Women, Mangalore (2012) *Attacking Pubs and Birthday Parties: Communal Policing by Hindutva Outfits, a Joint Fact Finding Report* (PUCL-K: Karnataka).

Ramusack, B. N. and Sievers, S. (1999) *Women in Asia: Restoring Women to History* (Bloomington and Indianapolis: Indiana University Press).

Scrase, T. and Ganguly Scrase, R. (2009) *Globalisation and the Middle Classes in India: The Social and Cultural Impact of Neoliberal Reforms* (London and New York: Routledge).

Sunder Rajan, R. (1993) *Real and Imagined Women: Gender, Culture and Postcolonialism* (London and New York: Routledge).

Talwar, V. (1989) 'Feminist Consciousness in Women's Journals in Hindi, 1910–1920' in K. Sangari and S. Vaid (eds), *Recasting Women: Essays on Colonial History* (New Delhi: Kali for Women).

Thapan, M. (2004) 'Embodiment and Identity', *Contributions to Indian Sociology* 38(3), pp. 411–444.

The Times of India (2012) 'Mangalore Attack: Girls Should Skip Parties, Karnataka Women's Panel Boss Says', *The Times of India*, 2nd of August 2012, avaliable on:

http://timesofindia.indiatimes.com/india/Mangalore-attack-Girls-should-skip-parties-Karnataka-womens-panel-boss-says/articleshow/15320099.cms

Unnikrishnan, R. (2013) 'Companies Bill: More Women in Corporate Boards Mean More Discipline, Diversity and Innovation', *Economic Times*, http://articles.economictimes.indiatimes.com/2013–08–13/news/41375258_1_indian-women-new-companies-bill-women-representatives, accessed 22 September 2013.

Yuval-Davis, N. (1997) *Gender and Nation* (London, Thousand Oaks: Sage).

11
Participation in the Internet Era
Rikke Frank Jørgensen

The UN Special Rapporteur on the promotion and protection of the right to freedom of opinion and expression has stressed that he believes the Internet to be one of the most powerful instruments of the 21st century for 'increasing transparency in the conduct of the powerful, access to information, and for facilitating active citizen participation in building democratic societies' (La Rue, 2011, p. 4). As an example, the rapporteur highlighted the Arab Spring of 2011, which illustrated the role of the Internet in mobilizing populations in their call for better respect for human rights.[1] This chapter presents four different perspectives on digital media as means of public participation, provides empirical examples across different arenas, and discusses the structures / actors that can restrict digital media as means of public participation. I argue that there is positive potential related to the public's increased ability to communicate and participate in public life, but also new challenges related to participation in the digital domain. One challenge is linked to the role and powers of the private actors that control the digital media. The communication infrastructure and online platforms where social life unfolds critically differ from the physical sphere. There is also a distinction between access to participate in policy processes, and access to the means to influence a particular outcome. Communication technology can alter and improve access for individuals and groups to participate in political life, but it does not necessarily alter the ability to influence a particular outcome.

The chapter provides a brief introduction to the notion of public participation, including how this relates to communication technology. It investigates the notion of public participation in the Internet era from four perspectives: first, participation as empowerment, the development perspective; second, participation as a human right, the rights

perspective; third, participation by civil society groups in political processes, the institutional perspective; and, fourth, participation by the
individual, the community perspective. Each perspective considers
how the use of communication technology can influence the means of
public participation, and thereby the public's ability to gain access to
policy processes and influence a particular outcome. Finally, the chapter
discusses a range of structures and actors that may limit this potential.

What is public participation?

The notion of *public participation* has many connotations and competing
definitions. According to Pateman: 'the widespread use of the term ... has
tended to mean that any precise, meaningful content has almost disap-
peared; "participation" is used to refer to a wide variety of different situations by different people' (Pateman, 1970, p. 1). According to Smith
(1983) participation refers to various procedures designed to consult,
involve and inform the public and allow those affected by a decision to
have an input into that decision. Drawing on this definition, Rowe and
Frewer (2000, p. 6) stress *input* as the defining feature that differentiates
participation methods from other types of communication. Public participation can refer to political participation in a narrow sense – voting,
political parties, lobbying, and so on – or to community/social participation in a broader sense – the various ways by which citizens engage with
community services.[2] Examples of the latter may include service users'
involvement in various community services, such as day care, schools,
or health and social services, or the participation of local community
actors and beneficiaries in development projects. Recent years have
seen a shift towards a more rights-based understanding of participation,
emphasizing participation as part of citizenship and closely related to
'good governance' (Cornwall et al., 2001). This shift implies a move
from beneficiary to citizen, from the project to the policy level, and
from consultation to decision-making. In line with this move towards
a more active understanding of participation, the notion is increasingly
related to empowerment – something that can redistribute power by
enabling people to gain more control over their lives (Cornwall et al.,
2001, p. 52).

More recently, communication technology has entered the equation
and fuelled new perspectives related to both participation and power.
Numerous articles and empirical studies have addressed the Internet's
potential to support democracy, revitalize political life, mobilize civil
society groups, provide new means of gaining access to and interacting

with the state, and so on (Benkler, 2006; Castells, 2009; Coleman and Blumler, 2009; Hindman, 2009).

One of the scholars to have attempted to develop a theory of power and the networked society is Castells (2009). Castells' work combines the conventional understanding of power, the action of humans on other humans to impose their will, with the transformative nature of power – the ability to make a difference (Hoff et al., 2006, p. 19). The latter implies a more dynamic focus related to influence in a broader sense. Castells emphasizes communication as the constitutive element of modern societies, and power is related to access or non-access to the networks of communication, as well as to mutual recognition within these networks (Castells, 2009). This implies that power increasingly rests in networks such as those of capital, information, business alliances, and so on; and that access to – and recognition within – these networks is crucial in order to gain access to decision-making processes and influence their outcome. From this perspective, a discourse of public participation in the networked society needs to address the ways in which communication technology can enable access to, and influence within, communicative networks (nodes of power), as well as the factors that might restrict these potentials for participation. Communication technology is examined below as an enabler of participation across the four perspectives outlined above: development, human rights, institutional participation and community engagement.

Development discourse

Since the late 1960s, development agencies and scholars have established a close link between participation and development. From this perspective, participation is often linked to local empowerment, for example, by transferring control of development programmes to the local context with the aim of improving the livelihood of poor, excluded or vulnerable groups. Such a perspective is illustrated in the definition of participation as 'collective and continuous efforts by the people themselves in setting goals, pooling resources together and taking actions which aim at improving their living conditions' (Mishra et al., 1984, p. 88).

Since the late 1990s, communication technology has been increasingly linked to the development discourse under labels such as 'information and communication technology for development' (ICT4D) or simply 'communication for development' (C4D). At the first UN World Summit on the Information Society (WSIS), convened in Geneva in 2003, and its follow-up Internet Governance Forum (IGF), in Tunis in 2005, the overall goal was to establish common principles for the role of communication technology in fostering development (WSIS, 2003a), including a global Plan of Action on these issues (WSIS, 2003b). Numerous civil society organizations from around the globe participated in these negotiations, including a network of women's groups from Uganda (WOUGNET), which had been a pioneer in deploying communication technology to strengthen the livelihoods and public participation of local women.[3]

WOUGNET is one example of many illustrating how civil society groups in a developing context use different media platforms to further their causes. In a context of poverty, gender inequality and limited infrastructure, WOUGNET created an online platform that more than 60 local women's groups have joined since 2001 to mobilize and share experiences. Research on WOUGNET concludes that an online presence has created new business opportunities for micro-organizations, whereas better-resourced organizations mainly use the platform as a space for networking and sharing information (Jørgensen, 2012, pp. 202–203). At the rural level, WOUGNET works with community radio and mobile phones to increase farmers' access to agricultural information, to engage in community debate, and to improve collective bargaining. As a result, more women in the community participate in public debate and run for local elections (Jørgensen, 2012, pp. 185–187). The case provides an empirical example of how a combination of the use of mobile phones, community radio and the Internet has enhanced public participation in a context of few resources and limited access to communication technology. However, it also highlights various challenges in the local context, which relate to the power dynamics in a community.

Several of the women in the WOUGNET project spoke about structures of gender inequality, especially in rural areas, and highlighted the fact that public debate and decision-making is largely dominated by men. Better access to community radio and mobile phones was thought to contribute positively to reducing this gender divide by creating spaces where men and women could debate and interact in new ways, albeit within an overall context of inequality. Factors that have a negative impact on participation include an unstable and limited power supply, infrequent radio signals, a lack of money to buy batteries for the radio and airtime for the mobile phone, the high level of illiteracy in the community, and dependence on training on the use of mobile phones and the challenges of building confidence among the women (Jørgensen, 2012).

In sum, the study found that communication technology had been instrumental in creating new means for women's public participation, such as in radio programmes and community meetings, and facilitated increased access to decision-making processes in the community. It also identified ways in which the women were increasingly able to influence decisions that had a direct impact on their livelihood: for instance, their ability to negotiate prices for local products and their ability to deploy new means of production. The study provides an example of how communication technology can contribute positively to local empowerment through increased participation at the local level.

Human rights discourse

From a human rights perspective, public participation is a right on its own as well as a right that is closely related to a number of other rights. The right to take part in the conduct of public affairs is enshrined in Article 21 of the Universal Declaration of Human Rights: 'Everyone has the right to take part in the government of the country either directly or indirectly through freely chosen representatives' (United Nations, 1948). It is also part of the International Covenant on Civil and Political Rights (ICCPR), Article 25. The Human Rights Committee has noted that the conduct of public affairs is a broad concept that 'covers all aspects of public administration, and the formulation and implementation of policy at international, national, regional and local levels' (United Nations Human Rights Comittee, 1996, para. 5). It further stresses that participation is supported by ensuring freedom of expression (ICCPR, Art. 19), assembly (Art. 21) and association (Art. 22), as citizens take part in the conduct of public affairs 'by exerting influence through public debate and dialogue with their representatives or through their capacity to organize themselves' (United Nations Human Rights Comittee, 1996, para. 8). The right to public participation therefore presupposes that the public is free to speak its mind, and to organize its voices in voluntary associations.

In the past ten years, the impact of the Internet on the enjoyment of human rights has risen increasingly high up the international agenda. This is backed by countless examples of new modalities for public participation, including but not limited to access to public information, new means and spaces for public debate, online alternatives to mainstream media, new ways of mobilizing groups and voices, and questioning government affairs. The Arab Spring, for instance, gave rise to the contested term 'Facebook revolution', indicating the role that social media played as a resource in organizing and distributing information among individuals and groups opposed to the regimes (Naughton, 2011).

At the seventeenth session of the United Nations Human Rights Council in June 2011, the United Nations for the first time debated a report specifically focused on the potential for and challenges posed by the Internet to the right of all individuals to seek, receive and impart information and ideas of all kinds (La Rue, 2011). Sweden's Foreign Minister, on behalf of 41 states, supported the report and stressed that 'the same rights that people have offline – freedom of expression, including the freedom to seek information, freedom of assembly and association, among others – must also be protected online' (Bildt, 2011). As a follow-up, the Swedish government initiated a resolution on the promotion, protection and enjoyment of human rights on the Internet, which was adopted by consensus at the Human Rights Council in July 2012 (United Nations Human Rights Council, 2012).[4] At the G8, the role of the Internet was highlighted in the Deauville Declaration,[5] which stressed that the G8 leaders are committed to 'encourage the use of the Internet as a tool to advance human rights and democratic participation throughout the world' (Art. 13). As part of the G8 meeting, Germany's Foreign Minister stated that freedom of expression and freedom of association are only protected in the 21st century if they are also protected in cyberspace (Westerwelle, 2011). Policymakers are thus increasingly embracing the notion of Internet freedoms, stressing that the online protection of human rights is crucial to advancing the Internet as a tool for development and democratic participation. According to then-US Secretary of State, Hillary Clinton, 'as technology hurtles forward, we must think back to that legacy [the Universal Declaration of Human Rights]. We need to synchronize our technological progress with our principles. ... Today, we find an urgent need to protect these freedoms on the digital frontiers of the 21st century' (Clinton, 2010).[6]

Several scholars have addressed the Internet's potential impact on participation in the public sphere and how this may influence democratic life. Benkler argues that the Internet and the emerging networked information economy have provided distinct improvements in the structure of the public sphere (Benkler, 2006, pp. 212–214). This is not least due to the information and cultural activities of non-market actors, which the Internet enables and which essentially allow a large group of actors to see themselves as potential contributors to public discourse and as potential actors in political arenas (Benkler, 2006, p. 220): 'The network allows all citizens to change their relationship to the public sphere. They no longer need to be consumers and passive spectators. They can become creators and primary subjects. It is in this sense that the Internet democratizes' (Benkler, 2006, p. 272). Coleman and Blumler

(2009) also argue in favour of the Internet's potential to improve public communication and enrich democracy. However, they emphasize that policy intervention is needed in order to realize this potential, mainly because the virtual sphere has not been integrated into the constitutional structures and processes of liberal democracies (Coleman and Blumler, 2009, p. 11).

One challenge for the Internet as enabler of human rights is the various means by which states restrict online freedoms, for example, by censoring or monitoring specific Internet expressions. State restrictions related to online public life are documented by, for example, the OpenNet Initiative (Deibert et al., 2008, 2010) and there are many groups working in this field.[7] Another challenge relates to the role and responsibility of private actors, including but not limited to Internet service providers (ISPs) and other Internet intermediaries. Since ISPs control the majority of the virtual public sphere, this gives them unprecedented influence over individuals' rights to freedom of expression and access to information. Violations may occur, for example, through the blocking, filtering and removal of content, which prevents legitimate information from being distributed and displayed, whether to comply with restrictive state demands or to avoid copyright law infringements. Restrictions may also occur through the disconnection of users or by blocking access to networks, particularly at the behest of governments that seek to suppress civil society (La Rue, 2011). Finally, illustrated by the recent debate on surveillance programmes in the United States, violations can occur through the massive collection and exchange of personal data.

The policy discussion on the role and regulation of ISPs has evolved since the mid-1990s and raises some important points related to the role and responsibility of such actors. ISPs are regulated differently across the globe. In the European Union (EU), ISPs are seen as facilitators of communication and regulated as common carriers governed by the standards of private communication. This provides limited liability for the ISPs as the individual speaker or publisher is responsible for his or her own communication.[8] In North African countries, by contrast, the ISPs are regulated as editors and held liable for content hosted on their servers, in a way similar to the editorial liability applied to other media.

In recent years, states have exerted growing pressure on ISPs. At the EU level, an increasing number of law enforcement powers have been delegated to the ISPs. This has been raised many times by civil society groups such as European Digital Rights (EDRI): 'Large chunks of the [European] Commission are actually inventing ways of pushing the enforcement of regulation, and therefore the understanding of law, into the private sphere.'[9] According to McNamee (2011), examples of this privatized law enforcement role include policing peer-to-peer networks and, without a court order, blocking websites presumed to contain illegal content. Civil society groups and scholars alike have criticized the Europe-wide practice of delegating powers to ISPs, since the decisions to penalize users and websites are taken administratively rather than judicially (Callahan, Gercke et al., 2009; Brown, 2010). Current practices mean that companies that are in the business of providing access to the Internet are de facto being used to implement public policy with only limited oversight.

In sum, the Internet is increasingly seen as a human rights enabler by scholars and policymakers alike. Participation in the online realm, however, raises a number of challenges. The increasing powers vested in the private companies that control the online infrastructure, as well as the platforms on which public life unfolds, means that participation in the online public sphere may be restricted by actors and in ways essentially different from the physical public sphere. These include censorship, the blocking or filtering of online information and debate, the removal of content, and the collection and exchange of personal data carried out by the state and private actors. The policy response to these challenges is still at an early stage.

Civil society discourse

The third perspective concerns civil society participation in policy processes at the national and international levels. The notion of civil society is subject to much debate. I draw on the work of Habermas, who emphasizes that 'civil society embraces a multiplicity of ostensibly "private" yet potentially autonomous public arenas distinct from the state' (Eisenstadt quoted in Habermas, 1996, p. 367). Although part of the public sphere, civil society is linked to the private sphere – to the network of interactions found in families and circles of friends as well as to looser contacts with neighbours, work colleagues, acquaintances, and so on (Habermas, 1996, pp. 365–366). This understanding of civil society is in line with the definition used by the former Centre for Civil Society at the London School of Economics and Political Science (Anheier and Carlson, 2002, p. 1), which defined civil society as the sphere of institutions, organizations and individuals located between the family, the state and the market, in which people associate voluntarily to advance common interests. A well-functioning democracy is often assumed to include a vibrant civil society that represents the demands and concerns of various groups in society. UN institutions have for many years nurtured links with civil society organizations when taking global initiatives. The first WSIS and its follow-up IGF, however, developed this link from primarily 'consultation' into new means of participation, which it termed 'multi-stakeholderism' (Hemmati, 2002). Multi-stakeholderism implies that states and international institutions are no longer the sole actors, and that business and civil society actors are included in policy-defining processes. The United Nations General Assembly Resolution 56/183 on the WSIS encourages 'intergovernmental organizations, including international and regional institutions, nongovernmental organizations, civil society and the private sector *to contribute to, and actively participate* in the intergovernmental preparatory process of the Summit and the Summit itself' (United Nations General Assembly, 31 January 2002, author's emphasis).

During the WSIS process, civil society groups developed a structure for this participation based on working groups, or caucuses, various thematic mailing lists and an online platform provided by the WSIS secretariat.[10] These were used to develop arguments and interventions, which were then presented by the individuals or groups present at the physical plenary sessions and working group meetings. The mass use of mailing lists facilitated participation by groups and individuals who were unable to travel to Geneva for the numerous meetings held during the preparatory process. In this way, online platforms supported global civil society advocacy and collaboration that would not otherwise have been feasible. In principle, anyone with Internet access could contribute to the ongoing debate on the various thematic issues related to the WSIS and civil society.[11] A recurrent theme in the civil society plenary meetings was the 'inside / outside' debate, which addressed the means and modalities for influencing policy processes such as WSIS. Some groups argued that more would be achieved if civil society positioned itself outside the formal process, to ensure some opposition to the compromise-oriented negotiation space that the plenary sessions and working groups represented.[12] Others argued that it was more constructive to take part in the process and collaborate with governments, while trying to advance the positions of civil society. A study on the involvement of civil society actors in the first phase of WSIS concluded that the WSIS process has made a valuable contribution to increasing civil society's access to, interaction with, and consultation on international regulatory practices (Cammaerts and Carpentier, 2005). However, the study also found that power imbalances remain too strong to justify use of the term 'participation'. In their analysis, the authors distinguish between the level of access to or consultation on the process, and the capacity to change or influence process-related outcomes (Cammaerts and Carpentier 2005, p. 11).

With regard to the former, civil society was recognized as a legitimate actor in the process and was to some limited extent allowed to speak in official meetings. Moreover, the alternative civil society declaration *Shaping Information Societies for Human Needs* was posted alongside the official WSIS declaration on the WSIS website.[13] In terms of influencing the outcome, however, the authors identify several restrictive mechanisms. Many civil society groups lacked the financial means required to participate in the process, resulting in a geographic and gender imbalance (Cammaerts and Carpentier, 2005, p. 23). In addition, the formal system for civil society accreditation proved to be a barrier for some organizations, such as Human Rights in China and Reporters Without Borders. Most importantly, civil society had no voting rights in the preparatory process or at the summit itself, as voting rights were only given to state actors. Participation was therefore limited to the role of partial observer with the right to submit written contributions and some restricted rights to speak (Cammaerts and Carpentier, 2005, p. 28).

In sum, the WSIS process is an example of how communication technology was used to facilitate civil society's access and contributions to an international policy process. In this case, however, the virtual spaces deployed by civil society mostly served as a space for debate and collaboration between the groups active in the process, and as a mechanism to include groups that were not physically present. Research on civil society participation in the WSIS process gives no indication that these Internet-based platforms substantively enhanced the groups' ability to influence the summit outcome.

Civic participation (civic engagement)

A final dimension of participation is related to civic participation or civic engagement, which is often contrasted with political participation in the more formal sense. By civic participation, I mean the various ways citizens engage in and try to shape their communities at the local level. A large study of civic participation in the United States found that nearly half the adult population was disengaged from both the political and the civic realm. Those who did participate were slightly more likely to participate in traditional politics (20 per cent) than in civic activities (16 per cent) (Zukin, 2006, p. 188). It has also been suggested that there is a negative relation between the concentration of economic power at the local level and the degree of civic participation (Blanchard and Todd, 2006). In a study of the Catalan community, Castells found that while 1 per cent of those surveyed were involved in the activities of political parties, 33 per cent were involved in movements of various kinds and over 70 per cent believed they could influence the world through their social mobilization (Castells quoted in Howard, 2011, p. 56). The study also revealed that young Catalans who used the Internet became more autonomous with regard to political and media institutions.

The notion of civic media has been used as an umbrella term to characterize communication technology that empowers citizens to articulate, shape and reflect on local issues and concerns. One example of a platform for civic media research is the Occupy Research Network at the Center for Civic Media at Massachusetts Institute of Technology (MIT).[14] The project was set up to provide the Occupy Wall Street movement with tools and methodologies to research and reflect on its demographic characteristics: 'Occupy Research was started in the spirit of the movement, in which we apply the participatory ethic to the project. We decided to set up a place where people regardless of the field could share research and data sets' (Costanza-Chock quoted in Davis, 2011). Since its launch in September 2011, the Occupy Research Network has compiled a list of relevant tools and best practices for civic media research, and initiated a number of working groups on topics such as data visualization, as well as structured field reports and an investigation into race, gender and class dynamics; for example, a dataset was developed on the general demographic and political participation of the Occupy movement.[15] The survey showed that more than half the respondents had previously been involved in social movements. The respondents were engaged in a wide range of civic and political organizations, but they tended to have distinct degrees of involvement in non-profit organizations, social justice groups and other volunteer associations. Other sites of active community engagement included professional associations, cultural groups, churches or religious organizations, and affinity groups. Approximately half the respondents belonged to political parties, but only one-fifth were actively involved. When questioned about the ways in which the respondents had taken civic action in their communities over the past year, more than 90 per cent had signed petitions, and either boycotted or deliberately bought certain products for political, ethical or environmental reasons. More than two-thirds had contacted or attempted to contact a politician or civil servant to express their views, and almost two-thirds had taken part in demonstrations, joined an Internet political forum or discussion group, or attended a political meeting or rally in the past year. Finally, 40 per cent of respondents had contacted or appeared in the media to express their views.[16] The respondents were found to be heavy users of social media. The print and broadcast media were not used as frequently or as widely by respondents. More than 60 per cent reported using Facebook in the past 24 hours, and nearly 50 per cent had used the Occupy movement websites in the past 24 hours. 25 per cent of the respondents reported using newspapers, blogs or Twitter in the past 24 hours, whereas 20 per cent had used a live streaming video site, television or radio.

In sum, the Occupy movement – as an example of civic engagement – represents relatively high use of communication technology among participants to coordinate, distribute and advocate activities at the local, regional and global levels. However, the importance of these digital tools vis-à-vis the perceived impact of the movement was not covered by the research. The material gives no indication of how the respondents interpreted their ability to influence politics by means of their civic engagement.[17]

Conclusion

The chapter presents four different perspectives on public participation facilitated by digital media: first, as an enabler of women's participation in decision-making processes in a developing world context; second, as a facilitator of human rights related to public participation, such as freedom of expression, freedom of information and freedom of association; third, as a means to enhance participation by civil society groups in international policy processes; and, fourth, as tools used by citizens to mobilize and shape issues of concern. The examples all highlight the ways in which digital media have contributed positively to public participation, but also identify structures that challenge and impinge on this potential. Challenges such as gender inequality, poverty and lack of resources were identified, while recognizing that these are not particular to a digital context.

New ways of restricting online information and debate, by contrast, are specific to the Internet era. One particular challenge relates to the way in which states increasingly use private sector actors to implement public policy on the Internet without due process or safeguards. The recent UN Guiding Principles for Business and Human Rights (United Nations Human Rights Council, 2011) set a widely agreed-upon standard for the human rights obligations of private actors. Norms and standards are also being developed for Internet companies, for example, in the realm of the Global Network Initiative.[18] Further research, analysis and awareness-raising, however, lie ahead. This could include, for example, regular human rights audits of companies that hold specific positions of power in the online realm.

A further challenge relates to long-established regimes of formal power, such as the role of states in international policymaking vis-à-vis participation by civil society groups. The WSIS process illustrates how participation and mobilization by civil society groups were enabled and strengthened by means of digital media, but it also highlights that improved modalities for participation do not necessarily influence the policy outcome significantly.

In sum, digital media arguably substantiate rights that support the individual's ability to participate in public life, and in this way add to the modalities that constitute public life and public participation. The human rights compliance of private sector actors, however, is crucial if this potential is to be advanced rather than diminished in the years to come.

Notes

1. See also the APC Issue Paper, *Freedom of Expression, Freedom of Association and Democracy: New Issues and Threats*, which discusses the potential of and threats to Internet-enabled public participation on the basis of cases from around the world (Liddicoat, 2012).
2. An extensive body of literature argues that citizens' engagement with media, for example, the creative appropriation of web content, user-generated content, everyday media practices, and so on, is also an important mode of participation in the broader sense of the word. Carpentier (2011) provides a good overview of theories of participation in relation to media practices.
3. See www.wougnet.org, date accessed 12 October 2012.
4. For a critical perspective see, for example, Christensen (2011).
5. The Declaration is available at: http://www.g8.utoronto.ca/summit/2011 deauville/2011-internet-en.html, date accessed 8 May 2011.
6. Several scholars have contested the notion of Internet freedom. Morozov (2011, p. 318) critically examines the cyber-utopianism and Internet-centrism inherent in the notion.
7. Groups such as Amnesty International, Human Rights Watch and Reporters sans Frontières regularly document online human rights violations.
8. The EU directive on e-commerce (European Commission, 2000) operates with limited liability, implying that ISPs are not to be held liable unless they become aware of illegal content and fail to take action. There is, however, a legal grey area surrounding the notification procedure (Van Eecke and Truyens, 2009).
9. Executive director of EDRI (European Digital Rights), Joe McNamee, quoted in the *EU Observer*, 5 April 2011.

10. The author was part of this process as co-coordinator of civil society's Human Rights Caucus. An open archive of the activities of the Human Rights Caucus is available at http://www.iris.sgdg.org/actions/smsi/hr-wsis/, date accessed 20 June 2012.
11. For an overview of the topics and themes addressed by civil society see the virtual 'WSIS civil society meeting point' at http://www.wsis-cs.org/caucuses. html, date accessed 20 June 2012. For an elaboration of the way in which civil society groups organized and worked during the WSIS process see, for example, Ó Siuchrú (2004), Banks (2004), Cammaerts (2005).
12. The 'WSIS? We Seize!' campaign is one example of an alternative space and alternative action outside the official summit process. Available at http:// www.geneva03.org, date accessed 2 June 2012.
13. See http://www.itu.int/wsis/, date accessed 2 June 2012.
14. See www.occupyresearch.net, date accessed 2 June 2012.
15. See http://www.occupyresearch.net/2012/03/23/preliminary-findings-occu-py-research-demographic-and-political-participation-survey/, date accessed 2 June 2012. The survey covered 5074 individuals and was carried out primarily online.
16. See http://www.occupyresearch.net/2012/03/23/preliminary-findings-oc-cupy-research-demographic-and-political-participation-survey/ for a more detailed list of findings, date accessed 19 June 2012.
17. For further reading on the occupy movement see, for example, Graeber (2012) and Juris (2012).
18. See http://www.globalnetworkinitiative.org/, date accessed 11 January 2013.

References

Anheier, H. K. and Carlson, L. (2002) *Civil Society: What It Is, and How to Measure It*. CCS Briefing (London: London School of Economics and Political Science).
Banks, K. (2004) WSIS Phase II, APC Working paper, (Tunis: PREPCOM I, 23–26 June).
Benkler, Y. (2006) *The Wealth of Networks: How Social Production Transforms Markets and Freedom* (New Haven, CT: Yale University Press).
Bildt, C. (2011) 'Freedom of expression on the Internet: Cross-regional statement', Human Rights Council, 17th session, Geneva, 10 June 2011.
Blanchard, T. M. and Todd, L. (2006) 'The Configuration of Local Economic Power and Civic Participation in the Global Economy', *Social Forces* 84(4), pp. 2241–2257.
Brown, I. (2010) *Internet Self-Regulation and Fundamental Rights* (London: Index on Censorship), pp. 98–106.
Callahan, C., Gercke, M., De Marco, E. and Dries-Ziekenheiner, H. (2009) *Internet Blocking: Balancing Cybercrime Responses in Democratic Societies*. Report prepared within the framework of Open Society Institute funding.
Cammaerts, B. and Carpentier, N. (2005) 'The unbearable lightness of full participation in a global context: WSIS and civil society participation', 8. Media@lse. (London: London School of Economics and Political Science).
Carpentier, N. (2011) *Media and Participation: A Site of Ideological-democratic Struggle* (Bristol, England: Chicago Intellect).

Castells, M. (2009) *Communication Power* (Oxford and New York: Oxford University Press).

Christensen, C. (2011) 'Discourses of Technology and Liberation: State Aid to Net Activists in an Era of Twitter Revolutions', *Communication Review* 14(3), pp. 233–253.

Clinton, H. R. (January 21, 2010). 'Remarks on Internet Freedom', from http://www.state.gov/secretary/rm/2010/01/135519.htm, date accessed 6 September 2011.

Coleman, S. and J. Blumler (2009) *The Internet and Democratic Citizenship: Theory, Practice and Policy* (New York: Cambridge University Press).

Cornwall, A. and Gaventa, J. (2001) *From Users and Choosers to Makers and Shapers: Repositioning Participation in Social Policy* (Brighton: IDS).

Davis, P. M. (2011) 'Who Are the 99%? Occupy Research Aims to Find Out', http://www.shareable.net/blog/who-are-the-99-occupy-research-aims-to-find-out, date accessed 8 December 2011.

Deibert, R., Palfrey, J., Rohozinski, R. and Zittrain, J. (eds) (2010) *Access Controlled: The Shaping of Power, Rights, and Rule in Cyberspace* (Cambridge, MA: MIT Press).

Deibert, R. J., Palfrey, J., Rohozinski, R. and Zittrain J. (eds) (2008) *Access Denied: The Practice and Policy of Global Internet Filtering* (Cambridge, MA: MIT Press).

European Commission (2000) 'EU directive on e-commerce' (2000/31/EC). Brussels.

Graeber, D. (2012) *Inside Occupy* (Frankfurt: am Main, Campus).

Habermas, J. (1996) *Between Facts and Norms* (Cambridge: Polity Press).

Hemmati, M. (2002) *Multi-Stakeholder Processes for Governance and Sustainability: Beyond Deadlock and Conflict* (London; Sterling, VA, Earthscan Publications).

Hindman, M. S. (2009). *The Myth of Digital Democracy* (Princeton: Princeton University Press).

Hoff, J. et al. (2006) 'Introduction' in H. K. Hansen and J. Hoff (eds), *Digital Governance://Networked Society* (Copenhagen: Samfundslitteratur Press/NORDICOM), pp. 9–43.

Howard, P. (2011) *Castells and the Media* (Chichester: Polity Press).

Jørgensen, R. F. (2012) 'Framing the net: How discourse shapes law and culture', Unpublished thesis, Department of Communication, Business and Information Technologies. Copenhagen, Roskilde University.

Juris, J. S. (2012) 'Reflections on #Occupy Everywhere: Social Media, Public Space and Emerging Logics of Aggregation', *American Ethnologist* 39(2), pp. 259–279.

La Rue, F. (2011) 'Report of the special rapporteur on the promotion and protection of the right to freedom of opinion and expression', United Nations General Assembly A/66/290, Human Rights Council.

Liddicoat, J. (2012) 'Internet rights are human rights: Freedom of expression, freedom of association and democracy, New issues and threats'. *APC Issue Paper.*

McNamee, J. (EDRI) (2011) *The Slide from 'Self-regulation' to Corporate Censorship* (Brussels: EDRI).

Mishra, S.N, Sharma, N. and Sharma, K. (1984) *Participation and Development* (Delhi, India: NBO Publishers' Distributors).

Morozov, E. (2011) *The Net Delusion: The Dark Side of Internet Freedom* (New York: PublicAffairs).

Naughton, J. (2011) 'Yet Another Facebook Revolution: Why Are We So Surprised?', *The Guardian*, 23 January 2011, http://www.guardian.co.uk/technology/2011/jan/23/social-networking-rules-ok, date accessed 12 July 2011.

Ó Siochrú, S. (2004) 'Will the Real WSIS Please Stand Up?: The Historic Encounter of the Information Society and the Communication Society', *Gazette* 66(3/4), pp. 203–224.

Pateman, C. (1970) *Participation and Democratic Theory* (Cambridge: Cambridge University Press).

Rowe, G. and Frewer, L. J. (2000) 'Public Participation Methods: A Framework for Evaluation', *Science, Technology and Human Value*, 25(1), pp. 3–29.

Ruggie, J. (2011) 'Guiding Principles on Business and Human Rights: Implementing the United Nations' "Protect, Respect and Remedy" Framework', Report of the Special Representative of the Secretary-General on the issue of human rights and transnational corporations and other business enterprises (New York: United Nations).

Smith, L. G. (1983) *Impact Assesment and Sustainable Resourse Management* (Harlow, UK: Longman).

United Nations (1948) *The Universal Declaration of Human Rights* (New York: United Nations).

United Nations Human Rights Comittee (1996) 'General Comment No. 25: The right to participate in public affairs, voting rights and the right of equal access to public service (art. 25)', CCPR/C/21/Rev.1/Add.7 (Geneva United Nations).

United Nations Human Rights Council (2012) 'The Promotion, Protection and Enjoyment of Human Rights on the Internet', A/HRC/20/L.13 (Geneva: United Nations).

United Nations Human Rights Council (2011) *Report of the Special Representative of the Secretary-General on the Issue of Human Rights and Transnational Corporations and Other Business Enterprises* (New York: United Nations).

Van Eecke, P. and Truyens, M. (2009) *EU Study on the New Rules for a New Age? Legal Analysis of a Single Market for the Information Society* (Brussels: DLA Piper).

Westerwelle, G. (2011) 'Die Freiheit im Netz', *Frankfurter Rundschau*, http://www.fr-online.de/politik/meinung/die-freiheit-im-netz/-/1472602/8496970/-/, date accessed 14 July 2011.

World Summit on the Information Society (2003a) *Declaration of Principles* (Geneva: WSIS).

World Summit on the Information Society (2003b) *Plan of Action* (Geneva: WSIS).

Zukin, C. (2006) *A New Engagement? Political Participation, Civic Life, and the Changing American Citizen* (Oxford and New York: Oxford University Press).

12
Communication in Social Movements: A New Perspective on Human Rights

Cicilia M. Krohling Peruzzo

Introduction

Popular social movements, human rights, culture and communication are interrelated phenomena in the concrete space of their achievements that develop in accordance with the level of consciousness and capacity for social articulation of each specific epoch. Communication is expressed in personal and interactive group processes and through technological channels. It permeates social dynamics but also has its own specificities.

This chapter emphasizes the key features of communication in the context of social movements.[1] It questions the relationship between citizenship and community communication, and examines how the right to communication can be understood as a critical dimension of human rights. The chapter unfolds in four sections: communication in popular social movements; popular/[2] community communication and social mobilization; communication as a human right; and the intersection between education and community communication.

Communication in popular social movements

Popular social movements are articulations of civil society. They are segments of the population that see themselves as holders of rights and organize to claim them. Even if they are not effective in practice, the grassroots are organized and the dynamic of action itself tends to be institutionalized as a way of social legitimacy and consolidation. As organized forces, conscious and willing to fight, they are also experts in the process of social transformation. However, a number of factors (liberty, conscience and unity) and actors (individuals, churches, political representatives and organizations) must intersect in order for change to happen.

There are several categories of popular social movement. David Aberle (cited in Gohn, 2004, p. 267) classifies them as transformers of the reformers, the redemptive, and the alternative. In a Brazilian context, these categories are often classified in accordance with factors that motivate or guide their raison d'etre: (a) movements to improve working conditions and remuneration, such as the teacher's movements and other professional categories; (b) those who defend the human rights of social segments related to certain characteristics of human nature, such as gender, age, race and sexuality; (c) those who aim to resolve social problems that derive from inequalities that affect the population as a whole, such as transport for students, housing, land for rural workers, health, leisure, the environment, peace, violence against women and children, animal rights, and so on; and (d) political-ideological movements that fight for political participation, protest, and demand democracy or a change of regime.

Some are supported by institutions that encourage or host them, such as churches, political parties, schools and universities – such as *Pastoral da Terra,* a church group that campaigns on land issues, and *Movimento Fé e Política,* the faith and politics movement.

According to Maria da Gloria Gohn (2004), political-ideological movements emerge from the political circumstances of a nation, such as political uprisings, revolts, riots, revolutions, and so on, or – even though ideology pervades all movements – from ideologies such as anarchism and Marxism, which ebb and flow according to circumstances. However, social movements do not only occur at moments of struggle. The world has witnessed the formation of politically charged social movements that have emerged from seemingly spontaneous public demonstrations or branched off from existing social movements and have become more expressive with the articulation of virtual media and social networks. Examples include the Occupy Wall Street movement, which began in 2011 with protests against the financial corporations in the United States; *Yo Soy 132* in Mexico, which began as an isolated protest but ended up demanding structural change in Mexican society (2012); the *Democracia Real Ya* movement, which led to demonstrations by '*Los Indignados*' (2011) in Spain; and protests against dictatorial regimes in Egypt, Libya, Bahrain, Tunisia, Syria, Yemen, Algeria and Jordan related to the so-called Arab Spring.

In June 2013, there were large-scale public demonstrations and protests in Brazil. These started modestly – with demands for the cancellation of fare increases on the bus and metro, and for free public transport for certain groups – but grew progressively and were joined by different spheres, with grievances and demands around health care, education, political ethics, and so on. Together, they formed a political movement and represented as demand for change. On the one hand, this was facilitated by the articulation, debate and identification made possible by virtual networks. On the other hand, they incorporated the meanings and experiences of struggles by historic movements and social networks in Brazil. However, one of the most important traits of this heterogeneous movement was that it only appeared in urban public spaces.

The confluence of identities is a necessary component of the articulation and meaning-making processes of social movements (Castells, 2000, pp. 23–24). Political identities can be classified as: asserters, introduced by the dominant institutions in order to maintain domination; of resistance, created by actors, such as gangs, who feel threatened by the structure of domination; and transformers or builders of project identities, forged by actors to build a new identity that redefines their position in society and transforms the social structure.

This chapter deals only with the Brazilian popular social movements by subaltern classes that I characterize as transformers and builders of project identities, in line with the third category identified by Castells. This is something that the most recent protests in Brazil did not encompass. However, the idea of constructing project identities can be identified in earlier social movements such as the *Movement of Workers Without Land* (Movimento dos Trabalhos Rurais Sem Terra, MST). Brazil continues to develop its political forces, with the appropriate political redefinitions characteristic of a historical period that is restoring democratic norms, including the refinement of movements in praxis and the creation of new – and the growth of existing – non-governmental organizations (NGOs) which sometimes take on functions previously carried out by social movements. Some are combative and of a politically disruptive character, while others are concerned with finding solutions to violations of citizenship rights related to social welfare. From these comes the struggle for space to participate in normative arenas of negotiation, such as the so- called 'sectoral councils' in Brazil, working to formulate, deliberate and regulate policies and actions towards protecting the rights of children, adolescents and other social groups.

In short, the Brazilian context contains a diversity of movements that includes the MST, the National Movement for Human Rights (Movimento Nacional dos direitos humanos, MNDH), the

Organization of Brazilian Women (Articulação de Mulheres Brasileiras, AMB) and dozens of other women's organizations, the National Forum for the Democratization of Communication (Fórum Nacional pela Democratização da Comunicação, FNDC), the national movement for the Right to Housing (Movimento Nacional do Direito à Moradia, MNDM) and its branches in the states of Brazil, the various organizations of the ecological movement, and hundreds of other groups and NGOs that undertake a socio-educational agenda with young people, homeless people, and so on, aimed at resolving the concrete problems of social segments that suffer the consequences of a disregard for fundamental human rights.

The significance of these movements in the context of civil society in Brazil has been substantial. They help generate political awareness and social mobilization with enough strength to affect political structures and intervene in public policies. This was seen with the emergence of new social movements in Brazil in June 2013.

Globally, it is important to highlight the international mobilization around the World Social Forum (WSF), with its slogan, 'Another world is possible.' It propounds development in which the human being is both the motivating force and the recipient of the results. The number of people and organizations that have gathered in these forums annually since 2001 to discuss and propose alternatives is indicative of its importance as a collective, and global, political actor. The WSF has led to the emergence of related forums around the world, such as the Social Forum of the Americas, the Brazilian Social Forum, the European Social Forum, the Los Angeles Social Forum, the Catalan Social Forum, the Mercosul Social Forum, the *Tríplice Fronteira* WSF (at the borders of Brazil, Argentina and Paraguay), the Migration WSF, and São Paulo's south region Social Forum, among others. Among the innovative aspects of the WSF is the fact that it is constituted not as a bureaucratic mechanism, but as a social articulation in a network format.

The WSF is a space for dialogue and exchange of knowledge, as well as a source of inspiration for plans and modes of intervention that emerge from shared knowledge. The event has become a major arena for debate through panels, roundtables and conferences, but mostly through self-managed activities led by civil society organizations. To realize such activities, these organizations sign up and pay their own expenses, report on their experiences and open these reports up for discussion, which results in the exposition of a variety of initiatives undertaken with the ultimate goal of building social justice by changing the conditions of human existence and development.

In contrast to what is sometimes thought, large-scale processes of social mobilization are occurring in all societies behind internal demonstrations, such as those that recently took place in Europe, the Arab world and the United States. The mainstream media barely report on the phenomenon of the WSF, or on its regional, national and thematic social forums. When they do, they represent them in a biased, fragmented and edited version – a 'picturesque' version that emphasizes the more festive aspects but neglects to provide a comprehensive understanding. A counterpoint is provided by the community and alternative media in forms of autonomous expression by civil society.

Popular community communication and social mobilization

Communication is an important part of the process of mobilizing popular social movements. Such processes unfold in accordance with the organizations' abilities and the resources available in a given period of time. The WSF, for example, has grown to a considerable size because it knows how to use the Internet as a communication channel for coordination and mobilization. The MST went from small informational newsletters to using magazines and a starring role at the news agency *Brasil de Fato*. Ultimately, popular movements adjust to the given conditions in order to communicate. In Brazil, social movements have always used their own means of communication, known as popular, community, participatory or alternative media. They do this because of the need to speak to their specific audiences, and because of the restrictions on their freedom of expression when using the national system of communication. Whether evolving from the pamphlet to the newspaper and later to the blog and the website, or from the megaphone to community radio, from slides to video and later to the television and the open community channel on cable television,[3] such practices are indicative of how communication works to facilitate struggles, and as an expansion of citizenship to include the right to communicate.

In this context, empowering and autonomous communication processes are perceived as necessary channels of expression in the dynamics of popular mobilization and organization. Even under the control and coercive power of the Brazilian military regime (1964–1985) during its decline, running all the political risks arising from the State of Exception and its enforcement mechanisms, popular social movements and other progressive organizations dared to create alternative channels of communication. They exercised the right to communicate in practice – and continue to do so now – through alternative means of escaping control and police repression, and opposing legal mechanisms and impediments, as in the case of community broadcasting. When there was no community radio, loudspeakers were used and later they broadcasted through free radio. In the aftermath of the shutdown of a large number of community radio stations, some went to court to ensure the constitutional right to freedom of expression and obtained favourable judgments.

At the theoretical-political level, prompted by a call by the United Nations Educational, Science and Culture Organization (UNESCO) in the 1960s, the issue of democratic public communication policy was widely discussed in Latin America[4] and other countries of the so-called Third World in the 1970s and 1980s. The motivation was the control of the international flow of information, in an international economic order centred on the diffusion of industrialization strategies based on modernization theory, which was favourable to the interests of large corporations controlled in the developed countries. Through news agencies and the export of the products of the cultural industry, in addition to direct investment in resources in the media in Latin America, the world view and way of life of the United States and Europe spread as a form of cultural domination at the expense of the global circulation of information from Latin, African and Asian sources – even between the countries of these regions (see Matta, 1980; Beltrán, 1982; Wertheim, 1979). However, in the context of the structural contradictions in the economic, social, cultural and political inequalities of the model – which was endorsed by the official, public and private, national and regional, media – the practices of horizontal communication emerged.[5] These were community, participatory and democratic modes of communication accomplished through the active involvement of people as issuers and receivers of messages in non-profit, grassroots organizations or associations. Since then, there have been signs of a social demand for another perspective on the right to communicate, moving beyond access to information. Such a right entails not only the means of communication, but also the processes of organization and mobilization.

Community communication in Brazil, in the experiences gestated and collectively administered by community organizations and for the public interest,[6] denotes 'another communication', one that is 'owned' by organized sectors of the subaltern classes, according to the needs of social mobilization, talking with their audiences and expressing their world view in the hope of gaining a voice in society. From this perspective, it is a way of exercising the right to communicate in practice. It helps to build processes of group or interpersonal communication in the coordination of actions, such as the informal and non-formal education of youth, the self-promotion of women, the organization of rural workers, and so on. It creates the means or channels of communication, such as newsletters, websites, community radio, popular video and community channels on cable television.

There are countless examples that create processes and simultaneously make use – or not – of technological communicative means in the pursuit of social transformation. These include Radio Comunitária Cantareira,[7] WebTV Cidade Tiradentes[8] and Movimento Pombas Urbanas,[9] on the periphery of São Paulo, and Movemento Enraizados,[10] based in Rio de Janeiro with branches across the country. These are expressions of current movements for freedom of communication that have a long history in the Brazilian context and beyond. At the international level, a New World Information and Communication Order was proclaimed when UNESCO created the *International Commission for the Study of Communication Problems*, coordinated by Sean MacBride. The result of the Commission's work was presented as the MacBride Report, or *Many Voices: One World*,[11] in February 1980.

Communication as a human right

The issue of the right to communication has become increasingly prevalent in Brazil.[12] The subject has been addressed by some authors, such as Antonio Pasquali and Romel Jurado (2002) and Cees Hamelink (2002) who have submitted proposals as subsidies for categorization in the World Conference on the Information Society (WSIS) in 2003. The proposal by Pasquali and Jurado includes the right to communication as the right to freedom of opinion, of expression, of broadcasting, of information, and the right to access to and use of media and information technology. Cees Hamelink (2002) specifies the information rights, cultural rights, protection rights, public and collective communication technology rights, and participation rights[13] as composing the right to communicate. The legal precepts, historically achieved, which ensure access to information and the right to freedom of opinion, expression and creativity have been reaffirmed, while at the same time new perspectives are being emphasized. Among them, there is growing popular discontent about disrespect for minorities and human rights by the mainstream media,[14] as well as support for cultural rights and the protection of citizens' access to the channels of communication as protagonists, using advanced technology and social non-profit organizations.

Current mobilizations demand the right to access the power to communicate for citizens and their collective organizations, which represent organized segments of the subaltern classes: that is, access to mass communication and digital channels as broadcasters of their own content and independent managers of media in the service of communities and popular movements. In the past, social movements were content with – or were forced to settle for – artisanal, low-range means of communication. Today, it is essential to ensure access to channels that are modern, efficient and able to reach a wider audience simultaneously. There is a demand for the aggregate communication opportunities that current information and communication technologies (ICTs) offer, without neglecting more traditional forms still in use throughout the country.

These mobilizations also bring the right to communicate to the same level of importance as other rights, such as decent housing, education, health care, and so on. From this perspective, this entails specific phenomena: the right to *isonomia* (equality of rights) and the right to *isegoria* (freedom of expression and the right to be heard). At the same time, communication rights pave the way for the realization of other rights. In other words, communication can contribute to the processes of knowledge dissemination, organization and action to ensure the fulfilment of all human rights. These mobilizations expand the notion from an individual right to the collective right to communicate; the rights of groups, communities, collectives and social movements to demand the expansion of the public sphere beyond the bourgeois public sphere, allowing new visions of class and values, grievances and new demands that favour public debate, make social conflict transparent and, at the same time, build links and identification with the struggle for hegemony.

This indicates a movement that seeks the transformation of citizenship from individual civil and political rights to social and collective rights (Bobbio 1992; Vieira, 2000). For these authors, human rights can be grouped as first-generation (civil and political); second-generation (social, economic and cultural); third-generation (collective); and fourth-generation (bioethical) rights. While at first the movement pursued just the rights to information and freedom of expression, gradually these rights were understood in broader terms along with the advancement of citizenship – if not in legal terms, at least through social legitimacy.

The notion of a 'generation of human rights' is attributed to the jurist Karel Vasak, who referred to it in 1979 in the inaugural class in the Course of the International Institute of Human Rights in Strasbourg, according to Antonio A. Cancado Trindade (2000), his former student. Vasak is, therefore, the precursor of that expression by drawing an analogy to the motto of the French Revolution: liberty, equality and fraternity[15], as rights of first (the rights of freedom and individual rights), second (rights to economic and social equality), and third (rights to solidarity)[16] generations. In the words of the Trindade (2000)[17]: 'liberté, egalité, fraternité'.

On the other hand, the classification of rights into generations, widely propagated e.g. by Bobbio – has been criticized (Trinity, 2000; Scarlet, 1998; Piovesan, 1998; Lima, 2003) – considered without legal basis, without correspondence between the generation of rights and the historical process, as divisive or unrealistic for giving the impression of the overcoming of one generation to another, among other aspects.

This type of grouping was adopted considering its appropriateness to clarify the metamorphoses undergone by the perception of what is human right in time and place, or of the changes in the quality in the conception of citizenship. These generations are intertwined among themselves and social practices (Peruzzo 2005, p. 32), and are, therefore, historical and inseparable, and constituted as a spiral. They are not understood within a framework in which a generation of rights surpasses the other; on the contrary, one helps to give more density to the other, once they are constituted and advance in accordance with the transformations in society.

The right to communicate (Peruzzo, 2005) is currently more visible as a human right of the first generation, but it is embedded in the second, third and fourth generations. The right to communicate is embedded in the first generation of rights, which refer to the *civil dimension*, such as access to information, freedom of opinion, freedom of faith, and so on (Marshall, 1967; Bobbio, 1992; Vieira, 2000), and in the *political dimension* of citizenship – participation. Both these dimensions are realms in which communication is of critical importance. Moreover, the right to communicate is among the second generation of rights because these include a social dimension through access to assets such as historic and cultural heritage (Vieira, 2000; Bobbio, 1992). These rights tend to be better recognized, as in the case of education and housing, compared to the sphere of communication. Historically, the ruling classes and governmental authorities have controlled the operation of media systems in Brazil. However, media and communication technologies are public property and belong to all social classes. Third-generation rights advance the notion of the rights of 'the common people as human beings to the specific understood in diversity' (Bobbio, 1992, p. 23). In other words, they expand the notion of individual rights to human beings in the collective sense – the rights of groups, communities, collectives and movements, and the various forms of social organization in the public interest, respecting difference[18] in every sense, regardless of gender, race, age, faith, culture and physical disability.

Understanding communication as a human right in the context of third-generation rights represents an advance in the vision of the right to communicate and in the conceptualization of citizenship itself, both because of its acceptance as a collective right, and by giving more visibility to communication, which tends to be somewhat less conspicuous in the classical dimensions of citizenship, given that the priority is usually directed to the conditions of life.

The fourth generation of rights is related to bioethics (Vieira, 2000) and concerns the right to life and its forms of reproduction. According to Lima Neto (1998, p. 1), It entails the right of the person and of humanity to 'not have his/her genetic patrimony altered' in view of risks of deterioration and modification of the human genome addressed by the UNESCO's 29th General Conference on 11 November 1997 (Universal Declaration on the Human Genome and Human Rights, 1997, p. 1). In this context, the right to communication is also present in terms of information, privacy and integrity.

The quality or status of citizenship changes within these historic processes. Perhaps it is time to take a step forward to demand that communication is perceived as a specific generation of citizenship rights that might be called a 'fifth-generation right', or 'communication rights'. This is justified by the central role that the media, permeated by ICTs, especially the Internet, play in society. As a specific dimension of citizenship, a fifth generation of rights would concern democratization of the power to communicate in order to empower the subaltern classes to generate and make use of cultural and information production. It would mean strengthening the technological means of communication by the citizen and collective non-profit organizations as transmitters, diffusers, managers, facilitators and receivers – not just as receivers or consumers.

Communication rights, when understood as a dimension of citizenship, strengthen the notion of citizenship itself, and bring the concept up to date with the importance of communication in contemporary society. Moreover, such recognition would make communication more salient as a right for all to see, be they citizens, the institutions of executive power, such as the police – who regularly shut down community radio stations and restrict the constitutional right to freedom of expression – parliament, private companies, or the major beneficiaries of concessions to operate in the mainstream media.

The crossover between education and community communication

Community communication is one way of exercising the right to communication. It is the one closest to people, within their homes and other spaces of community participation. Terms such as 'participatory', 'popular', 'horizontal' or 'alternative' communication have been used to refer to this communicative process carried out by popular social movements and non-profit organizations in civil society in Latin America. Community communication emerged among actors who are organized to promote social mobilization and take concrete steps to improve political consciousness and the living conditions of impoverished populations. Therefore, community communication is best understood as having emerged democratically through popular groups in communities, neighbourhoods, online spaces, and so on, according to their interests, needs and abilities. Its content is made by and for the community (Peruzzo, 2008, p. 2). It is based on the active participation of members in the whole process.

This mode of communication has its roots in the actions of popular social movements characteristic of the late 1970s and the 1980s,[19] and is therefore shaped by a series of reactions to political control, the degrading conditions of life, and disrespect for human rights established in the country at that time.[20] It is, therefore, communication linked to broader struggles of impoverished but organized population segments aiming to resolve problems that affect people's day-to-day lives and to expand the rights of citizenship (Peruzzo, 2008, p. 2). It is carried out of necessity on a voluntary basis, with scarce resources and according to the needs and realities of each situation. It helps to expand the achievement of other rights of citizenship, as is indicated above, because it helps to generate knowledge and to change the concrete conditions of existence.

Community and popular alternative communication are configured in a variety of ways, such as verbal and gestural (interpersonal, group communication), print (brochure, newsletter, fanzine, poster, banners), sound (sound car and bike, speakers, community radio), audio-visual (video, street television, community channels on television and cable television) and digital (blog, website, virtual communities, networks, e-zines, online community stations). It is full of virtues as well as distortions. Generally, such distortions are related to the different interests that drive the creation of a community's means of communication. These could be of a mobilizing and educational character aimed at providing community service to improve the quality of life of population segments. Or they could be motivated by commercial interests, as some use community media, especially radio, as a way to make money. There are also interests of a religious nature, as well as of a personal or political/ electoral character. Other distortions occur due to the lack of financial resources, authoritarian leadership practices, political use, a lack of adequate preparation, and so on.

When guided by the public interest, however, community resources help to improve people's living conditions and knowledge through awareness-raising and the promotion of human rights, strengthening the exercise of citizenship by opening up space to broadcast citizens' voices and enabling them to participate actively in various phases of the communicative process, including planning the *production and diffusion* of content and management of the means of communication.

In regard to the educational dimensions of community communication, participants receive little specific training. They learn through practice and from each other, receiving sporadic help from partners and the occasional opportunity to attend short or longer courses. Often, unless it is processed by social agents attuned to the prospect of transforming society, this type of ad hoc training leads popular communicators to reproduce the patterns of large commercial media. Performance could be improved – as an aspect of communication for participatory and sustainable development – if there were specific training, in particular on respecting the dynamics and logic of community communication.

It is important to prepare people for the use of the techniques and technologies of communication. It is necessary to familiarize them in the language of audio-visual, digital and press media, help them master technical diagramming for newspaper production, handle computers, create and manage blogs, operate camcorders, and so on. In the process of acquiring such skills, a 'new right' is added – access to technical expertise and specialist communications. It is not just about 'updating' or the mastery of techniques and technologies. The challenge is how to incorporate a collective way of operationalizing them in order to surpass the parameters of so-called digital inclusion, and to generate processes of exchange of knowledge across generations, driven by the desire to share and enhance information and communication systems. Communication is more than means and messages, and more than broadcasting and receiving. It is part of social relations in the dynamics of the coordination of actions in the process of self-organization and the exercise of active citizenship.

This line of thinking interconnects with the perspective of cyber-cultur@, which proposes a 'redesign' of the world in order to collectively *rescue* knowledge about our history and identities as societies, which have undergone processes of domination, as an element in *understanding* the present and *tracing* our own paths to building 'another possible world' (see Chapter 2 in this volume). Such a perspective offers an understanding of the world that 'is not limited to pure decoding of the word...but extends itself in the intelligence of the world' (Freire, 1982, p. 11). It is not enough to know how to use machines and software; it is about knowing how to put them to the service of the collective construction of a world that makes human beings the means and the ends of development.

Final considerations

Despite the importance of the mass media and digital communications to the expansion of citizenship, community, and alternative communication, movement in this direction is tenuous given that it is this that enables the community, the neighbourhood and the popular movement to achieve leadership and empowerment by organized citizens.

The exercise of the right to popular, community and alternative communication is intertwined with the modes of *informal* education processed on a daily basis and through communication practices in the public sphere, and the *informal* education (participation in training and workshops offered by institutions) that occurs in the context of social struggles and enables a rich process in which education and communication mix. What remains is a demand to enhance all the above in *formal* education, where the school guarantees literacy beyond textual writing and reading.

In order to ensure the citizen's right to education, it is important to take into account that communication media also informally educate, making use of different means of expression. Knowing how to read them, interpret them, dominate their codes, and implement and operationalize them is related to the need to increase awareness of the right to communication. Among the best ways to understand the functioning of the media as a whole, its power to influence and the possibility of manipulation in its messages, is the praxis of media: that is, the implementation of concrete projects of communication and their assessment. Active participation in the diverse range of communication for social change, and in the sphere of a broader social mobilization, contributes to the expansion of citizenship status. In other words, it helps redefine the meaning of the public sphere by forcing its expansion to accommodate deliberative participation by the organized subaltern classes. The public sphere, to be truly public, presupposes democratization of the word, as exercised in *isonomia* and *isegoria* – equality of freedom of expression and the right to be heard.

The right to communication is multifaceted. It is imperative that its dimensions at the community level and the practices of social groups that mobilize to extend citizenship are given the same degree of importance as that of the mainstream media and cyberspace.

What does community communication have to do with governance? In a nutshell, it helps enable citizens to understand the world and organize themselves to transform the world, from the perspective of *a different type of development* – a participatory and sustainable development in which the economy is primarily structured to meet human needs.

Notes

1. This chapter is a revised, updated and expanded version of 'A comunicação nos movimentos sociais: exercício de um direito humano' *Dialogos de la Comunicación* 82, pp. 1–7. Translated Janaina Krohling Peruzzo.
2. The word 'popular' is derived from the word 'people' and is used to refer to the impoverished segments of the population, or to the subaltern classes.
3. With the proviso that the move away from an 'artisan' means of communication to high-technology does not mean abandoning the use of the simpler and older means. Rather, both coexist in the first decade of the 21st century.
4. First Intergovernmental Conference on Communication Policies in Latin America, Costa Rica, July 1976.
5. See, for example the work of Reys Matta (1977), Beltrán (1981) and author (2004, 2005, 2008), among others.
6. Not all experiences that call themselves 'community' outrun the tendency to reproduce the canons of the major communications media and the privatization of interests, which, in theory, are collective commodities.
7. Radio Cantareira FM http://www.radiocantareira.org/
8. Centro Ecológico Cultural Tio Pac http://agectiopac.wordpress.com/ http://gectiopac.ning.com/
9. Pombas Urbanas http://pombasurbanas.org.br/blog/?page_id=898
10. Enraizados   http://www.enraizados.com.br/index.php/radio-;   enraizados-web-uma-nova-maneira-de-se-comunicar/
11. Published in Brazil in 1983 by Editora da Fundação Getúlio Vargas, under the title *Um mundo e muitas vozes: Comunicação e informação em nossa época*.
12. Just as in the 1980s and 1990s, when the academy opened up space for debate on horizontal and alternative forms of communication, interest in this debate has now reawakened. The watchwords today are the 'right to

communicate', community communication and alternative media. Given the social phenomenon they represent, these modes of communication are everywhere and in a variety of formats never seen before.

13. See Peruzzo (2005) for more details about these proposals.

14. Such as civil actions filed by federal prosecutors against human rights violations by television companies, which led to fines, the withdrawal of a show from the schedules, or a right to reply. For example, *Tardes Quentes*, made by Rede TV and presented by João Kleber, contained a segment that violated human rights, in particular those of lesbians and gay men. The court ruled, among other things, that *Tardes Quentes* should make way for 30 hours of programmes produced by the organizations involved in the civil action. As a result, a one-hour show called *Rights of Response* was broadcast for 30 days. See http://www.intervozes.org.br/destaque-4.

15. See also Karel Vasak (FlaviaPiovesan in Lima 2003:1), who argues that 'the first-generation of human rights is the civil and political rights, based on freedom (liberté). The second-generation, therefore, is that of economic, social and cultural rights based on equality (égalité). Finally, the last generation is that of solidarity rights, particularly the right to development, peace and the environment, completing the triad with fraternity (fraternité).'

16. The judge and professor Paul Bonavides (2008) proposes to transfer the right to peace as a third-generation right in the framework proposed by Karel Vasak, to instead be included in a fifth generation in order to stress its importance and make the issue of peace more visible.

17. Lecture in the seminar entitled *Human Rights of Women: International Protection (V ConferênciaNacional de DireitosHumanos* – 5th National Conference of Human Rights) which took place on 25 May 2000 in Brasilia.

18. UNESCO adopted the *Universal Declaration on Cultural Diversity* on 2 November 2001, representing recognition and worldwide acknowledgment of the legitimacy of third-generation rights.

19. The decades preceding the 1970s were marked by the curtailment of participation in the light of the military dictatorship established in the country in 1964.

20. In the early decades of the 20th century, however, there were newspapers and other alternative media that served the interests of workers (see Peruzzo, 2004).

References

Beltrán, L.R. (1981) 'Adeus a Aristóteles: Comunicação e Sociedade', *Journal of the Program of Communication* 6, pp. 5–35.

Bobbio, N. (1992) *A Era Dos Direitos* (Rio de Janeiro: Campus).

Boletim FSM (2007) *Fórum Social Mundial*. Porto Alegre. Newsletter, 5 October 2007.

Bonavides, P. (2008) 'A Quinta Geração de Direitos Fundamentais', *Direitos Fundamentais & Justiça*, (April/June) 3, 82–93.

Bonavides, P. (1998) *Direito Constitucional* (7th ed.) (São Paulo: Malheiros).

Castells, M. (2000) *A Era da informação: Economia, Sociedade e Cultura: Poder da Identidade* (second edn) (São Paulo: Paz e Terra).

182   *Cicilia M. Krohling Peruzzo*

Freire, P. (1982) *A Importância do Ato de Ler* (São Paulo: Autores Associados / Cortez).

Fórum Social Mundial (2012) *Grupos Temáticos Rumo à Cúpula dos Povos* (São Paulo: World Social Forum), 11 January 2012, avaliable on http://www.forumsocialmundial.org.br/noticias_01.php?cd_news=3606&cd_language=1, date accessed 31 July 2012.

Fórum Social Começa Hoje e espera (2012) *Uol Notícias* (São Paulo, 24 January) http://noticias.uol.com.br/internacional/ultimas-noticias/2012/01/24/forum-social-mundial-comeca-hoje-e-espera-reunir-40-mil-em-porto-alegre.htm, date accessed 31 July 2012.

FSM (2007) *Fórum Social Mundial* (Porto Alegre: World Social Forum). Retrieved from http://fsm10.procempa.com.br/wordpress/?p=338, date accessed 31 July 2012.

Furtado, E. T. and Mendes, A. S.V. (2008) *Os direitos de 5ª. Geração enquanto direito à paz e seus reflexos no mundo do trabalho.* Unpublished paper presented in the 17th National Conference CONPENDI (XVII Congresso Nacional do CONPEDI), in Brasília, November 20–22 2008. *Anais.* Retrieved from www.conpedi.org.br/arquivos/anais/brasilia/02_335pdf, date accessed 27 March 2013.

Gohn, M. da G. (2004) *Teorias dos Movimentos Sociais: Paradigmas Clássicos e Contemporâneos.* (4th edn) (São Paulo: Loyola).

González, J. A. (2010) *Cibercultur@ como Estrategia de Comunicación Compleja desde la Peperiferia.* Ciudad de México: Labcomplex-CEICH/UNAM (n.d.). Retrieved from www.labcomplex.net, date accessed 28 February 2010.

González, J. A. (2008) 'Digitalizados por decreto. Cibercultur@: inclusão forçada na América Latina', *Matrizes – Journal of the Graduate Program in Communication Sciences* 2(2), pp. 113–138.

Hamelink, C. (2002) *El Derecho a Comunicarse.* Boletim PADH (Ecuador: Universidad Andina Simon Bolívar).

Lima, G. M. (2003) 'Críticas à Teoria das Gerações (ou mesmo dimensões) dos Direitos Fundamentais', *Jusnavigandi*, p. 1. Retrieved from http://jus.com.br/revista/texto/4666/criticas-a-teoria-das-geracoes-ou-mesmo-dimensoes-dos-direitos-fundamentais, date accessed 26 March 2013.

Lima Neto, F. V. (1998) *Direitos Humanos de 4ª.Geração.* DHnet – Direitos Humanos na Internet. Retrieved from http://www.dhnet.org.br/direitos/textos/geracaodh/4_geracao.html, date accessed: 25 March 2013.

MacBride, S. (1987) *Un solo Mundo, Voces Múltiples* (México: Fondo de Cultura Económica). Coleção Popular. Retrieved from http://unesdoc.unesco.org/images/0004/000400/040066sb.pdf, date accessed 27 January 2008.

Números do FSM (2010) *Fórum Social Mundial.* Porto Alegre. World Social Forum. Retrieved from http://fsm10.procempa.com.br/wordpress/, date accessed 31 July 2012.

Pasquali, A. Jurado, J. (2003) *Propuesta de Formulación del Derecho a ala Comunicación.* June 2003. Avaliable on www.movimientos.org/foro_comunicacion (documentos), date accessed 12 February 2003.

Peruzzo, C. M.K. (2004) *Comunicação nos Movimentos Populares: a Participação na Construção da Cidadania* (3rd edn). Petrópolis: Vozes.

Peruzzo, C. M.K (2005) 'Direito à Comunicação Comunitária, Participação Popular e Cidadania', *Revista Latinoamericana de Ciencias de la Comunicación* 2(3), pp. 18–41.

Peruzzo, C. M. K (2008) 'Movimentos Sociais, Cidadania e o Direito à Comunicação', *Revista Fronteiras* 11(1), pp. 33–43 (São Leopoldo: UNISINOS).

Peruzzo, C.M.K, Tufte, T. and Veja Casanova, J. (eds) (2011) *Trazos de una otra comunicación en América Latina* (Barranquilla: Universidad del Norte).

Piovesan, F. (1998) *Temas de Direitos Humanos* (São Paulo: Max Limonad).

Process FSM (2008) *Chamada Para um Dia de Mobilização e Ação Global*. Fórum Social Mundial. Porto Alegre: World Social Forum (n.d.), Retrieved from: http://www.forumsocialmundial.org.br/dinamic.php?pagina=chamada2008>, date accessed 29 June 2008.

Ramos, M. C. (2005) 'Comunicação, Direitos Sociais e Políticas Culturais' in J.M. Melo, and L. Sathler (eds), *Direitos à Comunicação na Sociedade da Informação*. (São Bernardo do Campo: UMESP), pp. 245–253.

Reyes Matta, F. (1980) *A Informação na nova Ordem Internacional* (Rio de Janeiro: Paz e Terra).

Reyes, Matta, F. (1977) 'From Right to Praxis: A Model of Communication with Active Social Participation', Paper presented at the International Seminar on Third Word of Communications and Participation, Amsterdam, 5–8 September 1977.

Sarlet, I.W. (1998) *A Eficácia dos Direitos Fundamentais* (Porto Alegre: Livraria do Advogado).

Trindade, A. C. (2000) *A Proteção Internacional (Human Rights of Women: the International Protection*. Lecture presented in the Seminar *Direitos Humanos das Mulhere- V Conferência Nacional de Direitos Humanos* (5th National Conference of Human Rights. 25 May 2000). Brasília: Câmara dos Deputados.

Vieira, L. (2000) *Cidadania e Globalização* (fourth edn) (Rio de Janeiro: Record).

Wertheim, J. (1979) *Meios de Comunicação: Realidade e Mito* (São Paulo: Nacional).

13
Citizen Engagement through SMS? Audiences 'Talking Back' to a Reality TV Edutainment Initiative in Tanzania

Ylva Ekström and Linda Helgesson Sekei

Introduction: from reproductive health to economic empowerment

'It is all well and good to learn about HIV/AIDS and reproductive health, but we need jobs!' This was the audience feedback given to Femina HIP, a civil society media platform in Tanzania. Since 2001, Femina HIP has provided information and provoked discussion about sexual and reproductive health, HIV/AIDS and healthy lifestyles, with youth as its major target group. In response to the demand for information related to livelihoods, Femina organized a youth conference in 2008 under the theme 'Empowering Youth for Employment'. The conference was attended by youth from around the country, and it was soon clear that the demand for developing skills in entrepreneurship, business and income-generating activities was enormous (Helgesson and Ernest, 2008). In response, the economic empowerment initiative 'Ruka Juu' (Jump Up) was launched in early 2011.

Femina has developed the concept of 'Combination Prevention' in which economic empowerment is seen as a prerequisite for healthy lifestyles, gender equality and citizen engagement. Femina HIP is engaged in the production of a variety of communication activities that together create a multimedia platform, which aims to stimulate open talk, critical thinking and social change in order to foster healthy lifestyles and positive, responsible attitudes to sexuality, HIV/AIDS and democratic culture.

Femina's objectives over the years have included the production and dissemination of 'long-term, recurring, as well as one-off media products that communicate factual information on healthy lifestyles, sexuality, and reproductive health and rights including HIV/AIDS, and promote life skills, audience voices, entrepreneurship and positive role models for behavior and wider social change' (Femina HIP, 2006, p. 6). At the heart of all its activities is the *edutainment methodology* (often called 'entertainment-education' in the literature), which aims to entertain while at the same time educating audiences about certain life essential topics. Arvind Singhal and Everett M. Rogers (1999) define entertainment-education as

> the process of purposely designing and implementing a media message to both entertain and educate, in order to increase audience knowledge about an educational issue, create favorable attitudes, and change overt behavior. This strategy uses the universal appeal of entertainment to show individuals how they can live safer, healthier, and happier lives. (xii)

Femina aims for a *participatory production process* that uses real-life stories of ordinary youth, lets the audience talk back, and gives voice to the questions and concerns of local communities around Tanzania (Fuglesang, 2005). At the core of this chapter is an analysis of this participatory production process, based on an examination of audience members' interactions with Ruka Juu through their use of SMS.

Ruka Juu: edutainment through reality television

The main vehicle of the economic empowerment initiative Ruka Juu is a reality television entrepreneurship competition. The first season revolved around entrepreneurship and financial education, and was broadcast on national television in Tanzania between March and May 2011. The objective of Ruka Juu was to *inspire* young people to become more entrepreneurial and proactive instead of waiting for opportunities to come to them. Part of the objective was to *provide information* about the different aspects of entrepreneurship required to succeed in business, such as marketing, customer care, savings, access to capital, record keeping and planning. The main target group was young people in Tanzania aged 15 to 30, both in school and out of school, living in urban as well as rural areas. As part of a wider community, Ruka Juu also aimed to attract and be endorsed by the young people's families and communities as a secondary target audience.

During 11 episodes, the audience followed six Tanzanian entrepreneurs, all under 30, as they competed for the opportunity of a lifetime. Each entrepreneur was followed through a number of competitive challenges that explored money management, savings options, dealing with emergencies, finding working capital, business planning, and so on, with the aim of determining how the six could improve and grow their businesses. For the final challenges, all the contestants came to Dar es Salaam where experts from the University of Dar es Salaam trained them in entrepreneurship, business skills and financial education. Their last challenge was to present their business plans. The final episode was broadcast live and the winner, Idrissa, a barbershop owner from Kibaha, was awarded a prize of TSH 5 million (USD 3000) to invest in his business.

The contestants were evaluated by three judges and by members of the audience who were encouraged to vote for their favourite contestant by mobile phone SMS messaging. The rapid increase in mobile phone use and the presence of other social media in Tanzania provide new communication opportunities, and the audience was encouraged to engage with Ruka Juu by answering a 'question of the week' and sending spontaneous comments and questions. Like other Femina initiatives, a participatory production process and letting the audience talk back were part of the aim.

In conjunction with Ruka Juu, Femina launched the 'Sema na Fema' (Speak Up with Fema) initiative as part of its new social media agenda, and to create 'a more systematic way to work with SMS; to make it a more consistent part of the organization's participatory production processes, deepening conversation with the audience and encouraging our followers to participate in content production' (Femina HIP, 2011, p. 1). Femina found that alongside the new opportunities arising from the new technology, there were also challenges:

> The untapped potential for an even richer exchange with audiences was becoming more evident with mobile phone use on the rise in Tanzania. With Femina's deepening agenda around citizen engagement the 'reporting back' function has become even more important. The challenge has been how to get more value out of SMS communication. More specifically, how to better mine the content of the messages that were coming in, how to reach out to individuals via SMS and how to use the voices, 'the speaking up' Femina's audience, to improve media content, make it more user-driven and empower youth in the process. Sema na Fema is the beginning of this exploration. (Femina HIP, 2011, p. 1)

The Sema na Fema shortcode platform[1] serves as a new channel for the audience to interact with and 'talk back' to Ruka Juu, and creates a potential space for citizen engagement.

Aim and methods

The aim of this study is three-fold: First, to conduct a demographic analysis of the interacting audience in order to capture *who is communicating* with Ruka Juu through SMS. This raises questions about who has access to the new channel and who does not, and who chooses to use this new space for interaction and engagement and who does not. Second, to conduct a content analysis of *what is being communicated*. This leads to questions around what it is possible to communicate and what cannot be captured through this form. In addition, if the messages demand responses, to what extent has this been possible? Third, to identify the strengths and limitations of the approach taken in Ruka Juu of using mobile phone messaging for participatory communication. In essence, this discussion is important from a production point of view: that is, how information and communication technologies (ICTs) can be better utilized as tools for participatory development.

It is the particular mode of audience interaction, through SMS messaging, which is the focus of the empirical study presented in this chapter. The study serves as a preliminary evaluation of the results of using mobile phone communication as a participatory communication tool during the first season of Ruka Juu. It also aims to serve as a case study analysing and illustrating the opportunities and obstacles in relation to the use of mobile phone text messaging as a tool for participatory communication in an edutainment context. As such, the study makes an empirical contribution to the more theoretical discussion of the role of new ICTs – particularly mobile phone communication – in processes of participatory communication and social change. In particular, it makes a contribution within the expanding research field concerned with the interplay between reality television and social change.[2]

Femina provided access to its database of the 10,150 mobile phone numbers that had been used to communicate SMS messages. The most active phone number had communicated 2043 times, and the top 20 on the list had interacted more than 100 times each. Below, we call these *high-frequency interactors*, and the rest *low-frequency interactors*. We conducted a telephone interview with 20 high-frequency interactors and 30 low-frequency interactors.[3]

About 22,000 SMSs were received through the *Sema na Fema* shortcode platform between March and May 2011. Among these, around 10,000 were votes, 12,000 were responses to the weekly competition questions, and 150 were spontaneous comments on and questions to the show. We were given access to all these messages by Femina, including those that had been classified as invalid, and conducted a systematic analysis of the SMS responses to the show.

Context: youth and entrepreneurship meet media, communication and social change

Tanzania has a young population and the demographic picture provides a strong argument for why it is so important to focus on youth. According to the latest census, 71 per cent of the population is under 30 years old (URT, 2013). Every year, almost one million young people finish primary and secondary school. However, few manage to find a job in a labour market where only 6 per cent of the population aged 15 and above are formally employed (FSDT, 2009). Many will have to create their own jobs and opportunities for income. The Tanzanian Government, whose message to young people is not to wait for government employment, but to employ themselves and become entrepreneurs, encourages self-employment. Self-employment, entrepreneurial training and financial services such as credit schemes are promoted in the National Youth Development Policy (URT, 2007). However, as Helgesson (2006) shows, the support system for those seeking to undertake self-employment and become entrepreneurs is very limited, which puts young people in a vulnerable position. This is where Femina HIP has found its niche through the Ruka Juu initiative. It is thus at the intersection of research about youth actively engaging in media, ICTs and processes of social change, and research about youth and livelihoods that we situate this critical analysis and provide new knowledge.

Ruka Juu can be classified as what Tufte (2005) refers to as the third generation of entertainment-education. This third generation of edutainment focuses on societal problems and social change through empowerment and participation. This is different from the first two generations of entertainment-education, which focused on individual behavioural change related first to marketing and then to health. To focus on economic empowerment of youth indicates a shift in the focus. Ten years ago, interventions targeting youth were largely about HIV/AIDS and sexual and reproductive health – youth were told to avoid risky behaviour and not contract HIV/AIDS, in order to stay alive and be the future of tomorrow (Helgesson, 2006). To use edutainment to support young people to become entrepreneurs can be seen from different perspectives. One could argue that self-employment suits a neo-liberal perspective where the state is rolled back and the citizens are encouraged to take responsibility for their own lives, including creating their own employment. However, in a context where formal employment is extremely limited, supporting young people to become self-employed and thereby more economically active, can also be a way to include youth as important citizens and offer them a voice.

Other media initiatives in the Global South had been initiated prior to Ruka Juu, most notably 'Dream to Achieve' in Afghanistan, which started in 2008. This was a reality television entrepreneurship competition in which aspiring entrepreneurs presented their business ideas to successful business people in order to win prize money for start-ups. A successful edutainment example in East Africa is FIT Uganda, which began in 1999, in which a business development company teamed up with the International Labour Organization (ILO) to provide technical support to radio stations. The rationale was to develop commercially viable small business content in order to build an audience that was worthwhile targeting for advertising. The most famous programme is 'Nekolera Gyange' ('I run my own business') (Anderson and Hitchins, 2007). Another interesting example is the Kwanda Initiative in South Africa, a 'community makeover' reality television show broadcast from 2009 (Ramafoko et al., 2012). Like Ruka Juu, the aim was to inspire and empower the audience to make a difference to their lives. The Kwanda Initiative, however, focused on collective action with whole communities as contestants, competing against other communities to 'make our communities look better, feel better and work better' (Ramafoko et al., 2012, p. 160). Like Ruka Juu, the Kwanda Initiative had an SMS feedback system, but it also encouraged the audience to respond by letter.

Ekström (2010) discusses how people's lives, predominantly in the urban areas of Tanzania, are now saturated by media. Although not everyone has direct access to the whole range of media and information technologies, domestic and foreign cultural flows are mixed up with everyday discussions and serve as a resource in the ongoing project of identity formation, as well as in processes of development and social change. New media are largely social activities that people engage in together in each other's houses or in public places, and as a result they are no longer only for the privileged few who have direct access to all the modern communication technologies. Nor is it only an urban phenomenon. At the same time, however, it is important to remember that the flows and patterns of media production and consumption are far from equal, which is why thoroughly culturally and socially contextualized research in the field is necessary in order to understand the particularities of, in our case, youth engagement with the media in Tanzania. The need for a context-centred approach is also highlighted by Wasserman (2013), who argues that, although mobile phones can be used as a medium for *transmitting* messages, people also use the mobile phones for *transgressing* boundaries by adapting, adopting and integrating the technology into their daily lives. This may include practices such as local political satire, mobilization and activism, and developing alternative livelihoods through entrepreneurship activities.

Mobile phones, the Internet and various forms of social media are now frequently used by youth in Tanzania (see e.g., Uimonen, 2009). In an analysis of Internet use among students at the Tanzanian arts college of Bagamoyo, 'it becomes quite clear that transnational cultural flow is becoming more commonplace, even in peripheral corners of the world' (Uimonen, 2009, p. 277), but Uimonen concludes that 'the Internet enables more than transnational connectivity'. Her analysis of Internet use and patterns among Tanzanian students illustrates 'the extent to which the Internet mediates trans-local interaction, allowing people to maintain and explore social networks that spread beyond Bagamoyo, but not necessarily beyond Tanzania'.

Audience analysis: who is communicating?

We wanted to find out from the audience analysis who the people interacting through SMS texting with Ruka Juu really were. We carried out a telephone survey of 50 individuals behind the numbers used to send SMSs to the programme. In our selection of respondents, we decided to get in contact with 20 high-frequency interactors by calling the first 20 such numbers on the list. In addition, we called every hundredth number until we reached an additional 30 respondents.[4] We wanted details of age, gender, education, occupation, geographical location, type of message, relationship with contestant, and whether they had previously interacted with any of Femina HIP's products.[5]

The contestants apparently had an interest in communicating with Ruka Juu, not least by voting, and they were all found among the high-frequency interactors. The majority of the high-frequency communicators were men. Among the 20 high-frequency interactors included in the survey, only five were women. Among the 50 individuals included in the telephone survey, 60 per cent were men. It is interesting to note that while the target group for Ruka Juu was 15 to 30-year olds, many SMS communicators were somewhat older. Looking at how gender and age interplay in our material, we find that while in the target group for Ruka Juu (ages 15 to 30) the division was fairly even (16 males and 14 females), among the older SMS communicators (aged 31 to 45) males are slightly more predominant (13 males and 7 females).

Men over 30-years-old are an older group than would be expected in the context of Ruka Juu's target group. Whether this indicates that older men are overrepresented among those who watch Ruka Juu, or they appear more strongly because they are the ones who are able to communicate through SMS is impossible to say based on the available material. It is resonable to draw the conclusion that men slightly older than the target group have better access to mobile phones and more resources to spend on mobile phone communication with a television programme such as Ruka Juu. A large proportion of the Tanzanian population today has access to a mobile phone. There has been a rapid increase since 1998, when there were only 36,000 subscribers, to 28 million subscribers in 2012 (TCRA, 2012). However, many obstacles have to be overcome in addition to access to a mobile phone and the economic resources for a viewer to use SMS communications, such as technical skills, SMS/short-code literacy and, of course, access to a television and interest in the topic. Access to a mobile phone and limited economic resources were also highlighted as prohibiting factors in the Sema na Fema's Narrative Report (Femina HIP, 2011a), especially in relation to students, based on focus group discussions with in-school and out-of-school youth.

Our analysis of the interviews shows that a slight majority of the viewers who had interacted with Ruka Juu through SMS were men over the age of 30. There was a mix of educational backgrounds, from primary school leavers to university graduates. It was clear that the issue of *identification* with the show and the participants was important, and had contributed to a pattern of mobilization through: (a) *geographical identification,* by somebody from the same area as one of the contestants; (b) *vocational identification,* by those working in a similar business as one of the contestants; or (c) identification through a *personal relationship* with the contestants.

Although the sample size of the telephone survey does not provide statistically significant evidence, the survey nonetheless says something about who was inspired – and had the opportunity – to communicate by SMS with Ruka Juu. As a *reality edutainment* project, Ruka Juu gives the audience the opportunity to identify with real people. This in turn might trigger the audience to think about the opportunities presented in the show as 'real goals' and not just 'dreams', as may be the case when engaging with fictional or classic fictive edutainment. It also creates the idea of being able to communicate and interact with real people. Using mobile phones (and perhaps other forms of social media) can be a way to enhance the experience of a 'real' connection and interaction with the participants. It also creates an opportunity to combine mediated and 'real-life' communication with the participants in the programme. Ideas for future seasons of Ruka Juu might therefore be to make it possible for the audience to meet with participants, and to combine different modes of communication in the audience communication with the show.

As is noted above, it is clear that the issue of identification with the show was important. In addition, several of the most active telephone numbers belonged to people who were friends or relatives of a contestant, and some numbers belonged to the contestants themselves. Interestingly, very few respondents had previously interacted with any other Femina HIP product. Only five respondents answered that communication had taken place through Fema clubs, SMS or as a result of having read the magazines. Does this indicate that a new audience has been captured through Ruka Juu? Our findings show that people from outside the immediate target group interacted with the show. In addition, information from Femina shows that Femina's database of active phone numbers grew substantially through Ruka Juu, from about 3100 numbers at the start of the project to about 12,200 by the end (Femina HIP, 2011). This indicates that a new audience has been reached.

Any analysis of who has been communicating with Ruka Juu must take account of who has the opportunity to communicate through the particular format of shortcode SMS. An interesting question to examine is who is *not* communicating through SMS and why? The analysis showed that a number of groups fall outside the mobile communications arena: (a) students; (b) those who live in different geographical areas to the contestants; (c) those who do not have access to or own a mobile phone; (d) those who do not have enough credit on their mobile phones; and (e) 'SMS/shortcode illiterate' people, or at least their communication is not counted as valid. To find out whether these groups communicate, engage in and interact with the programme in any other way, a more holistic study of the communication patterns surrounding Ruka Juu would need to be conducted that includes both mediated and non-mediated, online and offline modes of communication.

Content analysis: what is communicated?

As is mentioned above, content analysis was carried out through a systematic analysis of the 12,818 numerical messages received through the shortcode system. The first part of the content analysis dealt with the weekly competition questions while the second part provided insights into the kinds of spontaneous comments, requests and questions that were communicated to the show. All the messages in this chapter have been translated from Swahili.

Femina's intention with the weekly competition question was to encourage interaction with the programme beyond voting and to call for creativity and critical thinking around entrepreneurship. The question of the week related to the theme of each episode, such as marketing, customer care, savings and the mobilization of capital. Three winners were selected each week, and their names were announced in the following episode. Table 13.1 shows the formulation

Table 13.1 Formulation of the weekly competition question and the number of valid and invalid responses

Episode	Question of the week	Valid	Invalid	Total
1.	What do you understand by the word 'entrepreneurship'?	561	773	1334
2.	Tell us one thing you would do to make your business attract more customers if you were surrounded by businesses similar to yours.	1026	43	1069
3.	Tell us one creative thing you would do with your business to stop customers leaving you.	240	368	608
4.	Why do you think HIV continues to spread in Tanzania?	468	799	1267
5.	Tell us why you think so many micro-entrepreneurs do not insure their businesses.	1180	790	1970
6.	What benefit is there in putting your money in financial institutions such as banks and Savings and Credit Cooperatives?	1052	586	1638
7.	What creative method would you use to get capital if you did not have enough savings?	565	384	949
8.	What will it take to inspire more women to become entrepreneurs?	1099	560	1659
9.	Tell us the main reasons why it is important to have a business plan.	959	101	1060
10.	How much money does Bwana Ishi have in his *kibubu*? [piggy bank]	1022	242	1264
	Total messages (excluding votes)	**8172**	**4646**	**12818**

Source: Femina HIP shortcode database.

of each 'Question of the week' as well as the number of valid and invalid answers received. There were more invalid than valid messages after some of the episodes. This could be an expression of shortcode 'illiteracy', because the message had to start with 'Ruka' followed by a space. If a message did not follow this rule, it would end up in the 'invalid' file of the database. Some of the messages that ended up in the alphabetical part of the database were also attempted votes. The short-code messages were limited to 160 characters, which is the capacity of an SMS message from a standard mobile phone – that is, not a smart phone. Unless the message was sent from a smartphone, any message longer than 160 characters was cut, and the second half of the message ended up in the invalid file. There were therefore many part-messages in the valid file and the invalid file.

A few examples are provided below to give a sense of the responses to the weekly questions. A typical response to the first question of the week 'What do you understand about the word "entrepreneurship?"' was: 'An entrepreneur is a person running a small business by following business rules with the aim of growing it.' Some of the people who answered the question identified themselves as entrepreneurs. The definition in the quote below is a common definition of an entrepreneur in Tanzania; that is, it is equated with somebody who is self-employed. This notion is related to the discourse around entrepreneurship in Tanzania, in which young people are encouraged by the government and other stakeholders to become (self-employed) entrepreneurs rather than to wait for employ-ment: 'My name is Rehema. I understand entrepreneurship as someone who has employed him/herself in order to look for resources. I am also an entrepreneur.'

The spontaneous comments typically fall into five categories: (a) praising the show and its participants; (b) searching for more knowl-edge about entrepreneurship and business; (c) calls to include geograph-ical areas not covered; (d) requests for contact with and comments on contestants; and (e) practical and technical questions. In the first cate-gory, there were positive messages after every episode that praised the Ruka Juu show. One message came after episode 10, and shows a true fan of the show: Ruka I REALLY LIKE FEMA'S SHOW, I HAVE WATCHED IT EVERY WEEK. I WOULD RATHER MISS FOOD THAN MISS THE SHOW. I PRAY FOR YOUR HEALTH DURING THE FINAL. TERY.

Some of the praise messages could have provided important feedback but, as the following message shows, they were cut short due to the shortcode message format on standard mobile phones: 'I have been a big fan of this show and it has attracted me for a long time. It was really run professionally and managed to make a person understand what was said by...' [message cut]

Regarding the *Search for knowledge*, this category includes requests for advice, information and material, including the Ruka Juu episodes. As these messages show, Ruka Juu has triggered interest in learning more about entrepreneurship and how to run a business:

> 'ruka, please advise me. I have 150,000 but I don't know what to do with it so it could grow. Ema from mwanza'.
>
> 'ruka dada bahati, I am really happy with the show, I have learned a lot but I am thirsty for entrepreneurship magazines if it is possible'.
>
> 'ruka MY NAME IS SADITI ISSA. I HAVE A QUESTION: FOR US WHO LIVE IN THE LAKE REGION, HOW CAN WE GET THE RUKA JUU DVDS?'.

Judging from the messages from the audience, there was a great demand for Ruka Juu to visit viewers' locations, which we have summarized in the third category – requests for geographical coverage. The audience questioned why their region was not being covered: 'ruka My question is why you did not involve Kagera region? What were the reasons? My name is Badru mstafa from Kashai'; and 'ruka my opinion is that when you are preparing shows like these you should involve the southern regions as well. Those who live there also need such services.'

The fourth category illustrates that the reality television format invites requests for encounters with contestants. As the first message below shows, members of the audience wanted to get in touch with the contestants. The second message is a comment about one of the contestants combined with a vote (the message starts with 'ruka 03', which is the way the audience has been instructed to vote).

> 'ruka can I please get rajabu's contact from kilindi, so I could learn how to create power! Kalinga daniel udom'.
>
> 'ruka 03 Benitha deserves the capital. Her education is an obstacle, but her plans are good and she is born bright. Welcome to our place, there is no power, please bring us brochures. I am Fibe'.

Messages in the fifth category often require an immediate and individual response. Many of these messages were found in the invalid part of the system. This may be because, due to the practical nature of the question, to which a quick answer was wanted, the members of the audience forgot about the required format and simply wrote the message.

'When is your show on air? And what time?'

'When is the deadline for answering the questions?'

'how should I write the message?'

'ruka JUU, please send me last weeks question. Where I live there is power problems, so I couldn't watch the show. HAPPINESS ELIAKIMU FROM KIGOMA'.

'ruka THOSE QUESTIONS WHICH AUNT BAHATI ASKS, WHEN SHOULD WE START TO RESPOND AND WHAT TIME? BECAUSE WHEN I WRITE THE ANSWER I GET A MESSAGE THAT I AM TOO LATE!'

'ruka I am sorry but where did I make a mistake? You said start with ruka then leave a space, write my message and send it to 15665. That's what I did, isn't it?'

The responses to the different questions of the week and the spontaneous questions and comments provide important insight into how the audience has understood the Ruka Juu episodes. However, it is important to note that the shortcode messages have limitations. They have to start in a specific way in order to qualify as a valid message, and they have to be the correct length, which means that the audience must become 'shortcode literate'. Many messages and votes were considered invalid because they were in the wrong format. We included the invalid messages in this report, but invalid responses to the question of the week and invalid votes were not entered into the Ruka Juu competition. As the large invalid message ratio shows, this rather complicated system of shortcodes needs to be improved either technically, by creating a less rigid system, or by educating the audience better about the shortcode format.

The limit of 160 characters from a standard mobile phone does not allow for long messages that include phrases of greeting, which are typical in Swahili and Tanzanian communications, long explanations or questions, and information about the sender. The message is simply cut after 160 characters and the rest of the message automatically goes into the 'invalid box' of the database. New technology such as smart phones that allow people to send longer messages allow more information to be included in the same message. However, smart phones are more expensive than standard mobile phones. This means that people with ordinary mobile phones are not able to express themselves at length in the same way as somebody with a smart phone. Of course, somebody without access to a mobile phone cannot communicate their views at all, which highlights the importance of maintaining other forms of communication, such as ordinary letters.

Another constraint is that some messages include questions that need direct answers or guidance. If such messages receive automated responses, this discourages future interaction. If Femina encourages the audience to interact with the show, this means that Femina needs to communicate back – sometimes immediately in order to resolve a technical question. An automated response is one way of doing this, but for many messages this is insufficient.

Many, but far from all, include their names and place of residence in the message. This information suggests that there is a countrywide representation among the senders. However, those who have included their names and place of residence often had their message cut as a consequence, due to the limit on space. Apart from name, place and gender, we cannot tell much about the audience from their messages. This is a lost opportunity to gather information about the audience. It also emphasizes the importance of the kind of research that has been conducted in this study, to find out more about the interacting audience. The short code messages provide a golden opportunity, since the messages, including the senders' phone numbers, are automatically stored in a database. They can therefore be used to communicate with the senders by getting back to the interactors and responding to their questions through individual SMS texts or phone calls. The database also allows researchers to examine the senders further.

Despite the shortcomings of the Sema na Fema platform, it provides an opportunity to send out 'bulk' messages, receive feedback in a systematic way, and correspond with the audience. According to Femina HIP (2011), the platform will have to be developed further to become the interactive tool it envisaged. It is our hope that this audience response survey will assist with planning for future seasons of Ruka Juu.

Conclusions: shortcodes and shortcomings but powerful 'real-life' identification

The aims of this study were to identify who was communicating, what was being communicated, and the strengths and limitations of the approach taken by Ruka Juu to use mobile phone messaging for participatory communication. The findings of the study can be summarized in four points: (a) Ruka Juu is engaging with certain groups through SMS and the short-code format in particular, and maybe even some new groups; (b) the SMS format – especially in shortcode form – does not allow for or invite much discussion; (c) we can better understand the patterns of mobilization from access to the short messages sent from mobile phones; and (d) it is clear from the SMS analysis that Ruka Juu has inspired and created increased interest in the themes covered by the programme.

The study also shows how the use of mobile phone messaging works as a tool to create a more participatory relationship with the audience. There are technical as well as economic obstacles to using this mode of communication to engage with an audience. Cultural as well as social patterns and habits need to be understood in order to increase audience participation. Voting is the main reason for interaction by SMS. The questions of the week seem to function more as a test of knowledge than to provoke discussion, and spontaneous comments are often more of a practical character than a contribution to a discussion.

The use of SMS needs to be appropriated (and to be studied) in combination with other tools or modes of communication. It could then reach and engage broader segments of the audience, and create more relevant discussion and a genuine sense of participation. During the first season of Ruka Juu, many important lessons were learned from research conducted about the initiative. Femina took this into account during the second season, which focused on agriculture: 'Ruka Juu: Young farmers in business'. From an audience interaction point of view, it is important to highlight that the Sema na Fema platform is one space among many in which interaction can take place. Not everybody has access to this space, and the format is not suitable for all types of communication. It is therefore worth emphasizing that face-to-face interaction through existing Fema clubs and out-of-school groups will continue to be crucial for the audience in the future, as will ordinary letters and emails through Femina's regular magazines. These media will remain important for communication for social change, just as online communication will need to be complemented by offline conversations in order for communication for social change initiatives such as Ruka Juu to be successful.

Notes

1. The shortcode platform is a virtual space for audience SMS messages. The audience can make comments, ask questions, give feedback and also vote by sending an SMS to a short code number. The messages and phone numbers are stored in a database.
2. The study also serves as a contribution to a larger impact evaluation of the Ruka Juu initiative with the aim of documenting, measuring and analysing

the impact of the show on the target audience as well as on the participating entrepreneurs (Helgesson Sekei, 2011). See also Ekström & Sekei (2012) for a separate audience interaction report.

3. We later discovered that the most active caller was the winner of the competition. Four other high-frequency interactors also turned out to be contestants.

4. It should be emphasized that the small sample of interactors we managed to call on within the scope of this study does not provide statistically significant results. Nonetheless, the findings can be seen as indications of patterns, trends and themes in SMS communications between the audience and Ruka Juu during its first season.

5. The survey questions were written in English but the research assistant who conducted the survey interviews translated the questions into Swahili and communicated with the respondents in Swahili.

References

Anderson, G. and Hitchins, R. (2007) *Expanding the Poor's Access to Business Information and Voice through FM Radio in Uganda: Making Markets Work for the Poor* (Bern: Case Studies Series).

Ekström, Y. (2010) *''We Are Like Chameleons': Changing Mediascapes, Cultural Identities and City Sisters in Dar es Salaam'*, Uppsala Studies in Media and Communication 5. (Uppsala: Uppsala University).

Ekström, Y. and Helgesson Sekei, L. (2012) *Audience Interaction with Ruka Juu: Participatory Involvement in a Communication for Social Change Initiative through SMS.* Unpublished research report by the authors in collaboration with Femina HIP and with support from the Nordic Africa Institute. (Uppsala, Sweden: Nordic Africa Institute).

Femina HIP (2006) *Five-year Strategic Plan Document, 2006–2010*, HIP Multimedi Initiative in Tanzania, (Dar es Salaam: Femina HIP Ltd).

Femina HIP (2011) *Sema na Fema: A Final Narrative Report on the Pilot Project* (Dar es Salaam: Femina HIP Ltd).

FSDT (2009) *FinScope 2009 Survey: The Demand for and Barriers to Accessing Financial Services in Tanzania* (Dar es Salaam: FSDT).

Fuglesang, M. (2005) 'SiMchezo! Magazine: Community Media Making a Difference' in O. Hemer and T. Tufte (eds), *Media and Glocal Change: Rethinking Communication for Development* (Gothenburg: Nordicom), pp. 385–403.

Helgesson, L. (2006) 'Getting Ready for Life: Life Strategies of Town Youth in Mozambique and Tanzania'. Unpublished doctoral dissertation, GERUM Kulturgeografi 2006:1, Umeå University.

Helgesson, L. and Ernest, J. (2008) *Empowering Youth for Employment: Study on Out-of-school Clubs and the Potential for an Expanding Agenda* (Dar es Salaam: Femina HIP Ltd.).

Helgesson Sekei, L. (2011) *Impact Evaluation of Ruka Juu 2011: An Entertainment-Education Initiative in Entrepreneurship and Financial Education in Tanzania* (Dar es Salaam: Femina HIP Ltd).

Ramafoko, L., Andersson, G. and Weiner, R. (2012) 'Reality Television for Community Development: The Kwanda Initiative in South Africa', *Nordicom Review* 33, pp. 149–162.

Singhal, A. and Rogers, E. M. (1999) *Entertainment-education. A Communication Strategy for Social Change* (New Jersey: Lawrence Erlbaum Associates).

TCRA (2012) *Quarterly Telecom Statistics: Quarter 4 (June 2012)* Tanzania Communications Regulatory Authority, www.tcra.go.tz.

Tufte, T. (2005) 'Entertainment Education in Development Communication: Between Marketing Behaviour and Empowering People' in O. Hemer and T. Tufte (eds), *Media and Glocal Change* (Gothenburg, Sweden: Nordicom; and Buenos Aires: GLASCO), pp. 159–176.

Uimonen, P. (2009) 'Internet, Arts and Translocality in Tanzania', *Social Anthropology/Anthropologie Sociale* 17(3), pp. 276–290.

URT (2007) *National Youth Development Policy*. Ministry of Labour, Employment and Youth Development (Dar es Salaam: URT).

URT (2013) *Population Distribution by Age and Sex. 2012 Population and Housing Census, Volume II*. National Bureau of Statistics (NBS), Dar es Salaam.

Wasserman, H. (2013) 'Mobile Phones, Popular Media, and Everyday African Democracy: Transmissions and Transgressions', *International Journal of Media and Culture* 9(2), pp. 146–158.

14

Accessing the Public Sphere in Africa through a Slum Radio Project

Nicky Morrison and Martin Davies

Habermas (1974) noted that a public sphere independent of reigning governments was established out of a space set within the coffee houses of enlightenment Europe. Deane (2005) argues that the radio revolution in many developing countries can be seen in a similar light: 'Many countries where information used to be subject to absolute government control have seen unprecedented public debate and the arguable emergence of a fresh kind of public sphere' (Deane, 2005, p. 181). Fraser (1990) suggests that the conception of the public sphere set out by Habermas effectively excluded the poor. A similar exclusion of the poor from the modern public sphere is arguably happening today, witnessed in the growing lack of interest by the media in public interest issues. Moreover, as the advertisers and sponsors who pay for the newly liberalized media increasingly set agendas, the capacity of marginalized groups in society to have their voices heard in the public domain is further weakened. A lack of access to the media not only undermines the ability of people in poverty to participate in democratic processes, but also inhibits societal change.

This chapter documents the way in which Amnesty International has sought to redress this balance through a specific initiative – the Slum Radio Project (SRP). The aim of the SRP was to gain access to the new public sphere in order to challenge perceptions and stimulate public debate around the underlying causes of urban poverty. It required key stakeholders who had never met to come together and ultimately cooperate so that radio content could be created and delivered to a target audience. The project also required the senior radio managers who controlled public debate on the air to see a value in using radio airtime to expose a specific public interest issue that had not previously been part of their agenda.

The purpose of the SRP was to highlight, in particular, the human rights abuses of slum-dwellers in Nairobi and Accra, and to make the middle classes in these cities and elsewhere in Kenya and Ghana aware of these realities. The middle classes are seen to be largely hostile to slums and those who live in them. At the same time, however, the middle classes are the section of society with the most political influence to pressure their own governments to assist these expanding poor urban communities. The SRP therefore targeted this section of society with information, discussions and live phone-in debates on the radio stations that they listen to, so that they could hear the views of those living in the slums and develop a greater understanding of their human rights issues.

Many media campaigns aim to spread their message far and wide. Their goal is to gain publicity by targeting the largest possible number of people, regardless of where they live. In these instances, it is often the 'World Wide Web' that is the vehicle for communication, and the public sphere is the community of interest that builds around a particular issue (Crompton, 2010). By contrast, the SRP chose to access a public sphere that was intentionally limited geographically but which, if accessed successfully, would mean a high probability that messages would reach the intended target. The project was designed to initially reach a certain sector of society in order to engender debate that would increase awareness as well as pressure on governments to take action and address slum dwellers' human rights issues. In addition, Amnesty International wanted the radio content created through the SRP to be shared with its wider members online, and ultimately to have a wider international impact.

The chapter outlines the reasons why Amnesty International chose radio as the means to access Africa's public sphere, summarizes how the SRP was implemented and evaluates its achievements, and considers whether such an initiative has the potential to be carried out elsewhere.

The issue: slum dwellers' human rights

Rapid urbanization in developing countries and specifically Sub-Saharan Africa is characterized by unprecedented population increases and uncontrolled expansion of cities beyond the limits and capacity of local authorities to provide basic infrastructure and social amenities. These sprawling cities also depict high levels of unemployment, urban poverty, deteriorating services, and a rapid growth of the informal sector. This kind of urbanization inevitably culminates in the creation of informal settlements or slums, with individuals developing their own housing on often hazard-prone land that the government has not legally allowed them to occupy. The threat of forced evictions therefore hangs over the inhabitants as they live in a state of impermanency as well as worsening and precarious living conditions (Owusu et al., 2008). At the same time, neo-liberal policies adopted in many of these developing countries has resulted in central and local governments increasingly relinquishing their responsibility for housing development. Not only have public sector cutbacks exacerbated the chronic shortage of urban housing, such policies have also compounded the growth of informal housing provision (UN-Habitat, 2003).

More than one billion people live in the estimated 200,000 informal settlements that can be defined as slums. Forecasts indicate that the number of slum dwellers will increase to about two billion by 2030 (Amnesty International, 2010). People living in slums face a number of violations of their human rights, such as inadequate housing, a lack of basic services, overcrowding, high levels of violence, high maternal mortality rates, a lack of sanitation, drainage and electricity, little or no access to healthcare, police and gang violence, and the sexual abuse of women and girls. In particular, slum dwellers live with a sense of foreboding that at any moment they may lose their homes, possessions and livelihoods as a result of a forced eviction (Gruffydd Jones, 2009).

Slums are often seen by the rest of the urban population to be places that are riddled with crime. The general perception is that slums impede national development, pose a menace to society and form a breeding ground for deviance, armed robbery and prostitution. Society often does not know how to deal with slums, other than by getting rid of them with little or no concern for those who live there.

Amnesty International is working to protect the human rights of slum dwellers through its campaign, 'Human rights live here.' At the heart of this campaign is a drive to create greater public awareness of slum dwellers' living conditions and the violations of their human rights. It aims to change some deep-rooted negative perceptions in order to facilitate a human rights dialogue around the obligations that society has towards slum dwellers and the slums they live in (Amnesty International, 2010).

Research undertaken by Amnesty International has shown that if educated and middle class populations in Africa were to change their opinions about slums and slum dwellers, they would be the best placed to influence their government to take concrete actions to ensure that the human rights of slum dwellers are respected and implemented. The organization's research has also shown that educated and middle class people in Africa are heavily influenced by the content delivered through mainstream radio stations (Amnesty International, 2010).

Amnesty International sought to accelerate its campaign in Kenya and Ghana. It commissioned radio experts in Africa, Between the Posts Productions (BtPP), to coordinate the delivery of the SRP in Nairobi and Accra over a six-month period. Amnesty International wanted the middle classes of these African cities to become concerned, even outraged, about the rapidly expanding slums around them, and to become involved in a debate about how to manage this problem and improve the human rights of the poorest members of society who lived in them. The aims of Amnesty International were summed up by its director in Kenya, Justus Nyangaya:

> People who had not been exposed to slum issues have now become exposed to these issues through the Slum Radio Project. Many were wondering if these living conditions still occur in Kenya. They found out that they did and this raises a sense of outrage. We want this outrage. We want slum dwellers to be treated with dignity... and we want change.[1]

Why radio?

Radio is the medium that has the greatest impact in Africa (Mytton, 2000). According to the Inter Media Knowledge Center (2010), radio is accessed on a regular basis in Ghana and Kenya by more than 90 per cent of the adult population. In addition, Inter Media (2010) suggests that radio is the most trusted medium. Africa has an oral history and, in societies where there are still high levels of illiteracy, radio holds a prominent place.

Radio services have a long history in Africa. Kenya's and Ghana's national public radio services were established in the 1930s. In terms of representing the public sphere, radio throughout Africa underwent a golden era of growth and expansion in the late 1980s and the 1990s. The Cold War had ended, Nelson Mandela had been released from prison in South Africa, and across the continent there was a wave of inclusivity and liberalization that resulted in constitutional reviews and conferences designed to create more pluralistic and open societies.

Mytton (2000) states that there were just six independent radio stations in Africa in 1987, but by the turn of the century there were more than 450. A proliferation of radio stations, coupled with the advent of the phone-in and discussion programmes and the fact that the majority of people had access to radio sets, resulted in a rapid growth and opening up of Africa's public sphere. Ownership of radio sets and access to them remains high today – still much higher than television sets, for example – and, unlike televisions, radios do not require electricity. In a continent where electricity supplies are unpredictable, radio is seen as more reliable. Finally, because radios are also cheaper than televisions, they have greater accessibility and reach (Deane, 2005).

There are also other factors that suggest that radio is the best medium in Africa for raising public awareness and creating a debate within the public sphere. As Deane (2005) observes, the increase in mobile phone ownership in Africa has worked in tandem with radio to create a good platform for discussion. Mobile phones not only enable the public to communicate and debate with those broadcasting radio content, but also function as radios themselves, as many phones on the market in Africa also include basic FM receivers.

The rapid urbanization of African cities, of which slum sprawl is a part, creates the conditions that allow millions of urban radio listeners to be reached. The same failure in the planning system that has led to informal settlements emerging in these cities has also resulted in inadequate road systems. Without an effective mass transit system, large numbers of the middle class target-audience are trapped in their cars, with their car radios as the most convenient medium for accessing information, particularly during the ever-congested rush hour.

SRP coordinators negotiate access to radio stations

In order to gain access to the public sphere, the coordinators of the SRP needed to target the radio stations that reach middle class audiences. These stations include both state broadcasters and independent, commercial radio stations that target the wealthier sections of the radio market. Stations from both sectors sell airtime to advertisers and sponsors, which therefore directly influence the public debate and the use of airtime (Deane, 2005). In Kenya, in particular, this airtime in the private sector is some of the most expensive in Africa.

The aim of the SRP was to work with these radio stations to deliver content about slum issues over a limited six-week period. The coordinators aimed to work with the stations to design content that was varied in its format, duration and style, and that could run at different times of the day and week during this limited time frame. The plan was that the stations would promote this series of programmes on air and raise their listeners' awareness that an important public interest issue was being delivered to them that could not be ignored.

It is not easy, however, to gain access to a radio station's airtime, particularly to run a radio campaign like the SRP over a period of weeks. Air time is a station's advertising space and, in addition to selling short advertising slots, they often sell entire blocks of airtime, of perhaps one or two hours, to commercial sponsors. The state sector also sells commercial time and can be sensitive about content that might be perceived as critical of the government.

As Deane (2005) suggests, the dynamic between the media and profit, and particularly advertising, means that the concerns of the poor tend to be ignored because they do not constitute a market of any value for advertisers. In their discussions with those who control the media – that is, the senior managers at the radio stations – the SRP coordinators found that there was in fact an interest in issues concerning poor living conditions in slums in Nairobi and Accra. The managers recognized the value of telling the slum dwellers' stories for a limited period, in order for their middle class listeners to better understand the wider community in which they lived and some of the underlying dynamics that drive their society and the economy.

In most cases, the radio station managers and their editors acknowledged that they would have liked to be doing more reporting on the slums, but did not have the necessary contacts or connections to make this possible. The SRP therefore offered them a way in, providing an opportunity to build more understanding, context and contacts to enable them to cover radio stories more effectively. The media organizations that agreed to work with the SRP were Radio Africa, Capital Radio and Standard Group in Kenya, and Joy FM and GBC in Ghana.

The SRP model did not involve paying for expensive airtime, but instead working out a value exchange that would be of benefit to both parties. Acquiring commercial slots and airtime would have created a one-off commercial exchange without the journalists in the respective radio stations becoming involved in the project. Nor would relationships have been forged between the journalists and the slum communities. The journalists in the field would not have gained an understanding of the situation on the ground, limiting their ability to follow up with subsequent radio features in the future, once the SRP had been completed.

It was therefore important for the SRP coordinators to ascertain what would be of interest to the radio station managers and, vitally, what they regarded as being of value in exchange for their valuable airtime. During the discussions, it emerged that training was valued highly by the station managers. While it has become relatively cheap to acquire the radio equipment needed to set up and run a radio station, training for staff is often not available at a price that the managers felt they could afford. The coordinators therefore offered journalism and production training skills to the various radio stations' employees, as well as training in human rights issues. Moreover, on agreeing to be involved in the SRP, the different radio stations gained access to the slums through community leaders. They also obtained relevant statistics and background information on the different slums so that the programmes produced were factually accurate and of high quality. Editorial and production guidance as well as production and technical support, particularly while the outside-studio broadcast programmes were being produced in the slums, were also provided.

The radio managers regarded all these offers as valuable, but the key factor that led each station to agree to take part in the SRP was an acknowledgement that slums were a growing issue within the catchment area that the radio stations served. In Nairobi, for example, more than half the population now lives in slums. There had been recent high-profile cases of forced evictions in the slums of both Nairobi and Accra, which had received national media attention. The radio managers were therefore eager for their stations to better convey these human rights abuses and for their employees to fully understand such events and report them as accurately and widely as possible. The SRP provided the necessary support to enable the radio stations to achieve these tasks.

SRP phases

In order to deliver the project as effectively as possible, a clear work plan was established at the outset between Amnesty International and the project coordinators, and overseen by the adviser to the project. The SRP had five phases, each with distinct timeframes to ensure that the project maintained its momentum and achieved the greatest impact on the ground.

Phase 1: preparation of the SRP

In addition to securing the involvement of the different radio stations in both Nairobi and Accra, it was necessary to meet with community leaders in the slums to ascertain how they would like to engage with the project. This was crucial to ensure that the myriad of stakeholders they represented would also be committed to the project, and that the process of delivering the SRP would not disturb the community but instead be beneficial and accurately represent its interests.

Phase 2: training, briefing and launching a network of key stakeholders in Nairobi and Accra

Training was provided on journalism and radio reporting, focusing on how to create compelling and sustainable editorial angles, and on human rights issues in the slums. In each location, key community leaders from the slums were involved throughout, to answer questions about the realities of living in the slums and to enable them to gain a greater understanding of the project and establish trust between them and the journalists involved. There was also a launch of the SRP in each location, bringing together all the relevant stakeholders. This network consisted of Amnesty International's local officers, BtPP, the radio stations' senior managers, journalists, the different slum community leaders and the slum dwellers themselves.

Phase 3: editorial shaping and reporting trips into the slums

The different radio station managers nominated staff to be trained and undertake the gathering of the material. Ahead of this content gathering, the coordinators held editorial meetings with the stations to discuss the types of stories that could be available and explore the type of narratives the journalists were interested in. This enabled the coordinators to maintain some editorial influence over content creation and ensure that human rights issues were being considered.

Phase 4: on-air and outside broadcasts

The SRP was on the air for six weeks. The radio stations involved were encouraged to run the radio content as a six-week season, with an intensive week of action towards the end. This intensive week coincided with a week of campaigning undertaken by Amnesty International, with the aim of raising awareness and communicating the human rights message as powerfully as possible. A key element of this intensive week was a live outside broadcast from the slums, which was the first time that this had been contemplated.

Phase 5: review of the SRP's achievements

A log was made of all the material produced by the SRP, listener feedback and the extent to which the content was disseminated through other media outlets, including Facebook, the Internet and television coverage. A survey of participating journalists and their station managers was also conducted to gather their views on the success of the initiative and how to maintain its momentum. An evaluation of the project's immediate and long-term impact was undertaken by the project coordinators, in conjunction with the adviser to the project.

The SRP approach

A number of innovative and ground-breaking approaches were adopted by the SRP coordinators, in order to penetrate the public sphere effectively and have the greatest impact on changing listeners' perceptions of slums. These included setting up outside broadcasts within the slums, strengthening the message by telling individual slum dweller's stories, while at the same time gaining international media coverage to gather momentum and galvanize support for Amnesty International's campaign.

Outside broadcasts

The different radio stations ran a vast array of radio content on slum and human rights issues throughout the six-week season. The format that·penetrated the public sphere most effectively, however, was interactive discussion programmes hosted inside the slums. As Deane (2005) notes, phone-in programmes are an effective way to communicate with listeners, allowing listeners to communicate back using mobile phones, thereby creating a dynamic interactive discussion that galvanizes interest and action. The SRP coordinators wanted to take this concept one step further. Technological advances in recent years mean that radio stations can now broadcast away from their fixed location using systems with negligible transmission costs. This technology enabled the project to host programmes in the heart of the community, where the story was happening.

Producing outside broadcasts meant that the programmes could fully connect with the issues in these communities, capturing in essence the flavour of life there and gaining access to radio guests. It also meant that, for the first time, the media organizations serving the middle class communities were coming to the slum dwellers rather than the other way round.

Ahead of the project, as an incentive to radio stations to cooperate, the coordinators offered to set up temporary studios in the slums and to cover all the production costs of this airtime. Four of the five stations agreed to undertake an outside broadcast, producing a total of nine hours of airtime in the two countries. Although the different radio stations possessed the relevant technology, they had used it solely to broadcast from sports fixtures and similar venues.

A further advantage of creating programmes and outside broadcasts of this nature is that they tend to receive additional promotion. Having put the resources, planning and time into setting them up, they are then debated by the radio station both on and off the air. Consequently, not only did listeners hear that these programmes were going to happen, but a sense of excitement was generated at each station, which created further publicity for and awareness of the SRP. Moreover, presenters, producers and technicians welcomed the challenge of working on something new.

The best example of what could be achieved through the SRP was the programme-making undertaken by Radio Africa in Kenya. The SRP was delivered the most effectively by this radio station, primarily because there was buy-in from the top of the organization, from the senior editorial staff to the journalists who reported from the slums, the presenters who held the programmes together and the technicians who found technical solutions to broadcast live from the Mathare slum in Kenya. The level of coordination and cooperation throughout the different layers of the organization meant that each person was given incentive to make sure that the outside broadcasts and the SRP in general were a success.

Radio Africa welcomed the idea of a series of programmes on human rights issues in slums, and promoted their series as 'step into the slums'. They produced content that was aired by two different language services, creating more than 150 short items, which were broadcast over the six-week period. These stories were scheduled to air before the news, both during the breakfast show and then during the evening drive-time programme, which are the peak listening times. The radio station brought in live guests from the slums for their breakfast shows and heavily promoted the fact that they were going to broadcast their breakfast show in Swahili, live from the slums one morning. The outside broadcast programme maintained the regular slots for news, sport and travel, which meant that regular listeners tuning in would be encouraged to stay with the programme.

The outside broadcast from the slums included emotive stories from the slum communities. For four hours, listeners heard from people who had witnessed a slum fire claiming lives nearby as the programme went on air, women who teach other women how to defend themselves from sexual assault, or celebrities who had come from the slum and effectively become role models, as well as broader discussions on the effects of poverty and a lack of resources as well as human rights abuses.

Ghana's government station, GBC, chose a different but equally effective outside broadcast format. It took the decision to set up the outside broadcast as a public debate about slum clearance and evictions, and invited different guests on to the live show to air their views. Slum community leaders were given the opportunity to question the local authority's spokesperson from the Accra Metropolitan Assembly. Amnesty International's local officers were also on-hand to provide factual evidence of human rights violations. In effect, the radio station played a crucial role in helping community leaders to express their views and scale-up their efforts to hold the authorities to account over the forced evictions taking place in the slum. The live outside broadcast was transmitted across Ghana, giving the issues national publicity.

Conveying the stories of individual slum dwellers

While in Nairobi and Accra, the SRP coordinators met two young slum dwellers who appeared to have parallel lives that caught their attention. Abdallah, from Old Fadama slum, and Mustapha, from Kibera slum, were both in their mid-20s, graduates, ambitious and aspirational, and both by chance were Muslim. They were also articulate, chose to live in the heart of their slum communities, and passionate about promoting the rights of slum dwellers.

The coordinators approached them independently to act as the Master of Ceremonies at the launch of the Slum Radio stakeholder network in their respective cities. The intention was to show the media the potential of people living in the slums, but also to demonstrate that this was a project that was giving a voice to slum dwellers. These two young men became ambassadors for the SRP and heightened the realities of living in slums in a personalized way that different listeners could empathize with and, in so doing, alter their often negative perceptions of slum-dweller stereotypes.

Gaining international media coverage

The SRP ran simultaneously in Kenya and Ghana, and its coordinators wanted to find out if material from one location was of interest to media outlets and listeners in the other. Although the primary aim of the project was to use radio to target specific sections of society in specific locations, it was also vital to gain coverage from the international media in order to highlight the slum dwellers' human rights issues to a wider audience. Amnesty International, through the SRP coordinators, timed the project to coincide with a meeting of African Housing Ministers in Nairobi and a parallel event organized by Amnesty International to highlight its 'Human rights live here' campaign. The decision was made to have the outside broadcasts, in particular, coincide with the international meeting in order to create as big an impact as possible.

The meeting of Housing Ministers in Nairobi gave the SRP an opportunity to personalize the slum dwellers' plight even further. As part of its ongoing campaign, Amnesty International invited individual slum dwellers from different parts of Africa to attend a workshop as a way to raise awareness and publicity about the failure of African governments to enact international standards on human rights. While the Housing Ministers' meeting took place in Nairobi, the SRP coordinators worked with Amnesty International to invite Abdallah from Accra to become one of the delegates as part of the 'human rights live here' activation team. The project arranged for him to stay with Mustapha, who was leading his parallel life in the heart of Kibera slum in Nairobi. Until this point, these two young men were not aware of each other. The project coordinator therefore chose to build a narrative around the visit and use it as a way to personalize the human rights issues and further engage the media's interests.

The story was pitched to the international media. It was covered by Al Jazeera television, which filmed the two young men together in Kibera and during interviews given to the radio stations taking part in the SRP. This film effectively reinforced the SRP's message and gave the project international exposure. It also provided further radio content for the different radio stations in both Kenya and Ghana. Abdallah's visit was an effective way to compare the different living conditions in the two slums. He was interviewed extensively in Kenya, and in Ghana, both while he was visiting Kenya and on his return, making him a clear ambassador for the SRP alongside his counterpart, Mustapha.

An evaluation of the SRP's achievements

The aim of the SRP was to penetrate the public sphere in Kenya and Ghana, working on the premise that radio was the best means of reaching the middle classes. However, as other academics and practitioners have noted, it is impossible to accurately measure the impact of radio on listeners' attitudes and behaviour (Deane, 2005; Gordon, 2005; Servaes and Malikehao, 2005). Moreover, as with any awareness-raising campaign, evidence of behavioural change cannot necessarily be attributed to the campaign alone (Crompton, 2010).

In a limited time period, the SRP cannot instantly change middle class perceptions of slum dwellers and motivate them to take action with regard to human rights abuses. Closing the 'attitude-behaviour' or 'values-action' gap, where what people think is matched by what they do and how they act, is difficult to achieve (Crompton, 2010). The impact of the project, however, can be more readily evaluated in relation to measurable outputs: the volume of material that the SRP put into the public sphere and audience feedback. An evaluation of the way the project strengthened the radio stations' capacity to both understand human rights issues and transmit messages into the public sphere can also be made. Finally, to be truly effective, the project itself should sustain momentum beyond its duration. The coordinators therefore made a preliminary assessment of the SRP legacy in conjunction with the adviser to the project.

The volume of SRP radio content and listener feedback

The SRP's original target was that each participating radio station would produce eight pieces of recorded audio as well as a discussion programme of at least 15 minutes, focusing on human rights issues in the slums of Nairobi or Accra. The reality was that more than 180 items were broadcast, and nine hours of radio discussion time was produced. In this respect, the SRP's targets were exceeded. In addition, each of the radio stations actively used Facebook and their own websites to raise awareness of the SRP and effectively broaden the reach of the public sphere, as Deane (2005) suggests would be the case.

Feedback, both through discussions during radio programmes and off-air, was considerable, as reflected in quotes from the radio station managers:

> 'Listeners would call in ... to give their views and ... give ideas on other areas to cover. We even got nicknamed "slum galz"'

> 'The people around us recognized the project and made comments about the stories we had done and had been aired on our stations'

> 'We got people to understand our message that slum dwellers are just like us ... we got people to think differently'

The outside broadcasts undertaken by the radio stations became a particularly effective way of transmitting the message and stimulated the greatest listener feedback. This bold and groundbreaking experiment guaranteed that slum dwellers' human rights issues were given voice in the public sphere, and galvanized support among the radio listeners. It became a powerful tool for exposing human rights abuses, particularly cases of unlawful evictions, which could not be ignored by the respective governments.

Building the capacity of radio stations to deliver the SRP

Providing media training was a critical aspect of the success of the project, providing incentive to the different radio stations to engage with the project, and strengthening the capacity of the radio journalists to understand and convey the importance of human rights issues to their listeners. The training shaped their understanding of the issues and how to report them. As the different radio managers and journalists noted,

- 'staff got trained, conveyed the story, reached maximum numbers of people and good content went to air on radio stations.'
- 'the SRP gave us training and equipped us with radio skills and an understanding of human rights aspects and enabled us to take the stories of Kibera to wider society.'
- 'the training drew attention to human rights issues that are often ignored and we hitherto did not know of it also gave us insights into how to make feature stories and capture the listeners' attention.'

Moreover, capacity building was maintained throughout the project, primarily through the establishment of the SRP's stakeholder network. The aim was that this network would create a sense of ownership around the SRP and allow different stakeholders to communicate effectively and exchange information, often for the first time. Building these connections and establishing trust and reciprocity among the different stakeholders were critical elements in ensuring the SRP's impact as well as sustaining its momentum once the project was completed.

Creating a SRP legacy

Ensuring that the SRP will leave a legacy may be difficult to achieve without the resources, and the intensive coordination efforts and support on the ground from the project coordinators. It is hard to incentivize the different radio stations to continue transmitting on slum dwellers' human rights issues, particularly as their agenda is directly shaped by the demands of the advertisers and sponsors that pay for the airtime (Deane, 2005). Each of the radio station managers, however, had clearly seen the benefits of engagement with the project. Moreover, they provided guarantees that they would continue to keep slum dwellers' human rights issues on their agenda, raising awareness and campaigning through their respective radio stations.

- 'There are more angles our station has not developed. So even though the project is over, we will still be giving the slum dwellers a chance to air their views, and for us to take the responsibility of following up on issues with the relevant government authorities.'
- 'Now that listeners are aware of the issues of the slums, then a constant reminder will help keep the issues in their minds and start the process of demanding action from the government.'
- 'It has helped to bring out the issues in the slums and in so doing, eliminated negative stereotypes; it also showed that our radio station is not a station for elites.'

Transferable lessons from the SRP

There is potential to replicate the SRP model elsewhere. Table 14.1 highlights the necessary ingredients for similar slum radio projects to be successfully implemented in other countries.

Table 14.1 Necessary ingredients for successful SRP implementation

Resources and commitment from high profile international organization
Amnesty International
  – *The project is linked up with its broader campaigning work on human rights issues*
  – *Project gains credibility*

Dedicated leadership, coordination and support to provide the mechanisms to deliver the project (setting deliverable targets and work plan over agreed timeframe)
  – *Employ media experts (Between the Post Productions) to coordinate project*
  – *Employ adviser to monitor & evaluate the project's achievements & transferability*

Buy-in from radio stations' senior management – to place the issue on their agenda and continue campaigning after project's completion

Create incentives for key stakeholders to be involved – form a mutual exchange process to gain access to radio stations' airtime, for example by offering professional training in
  (a) *radio production and journalism skills*
  (b) *human rights issues*

Capacity building exercise
Establish a network of stakeholders
  – *to achieve a sense of ownership/ consensus / inclusivity/commitment*
  – *to develop trust/build relationships/connectivity/cooperation/reciprocity*

Continued

Table 14.1 Continued

Create innovative/ groundbreaking radio content: to convey the message as effectively as possible and have the greatest impact on listeners
  (a) *outside broadcasts produced in the slums.*
  (b) *invite slum dwellers as live radio guests to personalize stories.*
  (c) *deliver a live public debate on the radio with the different organizations held to account.*
  (d) *involve young aspirational slum dwellers to act as project ambassadors.*

Measure tangible outputs
  (a) *Log the volume of radio material produced*
  (b) *Monitor listener feedback*

Disseminate radio content to other media outlets to raise awareness/spread message
  Facebook, Internet, international television coverage

Sustain legacy
  (a) *Secure guarantee at senior management level that issue remains on the agenda*
  (b) *Ensure awareness campaigning continues and is translated into visible action*
  (c) *Develop a forward strategy to sustain project's momentum*
  (d) *Consider ways to secure ongoing funding sources and stakeholder interest*

Conclusions

Habermas's (1974) original depiction of a public sphere was one that evolved from the coffee houses of 17th and 18th century Enlightenment Europe. Individuals came together to freely discuss and deliberate on societal problems of the time, beyond the confines of government. New arenas for participation and new means of communication now exist, and the concept of the public sphere in Habermas's traditional sense has been recast in modern society. The SRP's aim was to infiltrate this new public sphere through the radio airwaves listened to by the middle classes and, in turn, to stimulate public debate in the shopping malls and coffee houses of 21st century urban Africa.

Both Kenya and Ghana have growing economies and a burgeoning middle class. They both have two of the fastest growing cities in Africa, in terms of population numbers. Much of this population growth, however, is from the urban poor. The SRP has gone some way towards putting the perspectives of the poor in the public sphere. As Deane (2005) notes, there remains a continual need to coordinate and target journalist-training programmes on poverty-related issues. The SRP not only supported and encouraged investigative reporting around issues of poverty, but also provided the mechanisms to effectively target the public sphere and raise public awareness around slum dwellers' human rights.

Radio matters because it transcends the narrow solidarities and particular affinities that shape the public sphere. It provides a medium for freedom of expression, where people and institutions can be held to account. In this instance, the SRP exposed the circumstances in which municipal governments have sought to evict slum dwellers, and posed questions that could not be ignored. The radio programmes created through the SRP were both bold and groundbreaking. The project was heralded, in particular, for its innovative use of outside broadcasts from the slums, conveying the life stories of individual slum dwellers and supporting young, aspirational individuals who ultimately became the project's ambassadors, both at home and abroad.

The SRP provided a means to connect slum dwellers with the rest of society, and in so doing, to influence public opinion and challenge negative labelling. The different radio stations, in effect, came out in support of the people in the slums and galvanized support. The SRP stakeholder network, which was established at the outset of the project and continued thereafter, has allowed relationships to be forged and created a consensus around the need to continually report on human rights issues.

Whether the SRP changed attitudes among middle class radio listeners in Kenya and Ghana, or instead cemented what they already believed and reinforced existing values, is hard to measure. What is significant about the project, however, is that it provided an opportunity and platform for slum dwellers' voices to be brought to the fore and strengthened networks of resistance against human rights abuses. It is difficult to evaluate what difference the project made, in particular whether any form of collective response has been accelerated or can be attributed to the SRP. Nonetheless, linking in with Facebook and the Internet, and gaining access to the international media through television coverage are clear achievements that help to guarantee that its message is extended beyond Amnesty International's initial target audience.

Radio represents just one place in which arguments can be brought to the surface and communities mobilized to act. At the same time, it provides a space where people and organizations can associate freely beyond authority. It is therefore a critical arena for promoting a better understanding of poverty-related issues as well as facilitating a constructive dialogue among different stakeholders. The quest to claim full citizenship rights for slum dwellers, and to develop alternative solutions to forced evictions, for example, continues. Radio and initiatives like Amnesty International's SRP have a part to play in scaling up collective efforts and ultimately addressing the broader issues of the marginalization of the urban poor.

Note

1. Interview with director of Amnesty International in Kenya, Justus Nyangaya.

References

Amnesty International (2010) *Human Rights Live Here: Annual Report* (London: Amnesty International).

Crompton, T. (2010) *Common Causes: The Case for Working with Values and Frames* (London: World Wildlife Fund).

Gruffydd Jones, B. (2009) 'Cities without Slums? Global Architectures of Power and the African City', paper presented at the 2009 *African Perspectives Congress: The African City Centre Re(sourced)*, University of Pretoria, South Africa, 25–28 September 2009.

Deane, J. (2005) 'Media, Democracy and the Public Sphere' in O. Hemer and T. Tufte (eds), *Media & Glocal Change: Rethinking Communication for Development* (Gothenburg, Sweden: NORDICOM and Buenos Aires: CLACSO), pp. 177–192.

Fraser, N. (1990) 'Rethinking the Public Sphere: A Contribution to the Critique of Actually Existing Democracy', *Social Text* 25(26), pp. 56–80.

Gordon, A. (2005) 'Radio in Afghanistan: Socially Useful Communication in Wartime' in O. Hemer and T. Tufte (eds), *Media & Glocal Change: Rethinking Communication for Development*, (Gothenburg, Sweden: NORDICOM and Buenos Aires: CLACSO), pp. 349–366.

Habermas, J. (1974) 'The Public Sphere: An Encyclopaedia Article', *New German Critique* 3, pp. 49–55.

InterMedia Knowledge Center (2010) *Audience Scapes*. Available at www.audiencescapes.org/country-profiles/kenya/media-and-comunication-overview/media-and-communication.

Mytton, G. (2000) 'A Brief History of Radio Broadcasting in Africa'. Unpublished paper available at www.transculturalwriting.com/radiophonics/contents/usr/downloads/radiophonics/A_Brief_History.pdf.

Owusu, G., Agyei-Mensah, S. and Lund, R. (2008) 'Slums of Home and Slums of Despair: Mobility and Livelihoods in Nima, Accra', *Norwegian Journal of Geography* 62, pp. 180–190.

Servaes, J. and Malikehao, P. (2005) 'Participatory Communication: The New Paradigm?' in O. Hemer and T. Tufte (eds), *Media & Glocal Change: Rethinking Communication for Development* (Gothenburg, Sweden: NORDICOM and Buenos Aires: CLACSO), pp. 91–104.

UN-Habitat (2003) The Challenge of Slums: Global Report on Human Settlements (United Nations, New York).

Afterword

Oscar Hemer and Thomas Tufte

The hype over social media has largely passed. Hardly anyone talks about Facebook or Twitter revolutions anymore. The euphoria of 2011, when the Arab Spring evoked expectations similar to those of the Eastern European revolution of 1989, has given way to disillusion and despair over the humanitarian disaster and deadlock in Syria – a 'backlash' that may also bring to mind how the horror of the wars in the dismantled former Yugoslavia soon overshadowed the celebration of the end of the Cold War.

The challenge of the present continuous, as media anthropologist John Postill (2012) has called it, or the tyranny of the imminent, becomes particularly conspicuous in the social sciences' attempts at keeping pace with the rapid technological development and transformation of the media environment. Just as the post-modernity debate of the 1980s made modernity aware of its own historicity, we ought perhaps to evoke a 'post-globalization' examination to put the recent claims to global transformational processes into historical perspective.

This volume can be regarded as part of one such endeavour. It is the direct result of a productive encounter between academics, artists, activists, master students and communication practitioners at the second *Örecomm Festival* in September 2012, under the headline *Reclaiming the Public Sphere – Communication, Power and Social Change*. But it is also the fruit of almost 15 years of cross-border collaboration in the field of Communication for Development and Social Change, centred around the master programme in Communication for Development (ComDev) at Malmö University and the research and consultancy work in the field carried out by scholars based at Roskilde University and Malmö University and Communication for Development practitioners in the region. This essentially interpersonal collaboration was formalized and institutionalized through the establishment in 2012 of the *Örecomm Centre for Communication and Glocal Change*.[1] The Örecomm cross-border group of researchers and practitioners has to date organized three thematic Örecomm Festivals, addressing some of the current challenges within the field of Communication for Development and Social Change (CDSC). The first Festival (2011) *Agency in the Mediatized World – Media, Communication and Development in Transition*, focused on agency and mediatization. The theme of the third Festival (2013) was *Memory on Trial – Media, Citizenship and Social Justice*. The over-arching aim of the festivals has been to constitute Communication for Development and Social Change as an interdisciplinary academic field, not by narrowing its focus, but on the contrary, by engaging in dialogue with neighbouring fields of research and enabling new cross-disciplinary approaches. It is moreover in the deliberate bringing together of all relevant stakeholders in CDSC, including public intellectuals, artists, media practitioners, development cooperation consultants and others, that we best explore, for example, as in this volume, how art, technology and public pedagogy connect to issues of communication, power and social change.

The three festival themes are closely related, and it is obvious that the notion of the public sphere is crucial to all of them, both as an arena for cultural and political agency, and for the exploration and articulation of individual and public memory. And, even though, from a historical perspective, we may feel inclined argue that there is nothing new under the sun, our conception of the public sphere has no doubt profoundly changed in the course of the past few years.

The twin phenomena of globalization and mediatization are posing interesting challenges to our understanding of participatory democracy and political action. On the one hand, national frame is largely being replaced or at least supplemented by transnational communications and cultural flows; on the other hand, mass media, which have formed the backbone of the public sphere, are now losing ground to new social media and other forms of what Manuel Castells (2009) has defined as 'mass self-communication'. An often-quoted editorial in *The Economist* (7 July 2011) even suggested that the era of mass media is coming to an end, bringing us 'back to the coffeehouses'.

But what are the implications of this on-going shift? Who are the new players in the public arenas of the present? What processes of power brokering are taking place? How do the communicative practices, the negotiation of power and the formation and negotiation of social relations all come together in and around public spheres? And how do public spheres relate to public *space* – be it physical cityscapes or virtual environments? These were the questions posed in the concept note of the festival and hence to the authors in this volume.

At the IAMCR conference in Istanbul in 2011, at the height of the social mobilizations that took both media researchers and Middle East 'experts' by complete surprise, it became obvious to us that the sudden explosion of academic interest in the relation between social media, civil society, civic action and social change was surprisingly not associated with CDSC. In other words: *While the crucial role of media and communication in processes of social change and development finally becomes evident, it is curiously detached from the field of communication for development and social change* – with a few exceptions, not even by the development agencies themselves, that were equally startled by the unleashed force of spontaneous civic engagement.

This observation is a cause of grave concern that calls for self-critique and reflection. Therefore, in addition to the idea of reclaiming the public sphere, which is at the core of this book, we become acutely aware of the urgency of also reclaiming core questions and concerns, which have been at the heart of CDSC throughout its existence. In the aftermath of the social uprisings of recent years, we have experienced an explosion in research and publications dealing with the dynamic relations between social media and social change (see e.g., Bennett and Segerberg, 2013; Gerbaudo, 2012; Hands, 2011; Kleine, 2013; Lievrouw, 2011; Milan, 2013). However, most of these publications emerge from within studies of political communication, media sociology, media activism and anthropology, with very limited connection to the history and development of CDSC as this has unfolded as a discipline. The role of the public sphere is oftentimes contested, but remains a key concern throughout these studies.

Reclaiming the public sphere may seem like somewhat of a hyperbolic statement that ought to be followed by a question mark. The statement implies that there once was a public sphere, in singular, that we once 'possessed', or at least to which we had access. That is, obviously, a truth that needs qualifying. The coffeehouses were not for everyone. The bourgeois public sphere comprised a privileged minority. Even the Habermasian ideal arguably secluded certain categories. Moreover, the public sphere has been intrinsically connected to the notion of a *national* culture and most often a nation-state. We need only to look a few years back in time to remember the heated debate about the perceived threat to the singular national public sphere by satellite dishes that enabled immigrants to watch TV from their 'home' countries. There is a certain degree of nostalgia attached to the perception of the public sphere as this shared frame of reference, as *collective memory*, in Scandinavia symbolized by the not too distant past of one public service TV channel which everybody watched. But that is hardly the public sphere that most of us would want to reclaim. Rather than retrieving *the* public sphere in a Habermasian sense, the new means of communication and political action are inevitably shaping and constituting new public spheres in the plural. Yet there is a paradox at play here. The proliferation of public spheres will undermine and at some point eventually dissolve the very idea of a public sphere: that is, a common arena for public debate (and participatory democracy).

While demonstrating the communication power of new media and ICTs, recent events, such as the Utøya massacre in Norway in July 2011 and former CIA employee Edward Snowden's revelations of the extent of global surveillance in 2013, have drawn our attention to the 'dark side' of the Internet and global connectivity, with its propensity for enhancing a narrowness of thought on the one hand and corporate or state control on the other. The blurred borders between our private and public selves in new forms of social media certainly add a new dimension to the notion of the *public* sphere.

The present is a moment of transition, and the challenge for us, as researchers and practitioners in the broad field of Communication for Development and Social Change, is to take a step back and reflect, analyse and understand, rather than impose recipes or strategies for change. Taking a step back thus implies (temporarily) escaping the tyranny of the present continuous.

Note

1. Örecomm was officially launched at the IAMCR congress in Stockholm in 2008, but attained legal status as a bi-national centre in 2012.

References

Bennett, L. and Segerberg A. (2013) *The Logics of Connective Action. Digital Media and the Personalization of Politics* (Cambridge: Cambridge University Press)
Castells, M. (2009) *Communication Power* (Oxford: Oxford University Press).
The Economist (2011) 'The End of Mass Media Coming Full Circle', *The Economist* 7 July 2011.
Gerbaudo, P. (2012) *Tweets and the Streets. Social Media and Contemporary Activism* (New York: Pluto Press).
Hands, J. (2011) *@ is for Activism. Dissent, Resistance and Rebellion in a Digital Culture* (New York: Pluto Press).

Kleine, D. (2013) *Technologies of Choice? ICTs, Development, and the Capabilities Approach* (London: The MIT Press).

Lievrouw. L. (2011) *Alternative and Activist New Media* (Cambridge: Polity Press).

Milan, S. (2013) *Social Movements and Their Technologies. Wiring Social Change* (Houndmills: Palgrave).

Postill J. (2012) *Digital Media and Social Change.* Örecomm Open Seminar, Malmö University, 16 March 2012

Index

GPSR Compliance
The European Union's (EU) General Product Safety Regulation (GPSR) is a set
of rules that requires consumer products to be safe and our obligations to
ensure this.

If you have any concerns about our products, you can contact us on

ProductSafety@springernature.com

In case Publisher is established outside the EU, the EU authorized
representative is:

Springer Nature Customer Service Center GmbH
Europaplatz 3
69115 Heidelberg, Germany